Quality Management (Princip]

GW00356881

Geoff Vorley MSc, MIQA
and
Fred Tickle BA, CEng, MIMechE, MIEE, MIQA

Founding Directors of Quality Management & Training Limited
Associate Lecturers at University of Surrey

Geoff Vorley

Fred Tickle

Quality Management & Training Limited

Quality Management & Training (Publications) Limited
PO Box 172 Guildford Surrey United Kingdom GU2 7FN
Telephone: +44 (0) 1256 358083 or +44 (0) 1483 453511 **Fax:** +44 (0) 1483 453512
E-mail: help@qmt.co.uk **Website**: www.qmt.co.uk

Quality Management & Training (Publications) Limited
PO Box 172 Guildford Surrey GU2 7FN

First Published by Whitehall Publications Limited 1991
2nd Edition Nexus Business Communications Limited 1993
3rd Edition Quality Management & Training (Publications) Limited 1996
Reprinted 1998
Reprinted 2000
4th Edition by Quality Management & Training (Publications) Limited 2001
5th Edition by Quality Management & Training (Publications) Limited 2002

British Library Cataloguing in publications data

A catalogue record for this book is available from the British Library

ISBN   1-904302-02-5

Printed and Bound in United Kingdom at the University Press, Cambridge

Quality Management (Principles & Practice)

Table of Contents

Introduction to Quality Management (Principles & Practice)

Quality Management (Principles & Practice) is now in its fifth edition. Why? It could be considered that quality management ought to be static - "*right first time*" and yet we are at issue five of this book (in eleven years!). Wasn't the book correct in the first place? Well, in defence, the subject has evolved, large changes have taken place since the fourth edition in 2001. Some key changes have been made - the latest revision of ISO 9000, Integrated Management Systems[1] (IMS), the Law and use of computers and the Internet in Quality Assurance, all of which are addressed in this new edition. ISO 9001 is now often used as the basis for organisation's second party certification (purchasing) standard, e.g. ISO TS 16949 automotive, AS 9100 Aerospace. There have also been significant sociological changes, with organisations placing much greater emphasis on employee involvement, on satisfying their customers and understanding on their customer needs. It is for this reason that additional information has been provided for reviewing and explaining various approaches that organisations have successfully employed. So why five editions? Well, put simply, the subject has evolved and will continue to do so.

Clearly the largest, most recent shift in QA thinking was ISO 9001. Many people have been predicting ISO 9001's demise but no obituaries have yet been written, in fact quite the reverse, it is expanding rapidly into many countries. ISO 9001 has its warts, as discussed in the section Limitations of the Management Systems approach but in spite of these problems it has consistently been retained by organisations. Cynics may say this is just because of fear - the effect on customers if ISO 9001 registration is lost. It is difficult to believe that hard nosed business people would retain the standard only for this reason. They retain the standard because it is of benefit (profit). As Abraham Lincoln said "*You can fool some of the people some of the time but you cannot fool all of the people all of the time*". So, as ISO 9001 has been around for fifteen years or so and has not been dropped, then the approach must have merit. So what is next, is there another ISO 9001 around the corner or some other major quality improvement technique? Well, just maybe - the focus on the customer and process improvement will continue to be key, although possibly achieved through much greater responsiveness as a result of the growth of the Internet.

---

[1] It may be argued that Integrated Management Systems (IMS) have no place in a book on Quality Assurance as they include issues (Health & Safety, Security, Environment, Training, etc.) which do not affect the quality performance of an organisation. However, possibly indirectly though these issues will at some stage affect quality, e.g. Training.

Nevertheless, it should be remembered that there are an enormous number of different approaches that can be adopted in achieving that elusive objective 'quality'. It is a never-ending quest with a whole variety of methods and techniques, some complementary, some conflicting (examination of the Quality Philosophy section will show that even influential individuals cannot agree as to what the correct approach is). The objective of this book is to give a rounded view of the various systems, techniques and approaches available, providing the opportunity to evaluate all these different approaches and to select the most suitable for a particular set of circumstances.

There can be no one solution or approach to achieving quality because it can never be completely achieved. There will always be new advances and improvements. A friend and colleague once said *"You know, this Quality Assurance thing's OK, but I'll give it a year or three and something else will come along!"* That statement was made some 30 years ago, which makes the statement approximately 28 years out, with time the statement will become even more inaccurate. There are representations of Egyptian masons measuring the sizes of blocks of stone to build the pyramids - so quality control (assurance) was undertaken in those days. With technology and the general public demanding ever higher quality and performance standards, then quality assurance will need to be in place. It may be in a different guise - process improvement etc. but nevertheless, will be just as essential today as it was in the past and will be in the future.

Quality Management (Principles & Practice) is part of the Quality Management series of books which includes; Introduction to Quality, Quality Management (Tools & Techniques) and Quality Management (Communication and Project Management). For clarity and continuity purposes, there is correctly some overlap between these titles. However, this book is expected to be a "stand alone" and comprehensive and practical reference to quality management.

The book has been split into nine basic sections[2]. Below is an outline of the contents of each section and what could reasonably expected to be appreciated having studied each section.

Management Strategy: This section is intended to provide sufficient information to:

N   understand the general introductory concepts associated with quality assurance,
N   be able to discuss the historical trend that quality assurance has followed and what the future direction could be,

---

[2]   Note: Where the suggestion "see section - ???" is made, the section can be located by reference to the contents list or index.

N   interpret key quality definitions and understand any jargon associated with Quality Assurance (QA),

N   understand the basic principles of quality management,

N   communicate 'quality' within the organisation and obtain feedback regarding acceptance and performance,

N   establish accountability and delegation of quality responsibilities,

N   describe what is meant by the learning organisation.

Total Quality Management: This section is intended to provide sufficient information to:

o   describe Total Quality Management (TQM),

o   understand the TQM approach and means of introduction and implementation and how it compares with the systems approach,

o   explain the concepts contained in BS 7850, the TQM standard and some techniques associated with TQM.

Quality Management Systems: This section is intended to provide sufficient information to:

o   understand Quality Management System (QMS) (specifically BS EN ISO 9000:2000), the systems or QMS model approach to QA and what QMSs are available and appropriate,

o   determine how these QMSs are interpreted, implemented and monitored (audited) in particular organisations (not only manufacturing organisations but service and software),

o   understand other QMS systems such as QS 9000 (the automotive standard),

o   explain what an the integrated management system approach is and how it involves other key areas of an organisation's business, e.g. Health & Safety, Security, Training, Environment etc.

Quality Audit: This section is intended to provide sufficient information to:

o   manage audit programmes,

o   know what qualification and skills auditors require,

o   perform an audit,

o   understand the contents of ISO 10011, the auditing standard.

Law: This section is intended to provide sufficient information to:

o   understand the rudiments of Criminal and Civil Law,

o   understand the contents and implication on the Quality Department and organisation of;

    •   the Consumer protection and other acts,

    •   EC Directives

    •   European Legislation

o describe procedures associated with product liability and product recall.

Customer Feedback: This section is intended to provide sufficient information to:
o describe schemes for identifying, measuring, monitoring, analysing and improving customer satisfaction,
o understand customer liaison and feedback systems, Stakeholder analysis,
o conduct national and international surveys of quality performance.

Management Philosophy: This section is intended to provide sufficient information to:
o motivate for quality,
o examine the quality philosophy and the various approaches suggested by influential individuals,
o discuss the views of the following Quality Philosophers; Crosby, Deming, Drucker, Feigenbaum, Ishikawa, Moller, Peters, Shingeo and Taguchi.
o understand the contents and relative merits of the following Quality Frameworks and Award schemes; European Foundation for Quality Award, Malcolm Baldridge Award, Deming Prize, Investors in People, Charter Marks and Kitemarks.

Computer Aided Quality: This section is intended to provide sufficient information to:
o understand Computer Aided Quality Assurance,
o understand how computers can be used in the quality environment and what the advantages and disadvantages are.

The book has been written with the intention of making the various techniques and approaches to quality assurance self explanatory. However, if the reader has any problems with the contents or has a quality problem or issue that they would like to discuss further, please do not hesitate to contact us. We can be contacted via the publishers, or email us on help@qmt.co.uk. We welcome the opportunity to discuss quality issues.

The book has been written by Geoff Vorley and Fred Tickle with contributions from Mary Brightman, Mary-Clare Bushell, John Lewis, Edda Saunders and Penny Simmons.

SECTION 1 - MANAGEMENT STRATEGY

Introduction to Quality Management

Traditional Quality Control

In the days when a craftsman saw the whole job through from start to finish, quality was synonymous with craftsmanship. The craftsman would see the job through from start to finish, being responsible for quality at every stage. With the advent of Taylorism, Fordism, Work Study and the division of labour, firstly between 'planners' and 'doers', and secondly between tasks themselves, de-skilling. This led, on the one hand, to a loss of personal involvement and a sense of pride in one's work and on the other a need for planning and coordination. This resulted in the formation of centralised inspection departments and quality being controlled by filtering out defective work during inspection stages. It was reactive and detection oriented. It also tended to suggest that quality problems were related to the manufacturing process, whereas studies on the origin of quality problems have shown that up to 60% of quality problems are design faults. If the traditional approach to controlling quality with the emphasis on monitoring a manufacturing or production process is employed, the best that can be achieved is to make the product perfectly wrong! Clearly there was a need to extend control of quality into other areas that could have an impact on the quality of the product or service.

Quality and Survival

Today, as never before, society is virtually totally dependent on technology and quality failures frequently have catastrophic consequences. Just take a look at **Figure 4**. Only 20% of our food is 'organic'. The balance of chemicals used in food production is extremely fine and we frequently hear of breakdowns in the system causing alarming outbreaks of food poisoning. Air traffic control depends totally on computers which can reach the point

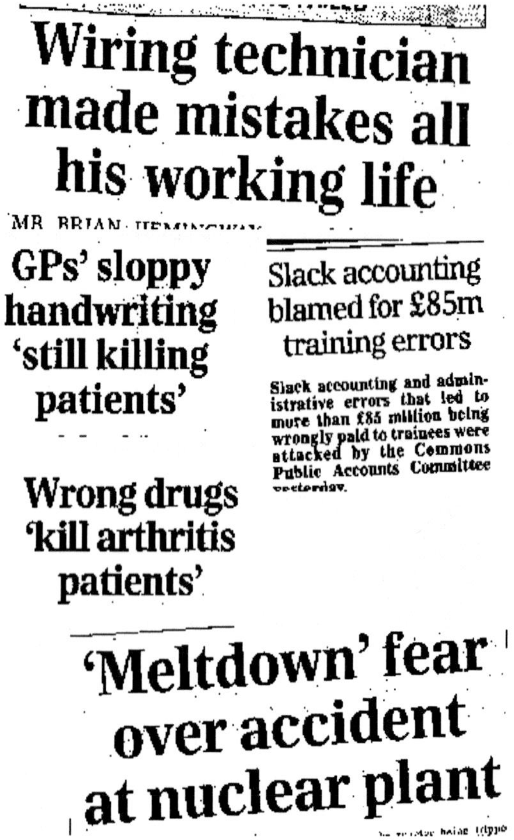

Wiring technician made mistakes all his working life

MR BRIAN HEMINGWAY

GPs' sloppy handwriting 'still killing patients'

Wrong drugs 'kill arthritis patients'

Slack accounting blamed for £85m training errors

Slack accounting and administrative errors that led to more than £85 million being wrongly paid to trainees were attacked by the Commons Public Accounts Committee vesterdav.

'Meltdown' fear over accident at nuclear plant

Figure 4 Some Quality & Survival Headlines

of overload. Currently 80% of the water authorities are failing to supply water which meets the required standards. Many treatments and cures for illnesses are totally dependent on technology. It is only in recent years that the long term damage to our environment has been realised. It can be seen from the above that it is not just the immediate customer or user who is at risk, we all are. More than at any other time in history we are relying on the correct and continuing operation of technological systems. How then do we ensure that everything that we design, make and service can be relied upon to operate every time it is required to do so?

Quality Sells

Why do people buy our products and services? Well, there are a number of reasons of which price is often the most significant and influential reason. However, there are other reasons which can sometimes be even more important; features, range of service, reliability, or quality. In order of importance, typically the sequence could be:

○   Price
○   Features of the product or range of services offered (possibly grade)
○   Reliability or Quality.

How could a supplier sell more?

Spend more on advertising? - It has been suggested that all advertising does is replace those customers who have been lost through poor quality of product or service.

Reduce the price?
Yes, get into a price-war - examination of the graph opposite in **Figure 5** suggests that this option is possible but there can be serious consequences. If you are company C then a price reduction is of advantage. This company can afford to reduce the market selling

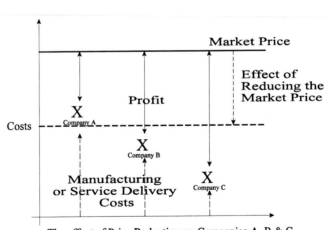

The effect of Price Reduction on Companies A, B & C

Figure 5 Price Reduction

price below the manufacturing or service delivery costs of its competitors, possibly making company A's position untenable. However, company A has problems. Its costs are too high to allow the company to embark on such a strategy. So much depends on the organisation's market position as to whether such a price war is appropriate.

Increase the range? Improve the grade of the product or service? Yes, improvement of the product or service will affect the marketability of the product. The competition will obviously be doing the same and what becomes a new or novel feature soon becomes what the customer naturally expects as standard. Also, these enhancements may merely move the product or service into a different market sector.

Improve the quality or reliability of the service? Reduce costs and improve the customers perception that this is a quality product or service. Advertising can improve the customers perception that this is a quality product but advertising is very expensive and is not always appropriate. Advertising, as stated previously, may only replace customers lost through poor quality. Consider this - it has been stated that if the customer's perception is that the product or service is of a better quality than the competitors, then the customer will pay up to 30% more for that product or service. Would you pay 30% more for a better quality product or service? Think about some recent purchases - coffee, stereo, garage services - and consider if you would have paid more.

All these issues need to be considered when attempting to grow and develop a business, and determining a strategy for price, advertising, grade of service, etc. is essential. One element of this strategy is where to place the greater emphasis. Which strategy requires the greater effort? Which will provide the best return on investment? More advertising, a price-war or a quality improvement initiative?

Quality Management

The complexities in technology and integration of designs have made total quality control by inspection alone unsuitable. Inspection can only determine the quality of an item in the as-made condition. To ensure reliability, which is the time-dependent dimension of quality, it is necessary to build-in quality at every stage. In recent years a new approach towards achieving quality and reliability has been evolving known as the systems approach to quality management. Since every stage of the product or service cycle is a potential source of failure we need to consider just what could go wrong at each stage. Quality is the degree to which this is successfully achieved for each of the above factors. It follows therefore, that quality achievement must be planned. This implies the examination of each stage of the process and careful consideration of the potential deviations and the methods and techniques necessary to prevent the occurrence of defective work. Quality management is proactive rather than reactive.

At this juncture it may be worth introducing the concept of *"Technical Debt"*. What is meant by this phrase? The *debt* refers to issues or possible problems, that are left over for other groups, departments or people to resolve downstream in the process or project. These issues maybe knowingly ignored e.g "we'll sort that out at the testing stage" or unknowingly ignored e.g left to the service deliverer to resolve. Another example could be unclear service contract terms making the service deliverables unspecific, "where is that requirement detailed in the terms of reference, quotation or order?" Nevertheless all these scenarios will contribute to the final Technical Debt of a project or process. Technical Debts can be debts left by the Sales Department of the nature "that's too much detail to be determined at the quotation stage, that will need to be resolved during design". They can be *debts* that may be left at the design stage "The Service or Support Departments will be able to modify or manipulate that, during installation phase". These are not necessarily mistakes or oversights, they are conscious decisions that have been made at specific stages in the project or process (possibly due to time or resource pressure) but nevertheless have not been communicated, agreed or thought through. The consequence of these issues, if allowed to accumulate throughout the process or life of the project, can be catastrophic for the final stages (particularly for those people attempting to manage these latter stages). Is it necessary to monitor this Technical Debt? If it is to be monitored how can Technical Debt be recorded, measured, agreed, controlled and resolved? Does quality management hold any answers to these questions? The sections in this book on quality management systems and customer satisfaction discuss means for controlling Technical Debt.

Quality Standards

Since the 1970s and '80s, standards and specifications have been emerging to provide either guides or even contractual requirements for quality systems.

In particular, the Ministry of Defence can require contractors to install and maintain quality systems in accordance with the Allied Quality Assurance Publications (AQAP 05-90 Series), depending on the content of the contract (see section on quality management system standards). ISO 9000 provides a similar set of specifications for industry in general. For each of the above there is provision for independent assessment to monitor compliance with the respective standards.

Management Strategy

System Review and Evaluation

Since the emphasis of quality management is that a properly designed and maintained system will result in the design and manufacture of quality products, it is essential that a regular programme of system checks is carried out. The actual observation and collection of facts about the operation of the system procedures is called a quality audit. The findings of such audits are reported to senior management for consideration and corrective action where necessary.

Quality Motivation

In spite of all the above attempts to organise for quality management in a systematic way, if an employee's attitude is wrong then efforts on coordinating the systems will have only limited success. Fostering a responsible attitude by everyone towards doing "it right first time" is the most effective means there is of assuring quality. For this reason many organisations have been looking for a number of years at various ways of motivating and involving employees in the quality of their work. There are numerous approaches that can be employed: Philip C. Crosby - Zero Defects; W. Edwards Deming - 14 Points; A. V. Feigenbaum - Total Quality Control; K. Ishikawa - Quality Circles and Joseph M. Juran - Breakthrough and Control.

The above approaches have been employed with varying degrees of success, depending on a number of factors, not least of which are the culture, systems and structure of the organisation.

Total Quality Management

Total Quality Management is the synthesis of the organisational, technical and cultural elements of a company. It is a "hearts and minds" philosophy which recognises that company culture (customs and practice) affects behaviour which in turn affects quality. It is not merely the performance of the product with regard to conformance to specification, reliability or even customer satisfaction, but the performance of every activity in the organisation. To this end every subsystem or function in the organisation is seen to have internal customers and suppliers as well as external customers and suppliers. Take the Purchasing Department. Who are the Purchasing Department's customers? Who are the Purchasing Department's suppliers? Well, its customers may include the production or process units who need raw materials and equipment supplied to specification, on time and to a price. In this sense the Purchasing Department is the supplier to the production or processing units. The suppliers to the Purchasing Department might be the outside suppliers or contractors who provide the material and services; the Goods Receiving Department with information regarding quality and on time delivery; the process units with information regarding quality and conformance to specification; the Training Department which supplies training services and facilities; the Computer Department which supplies computing facilities for planning and scheduling. Thus, the organisation becomes a chain or network of suppliers and customers. The principle underlying this approach is that every function or department is required to identify its immediate customers and is accountable for identifying the needs of those customers and ensuring the quality of service required by them. This in turn means that the function or department must ensure that its suppliers understand what is required and provide it.

From the above it follows that every function or department must operate its own quality management system and employ appropriate quality control techniques. In some departments this may mean the application of various techniques such as Statistical Quality Control, in others it may be Failure Mode and Effects Analysis or Cause and Effect Diagrams to solve problems. In other words, Total Quality Management embraces all known techniques and methodologies to create a management climate that encourages and inspires every member of the organisation to have conscientious commitment to quality.

Quality Definitions

In common with many management subjects, quality management has its own jargon. To assist in understanding some of the jargon this section has been provided to expand and explain some of the quality terminology. ISO 9000:2000 provides the following definition.

Quality: degree to which a set of inherent characteristics fulfil requirements - in simple terms this means 'fitness for purpose' or 'to satisfy a given need'. Requirements cover more than mere function. Even if aesthetics is included in function there are many other factors to be considered. For example, the method of distribution, initial and running costs, user awareness or knowledge, and other possible uses including reasonable misuse. Requirements also include implied and explicit needs such as legislative demand.

N   Quality is an approach not a programme or series of events
N   Quality is a accumulation of successful concepts, practices and techniques which can be applied at all levels in any organisation
N   Quality is not just for manufacturing. It is applicable across all other industries; health, financial institutions, government organisations, teaching establishments and social services
N   Quality is defined by the customer through their demonstrated satisfaction with the product or service
N   Quality is aimed at organisational excellence, anything less is a missed opportunity
N   Quality management effectively implemented improves business results in all areas; customer, people, society and financial
N   Quality embraces never ending improvement in performance
N   Quality improves customer satisfaction, reduces process time and costs, and eradicates mistakes and consequential rectification.

Grade: category or rank given to different quality requirements for products, processes or systems having the same functional use. The standard or specification that the product or service must achieve.

Quality v Grade: Table 1 opposite describes the difference between quality and grade. Both high grade (gold) or low grade (plastic) pens can be of high quality, if they meet the customer's expectations. Equally the pens can be low quality if they fail to meet the required customer's standard. Another example of the misunderstanding of the difference between quality and

Table 1 Quality v Grade

Grade	Quality	
	Good	Bad
High Grade	Gold pen that works perfectly	Gold pen that is unreliable
Low Grade	Ordinary plastic pen that writes smoothly	Ordinary plastic pen that doesn't write smoothly

grade is, a carpenter once said, "This quality thing is all well and good but I perform work on Board Rooms finished with oak panelling. I also fit out shops - down to a price - possibly using plastic fixtures and fittings. Now if quality means that the board room finish has to be put into shop fitting then that will put me out of business. No one will be able to afford my work". Here the carpenter confused quality and grade, although the board room is a high grade job, both jobs need to achieve the correct quality, be finished on time and at the agreed price.

Quality Assurance: *part of quality management that focussed on providing confidence that quality requirements will be fulfilled.* In other words, all those planned and systematic actions necessary to provide adequate confidence that a product or service will satisfy given requirements for quality.

Inspection: *conformity evaluation by observation and judgement accompanied, as appropriate, by measurement, testing or gauging.*

Specification: *document stating requirements.*

Quality Control: *part of quality management focussed on fulfilling quality requirements.* In other words, quality control is the regulation of individual activities that are performed to ensure the process performs reliably and consistently for quality. This control is not confined to manufacturing processes but extends to design processes, service processes, etc. In fact, any process that can affect the quality of the supplied product or service.

Figure 6 describes *a typical process* listing the activities from customer requirements, through product design and development, purchase of materials and process control, to delivery and subsequent service support.

The left-hand side of **Figure 6** indicates *some of the quality control methods* that would be appropriate for regulating each stage. For example, in the product development stage, the quality control methodology could include implementation of specification control, product design, product development, failure mode and effects analysis, design review and other quality control methods such as design validation and verification. Note that there is a series of dots under each suggested quality control method. The dots are to indicate that the list is not complete; there are numerous other quality control methods that can be employed. In fact, the action of designing the quality management system requires review and determination of which the multitude of quality control methods are appropriate for each process stage.

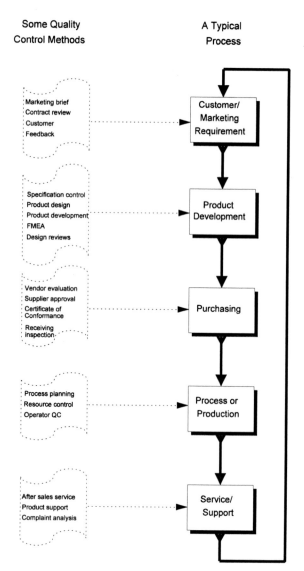

Figure 6 Quality Controlling a Process

Figure 6 does not show the other support activities that go to make up the complete quality management system - activities such as training, audit, feedback and control, data collection, etc.

How the appropriate quality controls could be determined and implemented needs to be established, i.e:

a) Determine the quality objectives for each process stage, e.g. one of the aims may be to ensure that the customer's requirements are completely understood by the completion of a marketing brief and contract review.

b) Institute a programme and plan to achieve the objectives, e.g. for a marketing brief and contract review to be completed, a planned and programmed introduction of how to complete a marketing brief and contract review will be necessary (training, procedures etc.).

c) Establish the quality control systems for each stage in the process, e.g. for the marketing brief and contract review - checks will be necessary on the completeness and accuracy of the brief and review.

d) Review and evaluate the implementation of the applied quality controls, e.g. for the marketing brief and contract review an audit will be necessary to confirm that the documents are being produced as per the procedures.

Rectification - Action taken to resolve a non-conformance, possibly bringing back within specification. See section - Interpretation of individual ISO 9001 requirements, specifically non-conforming material.

Corrective Action - Action taken to avoid the need for rectification happening again. See sections on Quality Improvement Initiatives & Techniques, specifically Problem Solving, Pareto Analysis and Cause and Effect Diagrams.

Preventive Action - Action taken to avoid the need for rectification or corrective action. Action taken to stop the problem happening in the first place. See Failure Mode Effects Analysis, Risk Analysis and Quality Planning.

Quality Plan - Enables the identification of preventive activities to provide early warning of any possible problems occurring or of them becoming major ones. Quality planning is used to anticipate any possible project or product risk areas so that the appropriate action can be taken to eliminate or mitigate any such difficulties. A quality plan differs from a quality manual and quality programme. A quality manual is project or product independent and a quality programme which usually describes the implementation of the quality system.

Listed below are some useful International and British Standards. Note, standards change and these were correct at the time of going to press.

Standard	Title & Remarks
ISO 9000	Quality management systems - Fundamentals and vocabulary. *Provides an introduction to the ISO 9000 family of standards and defines the fundamental terms and definitions.*
ISO 9000-3	Quality management and quality assurance standards - Part 3: Guidelines for the application of ISO 9001:1994 to the development, supply, installation and maintenance of computer software
ISO 9000-4	Quality management and quality assurance standards - Part 4: Guide to dependability programme management
ISO 9001 3rd party cert	Quality management systems - Requirements. *A model for quality management system. This is the requirement standard and used for third-party certification.*
ISO 9004	Quality management systems - Guidelines for performance improvements. *This guideline provides guidance for continual improvement of the quality management system.*
ISO 9004-4	Quality management and quality system elements - Part 4: Guidelines for quality improvement
ISO 10005	Quality management - Guidelines for quality plans. *Provides guidelines to assist in the creation, review, approval and revision of quality plans.*
ISO 10006	Quality management - Guidelines to quality in project management. *Guidelines to assist in the creation of project plans and controlling projects for quality. See Section Project Quality Assurance.*
ISO 10007	Quality management - Guidelines for configuration management. *Configuration management (more than change control) - controls all aspects of change including; drawings, processes, service, stock, purchasing, etc.*
ISO 10011 BS EN 30011	Quality systems auditing. *See also ISO 19011, Guidelines on Quality and/or Environmental Management Systems Auditing which is under development.*
ISO 10012-1 BS EN30012-1	Quality assurance requirements for measuring equipment. *Calibration systems*
ISO 10013	Guidelines for developing quality manuals. *Provides guidelines for creating, maintaining and customising of quality manuals to meet the specific needs of an organisation.*

Quality Management (Principles & Practice)

Standard	Title & Remarks
ISO 10015	Quality management - Guidelines for training
ISO/TS 16949	Quality systems - Automotive suppliers. *Sector specific guidance to the application of ISO 9001:1994 in the automotive industry.*
BS 4778	Quality vocabulary. Quality concepts and related definitions.
BS 5750-8:1991, EN 29004-2:1993	Quality systems. Guide to quality management and quality systems elements for services. *Note this is QMS applied to service e.g. Banks, Hotels, etc) organisations*
BS 5760	Reliability of constructed or manufactured products, systems, equipment and components
BS 6079	Guide to Project management. *Covering issues such as project; organisation, planning, budgeting and risk assessment. Useful for quality programmes, project auditing and quality assuring projects. See section Project Quality Assurance.*
BS 6143	Guide to the economics of quality. *Cost of quality, using the Process cost and Prevention, appraisal and failure model. See ISO/TR 10014:1998, Guidelines for managing the economics of quality and Section Cost of Quality*
BS 7373	Specification - guide to the preparation of specifications
BS 7850	Total quality management. *Guide to total quality management principles and improvement.*
PD 6584	Model for a supplier quality assurance assessment questionnaire. *Not strictly speaking a standard (PD - Published Document) See section Supplier Quality Assurance*

The Learning Organisation

Introduction

The role of the quality manager is changing rapidly. The idea that they are the person or department that solves all quality problems is slowly being changed. Their role is becoming coach and mentor, facilitating teams of problem solvers and resolvers. My old quality supervisor used to describe it as the "Maltese breast stroke". The normal breast stroke sucks in the quality problem, e.g. customer complaint and considers it the responsibility of the quality department to resolve. The person who caused the complaint learns nothing. With my quality supervisor's "Maltese breast stroke" approach, the actions are reversed and problems are dispersed (or pushed) to the appropriate person to handle. The person responsible resolves the problems and learns from their mistakes. However, when taking this approach not only must the responsibilities and processes be accepted and agreed but also the people dealing with the issues and problems must possess the necessary skills. The quality department itself is not outside of this training loop. Their personal development in the quality assurance field needs to be considered, so that they are conversant with, skilled in and can apply the very latest quality management tools and techniques.

ISO 9001:2000 also gives great opportunity and scope for this approach with its emphasis on human resources and training. The table opposite (which is an extract from ISO 9001:2000 requirements for Human resources) shows an excellent checklist which could be used to judge an organisation's commitment to learning.

Realisation of the Learning Organisation

The learning organisations are those that have established systems, mechanisms and processes that are used to enhance

Table 2 Human Resources ISO 9001:2000

Provision of resources	
i)	Implement, maintain and improve the quality management system
ii)	Enhance customer satisfaction
Human resources - Competence, awareness and training	
i)	Determine the necessary competence of personnel
ii)	Provide training
iii)	Evaluate the effectiveness
iv)	Ensure that its personnel are aware of the relevance and importance of their activities and the contribution of the quality objectives.
v)	Maintain appropriate records of education, training, skills and experience

their capabilities and those that work for it. This is to enable the achievement of sustainable objectives not only for themselves but also for their customers and the community in which they operate. Learning organisations can be categorised by their ability to:

i) adapt to their external environment,
ii) continually evolve and enhance their capabilities,
iii) develop group as well individual learning,
iv) apply the results of learning to the achievement of better results.

A learning organisation is not just about "training and education" although training is necessary to develop certain skills. The learning organisation is where a clear commitment is given to the development of higher levels of knowledge. An example of this can be seen in the four modules outlined in the table opposite.

Single loop learning is learning from your mistakes. A feedback loop is where a group of people may review the results from actions they have taken. This may be a as simple as teaching someone a task. Observe and complete the tasks, then

Table 3 Four Level Training Module

Level	Description
1	Learning facts, knowledge, tasks, etc. Single loop learning, which is applicable to understanding departmental processes and procedures.
2	Learning a new set of transferable job skills. Applicable where a completely new set of skills are required
3	Learning to adapt to new situations and threats. Double loop learning, which is partly feedback loop learning about the consequences of actions but also questioning the underlining strategy to achieve certain goals.
4	Learning to learn (regenerative learning). Applicable where organisations need to innovative and creative. Reinventing the organisations direction.

review any mistakes and update their skills accordingly. Obviously introducing some form of testing would avoid errors. In single loop learning we have discovered which certain variable, if changed, will have an effect on results. Consequently, we have learnt to monitor these variables and if an error occurs we know what action to take. This is fine until the underling variables no longer have the same influence. In this case, it is necessary to question the validity of the variables and their ability to control results, i.e. questioning the underling strategy.

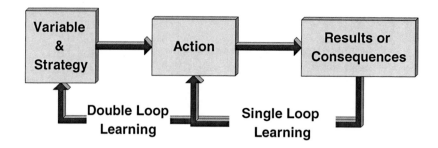

Figure 7 Double & Single Loop Learning

What does this mean in practice? Well, the Quality Manager may feel that the people within the organisation are incapable of solving quality problems or determining a course of action to find a rational solution. The Quality Manager confirms this theory by setting quality objectives that the group fails to achieve - Single Loop Learning or possibly, in this case, 'self fulfilling prophecy'. Consequently, the only sensible approach is for the Quality Manager to take on responsibility for problem solving. Double Loop Learning requires questioning this underlying thinking and experimentating with this situation to determine if it is possible to disconfirm or disprove the Quality Manager's original thinking.

E-Learning Role in the Learning Organisation

E-learning is Internet or Intranet enabled learning. This type of learning can be delivered in multiple formats such as Multimedia, video, etc. The objective being to provide a classroom environment at everyone's desk. This enables the management of the learning experience through the use of quizzes and multiple-choice type questions and online marking. Subsequently, determining and confirming the competence level achieved. In this way a networked community of learners and experts is developed.

> *"There are two fundamental equalisers in life – the Internet and Education. E-learning eliminates the barriers of time and distance creating universal learning on demand for people and countries"* – John Cambers President and CEO Cisco Systems

E-learning is important for a number of reasons. Technology and approaches change rapidly in the quality assurance field and for this reason it is important that the very latest quality management tools and techniques are understood and applied. Traditional training methods often have barriers of time, distance and socio-economic status. E-learning can go some way to eliminating some, if not all, of these barriers. E-learning also provides the opportunity for the individual to take charge of their own lifelong quality assurance learning.

There are huge benefits to be gained for both the organisation and the individual. For the business there is great productivity in terms of training delivery and reduced costs of training. Competence evaluation of the trained individual becomes almost automatic with the regular use of questions which confirm the ability and level of understanding of the delegate. Similarly, evaluation of the various delegates results can show the effectiveness of the training material to deliver the required information. Offering e-learning opportunities (particularly those which lead to a recognised qualification) can enhance employee loyalty, allowing them to enter into an employment-long learning experience. The organisation also has the opportunity to explain information clearly specifically for rapid adoption of new information and new programmes.

Below are three examples of e-learning applications which organisations have developed for their particular needs:
i) Technical Support Process: The e-learning modules explain the process and test the delegates ability to deal with and handle typical customer queries.
ii) Testers: The e-learning module explains the process, expected standards and associated accept and reject criteria. The module can then be used to examine the Testers ability to make sound judgements for a predetermined set of case studies.
iii) Management System awareness: All too often it is assumed that because the procedures are written down everyone will automatically know where to find the procedures and what they describe. The truth is often very different. E-learning modules guide the delegate through the scope and structure of the Management System and then test the ability to find information and understand processes and procedures.

There are, however, a number of challenges associated with e-learning. The generation of the material is extremely resource hungry as it is not just a matter of "putting a few slides together". Also tests have to be created - possibly of the type, true/false, multiple-choice, fill in the blank, etc. The students themselves need access to a computer, be computer (browser) literate and have keyboard skills. The student does not receive the "classroom experience" where free exchange of ideas and experiences can reinforce learning and aid competition.

SECTION 2 - TOTAL QUALITY MANAGEMENT

TOTAL QUALITY MANAGEMENT & QUALITY IMPROVEMENT INITIATIVES

"There is nothing more difficult to carry out, nor more doubtful of success, nor more dangerous to handle, than to initiate a new order of things. For the reformer has enemies in all who profit by the old order, and only lukewarm defenders in all those who would profit by the new order. This lukewarmness arises partly from fear of their adversaries, who have the law in their favour; and partly from the incredulity of mankind, who do not truly believe in anything new until they have had actual experience of it."

Machiavelli in 'The Prince' (1513)

Introduction

There are possibly as many definitions and approaches to improving quality performance as there are Quality Assurance Consultants. Some may argue that it is ISO 9001. This standard still has, however, several omissions, namely: economics of quality, motivation for quality, quality in marketing, product safety and product liability.

So can ISO 9001 be used as a quality improvement tool? Well possibly but total quality management is more of a motivational approach than a Quality Management System standard. Total Quality Management (TQM) and Quality Improvement Initiatives (QII) are aimed at motivating personnel for quality rather than giving guidance for the shape of a Quality Management System.

So what is Total Quality Management? Well, it is more of an objective or goal rather than a set of requirements, (as with ISO 9000) although both ISO 9000 and any quality initiative necessitate a structured approach to implementation.

Total Quality Management (TQM) does not happen by chance. It requires careful organisation, planning and programming. The TQM objective being the never-ending improvement of the quality performance of the whole organisation. Not just in the sense of the performance of its products (reliability, its ability to meet specifications and to satisfy the customer etc.) but the performance of every process and every person within the total organisation.

TQM achieves the objective of never-ending improvement by embracing:

"   Company-wide improvement by concerned and motivated personnel who are involved and participating in the application of Quality Improvement.

25

"   Concentrated effort in achieving customer satisfaction (both internal and external customers), by showing to all personnel that they can actively help in providing a better quality service.

"   Quality performance measures which will provide personnel with the means of assessing current performance and making a commitment to possible future performance targets or objectives.

Thus, TQM enables never-ending improvements in every facet of the company's activities; improving productivity, increasing employee participation, reducing costs and providing complete customer satisfaction at lower cost. Consequently TQM can provide a distinguished company image and a dedicated management and work force.

TQM is about fostering a state of mind for the employee that says, we cannot afford to stand still, we must make continuous efforts to make improvements, to make work more interesting and rewarding. Not necessarily with monetary rewards but making the quality of the working life more exciting. With economic pressures to be ever more efficient, the tendency is towards flatter organisational structures, fewer layers of management and less specialisation. The consequence of these new organisational arrangements will be that the normally expected promotional route, up through the management structure, will no longer be available. There will be a need to provide another outlet for the creative talent other than by providing promotion. There is a wealth of knowledge and talent available in an organisation. TQM is about providing the environment that allows that talent to develop and grow, harnessing that talent in a positive way and so improving the performance of the individual, team and organisation. When employees come to work, they do not hang up their intellect with their hat and coat on the way into work. TQM is about making positive use of that intellect.

There is a need to embrace change. Change to make improvements, making the processes more effective and efficient. Often people have a fear of change and improvement: fear that they will lose their job; fear of making or suggesting improvements because they will be seen as helping management or being too clever for their own good; fear of failure - failure to achieve the promised improvements. See Machiavelli in 'The Prince'.

There are three interlinked and overlapping elements that need to be considered and addressed in any Quality Improvement programme namely; Systems, Structure and Culture. Each of these elements cannot be dealt with in isolation, each element needs analysis and a strategy found., identified and implemented.

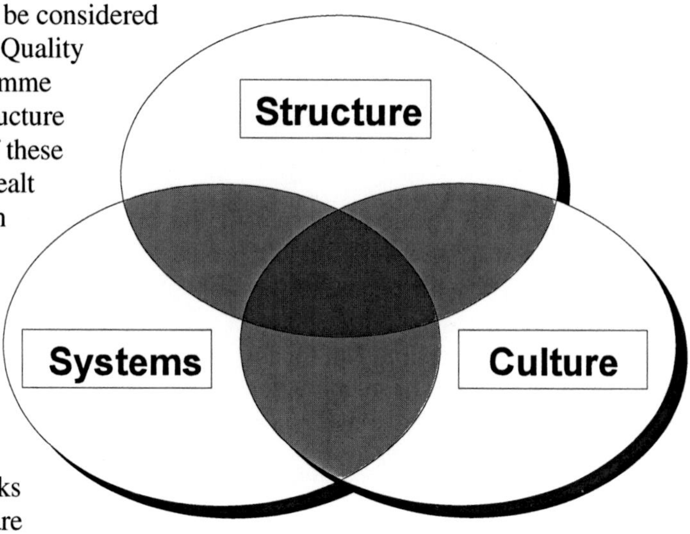

Figure 8 Structure, Systems & Culture

Systems: The way in which the various tasks within the company are organised, the manufacturing sequence or the way documentation flows around an organisation. Systems - the procedures that are followed to accomplish various tasks. There is often a concern when discussing process improvement - 'that means that we, the employees, need to work harder' - no, this is exactly what is not required, what is needed is for the employee to *Work Smarter not Harder.*

There are two erroneous comments that are often heard concerning Quality Assurance namely:

a.   "If you want the quality, you cannot have the quantity" - This is no longer true (if it ever was in the first place!). Achieving productivity improvements requires actively understanding and improving the process, eliminating waste and inefficiency. In this way the process quantity or output is improved and the quality element improvement is provided free.

b.   "If you want the project finished on time then you must provide more resources" - this is no longer valid. Studies comparing the ability to design and develop motor vehicles have shown that project teams 50% smaller than the norm have halved the motor vehicle's production time. The resultant motor vehicle was also more reliable and cheaper as well. Other studies into curable diseases have shown that diagnosing and curing diseases is not to do with money spent on the

> health service or social deprivation (although these can be factors) it is to do with the systems or the way in which the illness is identified and remedied.

It is necessary to closely evaluate all the organisation's systems and processes to ensure they are effective, efficient and adding value etc. (See Cost of Quality)

Structure: The formal relationships within the organisation - communication and reporting. The balance between grouping people with regard to their specialism rather than grouping people with regard to the tasks or process. For example, the usual approach may be to group all the buyers together and all the engineers together according to their specialism. The Quality Improvement approach may be to group people within a process or manufacturing cell which includes multi-disciplined personnel (e.g. combined buyer and engineer).

To some extent ISO 9000 describes the way organisations need to be *structured* and influences the *systems* employed. However, ISO 9000 may not be the most appropriate route for all organisations - it may hamper free thinking or a creative approach. There may be major advantages in the company assuming the responsibility for finding their own approach to Quality Improvement, (ownership of the problem). Consequently, TQM needs to involve all levels in the organisation, providing the catalyst to debate the issues and determine the most appropriate approach, which will affect the culture of the organisation.

The final element is often considered the most important.

Culture: The company policy and objectives: the management style (authoritarian or democratic); the employees' attitudes (negative against change or positive and receptive to new ideas and approaches); the employees' motivation for quality, change and improvement.

An example of the usual response to company policy may be - *"The company's prime objective is to make a profit."* The Quality Improvement response may be *"The company's prime objective is to satisfy its customers, everything else happens as a consequence of satisfying the customer."* The Management style may be *"I run a tight ship; there are few improvements that I can make to the tasks I control."* Quality Improvement style may be *"Employee involvement is essential if continual process and task improvements are to be made."* *"The employee must be actively encouraged to make improvements and entrusted with the power to make changes."* Employee attitude could be *"I can have no effect on the quality performance of the company because I work in the administration department, it's the people on the shop floor that influence quality. It is the responsibility of the quality department to control quality."* The

Quality Improvement approach is *"Quality is everyone's business, we all have customers who depend upon us and need to be satisfied, and we all have suppliers who must understand our needs and requirements."*

Since there are many definitions and views on Quality Improvement there are consequently numerous approaches to implementation. The more commonly recognised ones are listed below. This list is not exhaustive. The list includes a brief overview of each approach. More information regarding application and implementation of each of these approaches can be found by making reference in this book to the sections indicated at the end of each paragraph.

So the structure of this Quality Improvement section is as explained - firstly a list and overview of the most commonly recognised approaches. Next, each of these overviews are broadened out giving more detail in terms of: an introduction to the approach, how to motivate or sell the idea - benefits and how to implement or affect each approach. Note: This overview is not in any specific order.

Overview List of Approaches to Quality Improvement

a. Quality Improvement Profiles
    Evaluation of the company against some profile or example of what is considered good practice may identify short falls or gaps in the quality improvement initiative. It may also help point direction or strategy with regard to quality performance improvement and training needs. There are many such profiles, Crosby's Maturity Grid was an early example of such a profile. Today they can be much more sophisticated with profiles such as the European Foundation for Quality Management model which will be discussed later. See section on Quality Improvement Profile.

b. Customer Focus   Q F D .
    This approach has been mainly applied in the service sector (Banks, Hospitals, Hotels etc.) although interest has been shown in the manufacturing sectors. Typically the approach is characterised by slogans such as *"Delighting the Customer"*, *"Voice of the Customer"*, *"Customer Driven Quality"*. It is intended to focus attention on the external customer and improve the quality of service provided. This is achieved mainly by understanding the customer's needs and problems. Having established the customer's needs then comparing and contrasting company performance in meeting these customer needs both within the company and with the company's competitors. The techniques associated with this approach can be found by reference to the following sections of this book. Quality Function

Deployment (QFD), Customer Satisfaction Surveys, Hard & Software Standards (or Benchmarking), Product Enhancement.

c. Internal Customers
    Whereas Customer Focus deals with the external customer, there are also internal customers of our services. Internal Customers - the persons or departments within the organisation who are the consumers of our product. We need to ensure that our internal customer is completely satisfied with our level of service just as much as if they were an external customer. This approach is often characterised by the phrase *"The Internal Market"*. Approaches such as Departmental Purpose Analysis are used to evaluate departmental role and performance. See section on Departmental Purpose Analysis.

d. Economics of Quality
    "There's gold in the mine" - suggesting that rather than go out and win new business or obtain more orders, perhaps there's money to be made (saved) by looking inside the organisation. Techniques such as the Prevention, Appraisal and Failure model or the Process Cost model are methods by which the cost of quality for organisations or processes can be established and hopefully reduced. See section on Cost of Quality.

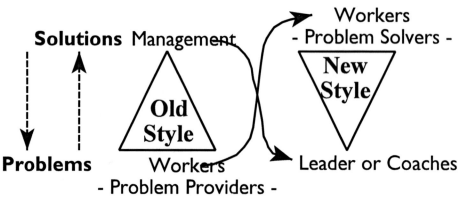

Figure 9 Management Style

e. Problem Solving - Team Approach
    This is possibly one of the more popular approaches to Quality Improvement, which embraces the idea of using teams to analyse and solve quality related problems. These team approaches are typified by the use of Quality Circles or Kaizen Teams. The concept is for small gradual change rather than

attempting step changes in performance. Step changes in performance are very difficult to manage and achieve. Things are much better achieved by small, gradual and continuous improvement. Quality Circles are teams of people who do similar work, learning to identify, analyse and resolve work-related problems. Kaizen Teams or Improvement Teams are multi-discipline teams whose role is to generate and implement schemes to improve quality and productivity. These techniques (Quality Circles & Kaizen Teams) do require a different style and thinking from management. As **Figure 9** shows, the old management style was for the workers to pass problems up to management and for management to pass the solutions down. This meant that decisions regarding problem solution were made at the furthest point from the source of the problem. Often without full knowledge and participation of those people who would have to implement the management suggested solutions. Quality Circles & Kaizen Teams turns this approach on its head. Now management suggests the problems[3] and has a team of problem solvers working for them. Managers, as leaders or coaches, supporting and understanding the needs of the teams in problem solving. Managers, being part of the solution not the problem. See section on Quality Circles.

f.   Quality Award Schemes
British Quality Foundation (BQF)(UK), European Foundation for Quality Management (EFQM) (Europe), Malcolm Baldrige (USA), Deming Award (Japan).

There are certain similarities in these award schemes and Quality Improvement profiles. Where Quality Improvement profiles may be self generated, self assessment, the award schemes (e.g. EFQM) listed here are nationally and sometimes internationally accepted profiles or models which organisations can use for self assessment. Possibly some organisations may choose to take the scheme further and enter a competition for the award. The primary purpose of these award schemes is as a means of self assessing or benchmarking organisations against some concept of good practice. These schemes are considered to be *a concept of good practice* as these models have become generally both nationally and internationally well accepted. Other models of good practice can be ISO 9000 but this standard, as explained previously, has certain limitations. It is these limitations which the award schemes have attempted to address.

---

3   Although Quality Circle Teams generally chose their own problems or agenda.

g. Business Process Analysis
    Organisations are full of processes but unfortunately organisations are not
    always structured to optimise these processes. Organisations are often
    structured on the basis of functional (specialised) departments. This can lead
    to process inefficiency, unclear responsibilities and lack of focus. One way
    to evaluate organisations with a view to optimising key processes is to use the
    business process analysis techniques. This involves structuring the
    organisation along process rather than functional lines. Making the process
    key rather than the departmental functions. This approach has led to dramatic
    savings in process, lead and running times and costs. Even to the extent that
    some quality philosophers see this as the next major breakthrough in quality
    performance levels.

Each of the above approaches to Quality Improvement has now been enlarged giving
additional information and detail.

Total Quality Management BS7850

Total Quality Management Profiles

The following is a typical approach to the application of Total Quality Management (see **Figure 10**). The numbers in brackets refer to the appropriate BS7850 requirement.

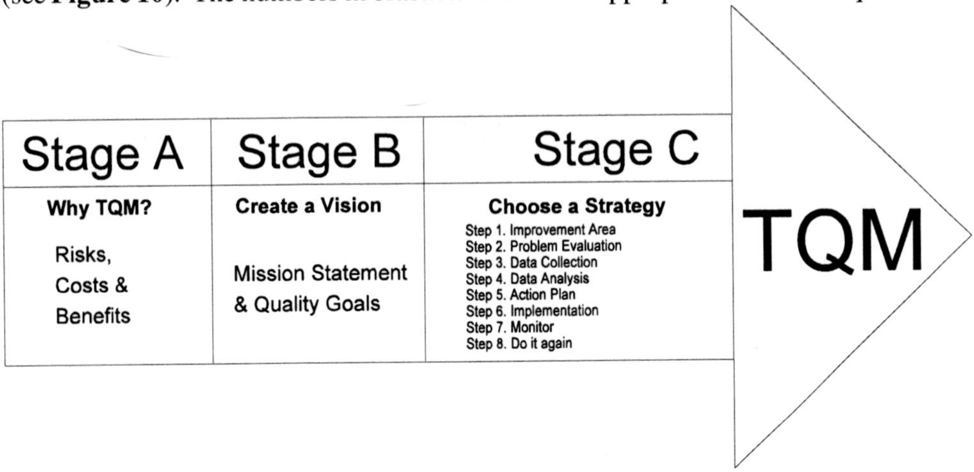

Stage A	Stage B	Stage C	TQM
Why TQM? Risks, Costs & Benefits	**Create a Vision** Mission Statement & Quality Goals	**Choose a Strategy** Step 1. Improvement Area Step 2. Problem Evaluation Step 3. Data Collection Step 4. Data Analysis Step 5. Action Plan Step 6. Implementation Step 7. Monitor Step 8. Do it again	

Figure 10 An Approach to Quality Improvement

STAGE A   *Why Quality Improvement?*

In this stage it is necessary to explain and introduce Quality Assurance. This includes background material regarding what is; quality assurance, quality control and some of the modern quality assurance philosophies as described by Deming, Feigenbaum, Crosby and Juran. (Much of the above has already been covered in the introduction and previous sections of this book.) This information could be drawn together in a presentation detailing such issues as Cost of Quality, Cost of conformance and non-conformance and audits that may have identified Quality Losses. The risks, costs and benefits to be gained from a Quality Improvement programme. (BS 7850 5.1 General & 5.2 Creating appropriate organisational structure).

STAGE B   *The organisation's vision for the future.*

During this stage it is necessary to explain the concepts embodied in Total Quality Management and to gain commitment from top management to embark on a Quality Improvement programme. If the top management are not able to provide total commitment to the Quality Improvement programme then don't start. *If anything less than total management commitment is obtained then the Quality*

Improvement programme will fail. This requires an understanding of the structure, the systems and the cultural needs of the organisation. To assist in determining these needs the Quality Improvement profile can be employed. (See Quality Improvement Profile section). The Senior Management team also needs to be clear regarding what the organisation's goals and objectives are - a clear understanding of the key issues facing the organisation. The organisation's goals can be outlined in a Quality Goals and Mission Statement. In order for the Total Quality Management Teams to have a clear understanding of what is intended to be achieved, a defined and agreed statement is required from Senior Management indicating positively what the Quality Goals are. Establishing these Quality Goals is usually agreed at a meeting of the Management Team. As stated previously, in establishing the Quality Goals, the Quality Improvement profile can be used to help determine the key areas of concern. Once defined and agreed, the statement should be communicated to all employees. Some examples of possible Quality Goals and Mission Statement could be:

Improve on time delivery to 95%	Currently running at 80% on time delivery
Improve response and lead time by 30%	In all areas: Engineering products into production. Purchasing in placement and delivery of orders. Administration in processing documentation.
Clean work place policy	In offices as well as work shops
Improve reject performance by 30%	In all areas: Engineering - number of drawing change notes. Purchasing - number of supplier rejects.

The organisation's wide strategic quality goals will require translation into departmental or sectional goals, i.e. how can each department contribute to these total company goals? What are the implications for the individual departments in achieving these goals? It may at this stage be appropriate to employ the technique Departmental Purpose Analysis. (See section on Departmental Purpose Analysis). (BS 7850 5.3 Implementing Process Management Concepts, 5.4 Measurement of Performance & 5.6 Training)

STAGE C   *Choose a Strategy*

This is one of the key stages in embarking upon a Quality Improvement programme. It can involve an improvement team approach, including the appointment of the Quality Improvement council and executive committee, necessitating the training and education of a Group Leader and Quality Improvement Groups. It is not possible to be prescriptive about the approach to Quality Improvement, it may involve the 'Eight Step approach', organising the quality improvement teams and implementing Quality Improvement. Alternatively, the Management may decide that a completely different approach is required and the improvement team style is really not appropriate for their organisation. The Mission Statement and Quality Goals may demand or suggest that a different route be taken. Deming in his 14 points does not provide solutions only issues that need to be considered and fully addressed within the Quality Improvement programme. Management needs to own the approach for the implementation of TQM and providing a ready-made solution does not enable Management to feel part of the improvement process. So it is with some caution that the following improvement team approach is suggested or adopted. What is important is that Management selects an approach that is much more appropriate to their own set of circumstances. (BS 7850 5.5 Introduce Improvement Planning, 5.6 Training).

Typical Improvement Team, Problem Solving Approach

Step 1   Identification of the improvement areas (within the scope of the Quality Goals)

Step 2   Problem evaluation, understand the background to the chosen area for improvement. (Where are we now?)

Step 3   Data collection, acquisition of information and data appertaining to the improvement area

Step 4   Data analysis, review of the information and data obtained to determine its relationship or effect on the chosen improvement area

Step 5   Development of an action plan which culminates in real improvement in quality performance

Step 6   Implementation of the action plan

Step 7   Monitor the effectiveness of the action plan, including feedback, reviewing and testing of the proposed quality improvements

Step 8   Repeat the exercise again.

Total Quality Management Profile

There is no fixed or absolute approach to TQM, it can be dependent on the needs and requirements of the particular organisation wishing to embark on a TQM programme. The following TQM profile has been developed as a means of assisting with formulating and establishing an agreed approach to TQM implementation.

The purpose of the TQM profile is not to score or derive a mark, greater importance should be placed on the completion of the profile and determining the appropriate action rather than a numerical value of the score obtained.

The profile can be used to:
- i) Establish the level of commitment at all levels within the organisation (including top management)
- ii) Establish the effectiveness of the existing Quality Management systems and structure
- iii) Determine the level of awareness, quality education and training needs
- iv) Ascertain possible areas for application of TQM techniques
- v) Ascertain the areas in need of the application of TQM techniques
- vi) Determine which TQM techniques are appropriate
- vii) Determine the level of application of TQM
- viii) Establish possible improvement areas
- ix) Provide a catalyst to promote further discussion
- x) Provide a guide for establishing the TQM approach
- xi) Identify areas for further work or improvement
- xii) Measure real quality performance improvement
- xiii) Assess whether the organisation as it stands is a Total Quality Organisation or how close the organisation is to being a Total Quality Organisation

The method of determining the organisation's TQM profile is by completion of **Table 5** (it is preferred that the TQM team individually complete the questionnaire). The first column describes the category to be judged. The second column is for the score awarded on the basis of:

Question a. *What is the organisation's policy or what does the formally documented Quality Management System state or declare with regard to each category?* A scale of one to ten is used. One would indicate no statement or approach. Ten would indicate a clear statement or approach.

Question b. *What do you believe is the case?* A scale of one to ten is used. One would indicate no implementation of the statement or

| | approach. Ten would indicate the statement or approach is fully implemented |
| Question c. | *What do you believe should be the case?* Again a scale of one to ten is used. One would indicate that the approach is of no value or significance. Ten would indicate the approach is of great value and significance. |

The third column provides a guide to assist in awarding the appropriate score for each category. *Note, where high scores have been awarded for "what you believe should be the case" this must be supported by documentary evidence.*

The TQM profile is first completed on the basis of each question in turn, i.e. a, b then c.

The completed questionnaires are then collated and analysed for trends and common views.

This analysis can then be employed to:

"   Identify any weaknesses in Quality Philosophy
"   Assist in agreeing and establishing the strategic plan
"   Identify the key cost of quality areas
"   Identify any organisational quality education short comings
"   Assist with agreeing an approach to attaining employee involvement
"   Assist with agreement to process improvement programmes
"   Assist in determining key performance indicators.

Table 5 Total Quality Management Profile

Category	Question			Guide & (BS7850 requirement)
	a.	b.	c.	
1. Quality Philosophy a. Management Commitment b. Mission Statement c. Quality Goals d. a, b & c agreed, communicated and accepted				Is there a clear quality philosophy? Has Management given a clear and unequivocal mission statement with regard to quality? Has this statement been turned into Quality Goals and are the statement & goals clearly understood and implemented at all levels? Do the controls include understanding the needs of internal and external customers? (4.1 & 4.2 General & Commitment)
2. Strategic Plan developed for the implementation of the TQM scheme				Is there a clear documented programme indicating tasks, responsibilities, time scale sequence, ownership, etc. cascaded down to departmental or unit level? (4.2 Commitment, 4.9 Alignment of corporate objectives and individual attitudes)
3. Quality Losses a. Waste b. Prevention, Appraisal & Failure (Internal/ External) c. Process Failure				Are all the categories which go to make the total cost of quality known, quantified and an action plan established for the reduction in the cost of quality? (4.4 Quality Losses)
4. Employee Involvement a. Provided with the power (empowerment) b. Operator Quality Control c. Team development and involvement d. Problem identification				Are employee teams involved in the decision making process, actively encouraged to identify problems and make improvements, made aware of the basic tools and techniques for achieving process improvements and have the power to implement the improvements? (4.5 Participation by all, 4.8 Problem Identification, 4.10 Personal accountability)
5. Process Improvement Programmes; Measured, Implemented, Coordinated and Effective				Has the improvement programme been organised? (4.6 Process measurements)

Total Quality Management & Quality Improvement Initiatives

Category	Question			Guide & (BS7850 requirement)
	a.	b.	c.	
6. Performance Indicators a. Internal Customer/ Supplier Relationships established b. Performance Measurement Criteria established c. Performance Measurement criteria understood d. Performance measured and data collected e. Performance targets achieved				Have departmental performance indicators been established? Are departments doing the RIGHT thing? Are departments doing things RIGHT? Can the department do the RIGHT things better? (4.7 Continuous improvement)
7. Customer Satisfaction (External Customers)				Are the customer needs clearly understood? What is the level of customer complaints (are they measured)? Have customer satisfaction surveys been carried out and what action has been taken? Has a Quality Function Deployment study been performed? (4.3 Customer satisfaction)
8. Quality Education Management & Supervisory, Quality awareness, Team Building, Skills, Process and Task competence, Problem solving tools and techniques (see table 6).				Are any of the subjects listed opposite applicable, relevant or have value in any future TQM programme? Which of the techniques listed could be most effectively employed in any TQM initiative? How well and widely are the techniques understood and used? Are personnel trained in the use of any of these techniques? (4.11 Personal development)

Summary of Findings

Having established the Mission Statement and Quality Goals for the organisation and completed the TQM profile, this information requires analysis to determine:

"   Are the Mission Statement and Quality Goals still relevant having completed the TQM profile?

"   Are the questions on the TQM profile relevant? Should some additional questions be asked?

"   How does the company's position (what you will do) compare with actual practice (what you are doing)?

"   How does the company's position compare with what should be happening?

"   Is there a consistent pattern emerging from the profile?

"   What action is now apparent combining the Quality Goals with the TQM profile?

Now summarise all the above in an action plan which may be similar to the Improvement Team Approach (see Stage C) or may reflect the Management Team's view of the correct approach.

Quality Improvement Techniques

In order for improvement teams to follow the above Quality Improvement approach, it is necessary for the groups to be trained in some of the techniques and methods, which can be applied in achieving a Total Quality Organisation. Just some of these improvement techniques are shown in the Quality Improvement Technique Selection Table.

Having gained an understanding of these techniques and where these techniques can be used to their best advantage, it is then possible to commence the implementation programme. This requires the monitoring, review and supervision of the progress of the Quality Improvement Groups culminating in the company wide quality performance improvements and achievement of customer satisfaction.

Table 6 Quality Improvement Technique Selection

Section	Identify Improvement Area	Evaluate Improvement Area	Collect Data	Data Analysis	Develop Action Plan	Implement Action Plan	Monitor Action Plan	Remarks
Activity Sampling		M	M	M				Statistical technique for monitoring
Brain Storming	M	M			M			Generate ideas
Business Process Analysis	M	M		M	M	M	M	Process Analysis method
Cause and Effect Diagrams		M			M	M		Logical approach to Problem Analysis
Check Sheets			M			M		Method for recording data
Customer Satisfaction	M	M	M					Method of monitoring customer reaction
Department Purpose Analysis Customer/ Supplier Relationships	M	M	M					Method of analysing the purpose of a department or section
Document Inspection	M							An inspection method for checking software & documents
Failure Mode and Effects Analysis	M	M			M			Logical method of identifying possible system failures
Histograms				M				Method of displaying data

Quality Management (Principles & Practice)

Section	Identify Improvement Area	Evaluate Improvement Area	Collect Data	Data Analysis	Develop Action Plan	Implement Action Plan	Monitor Action Plan	Remarks
Non-Value Added Activities	M							Approach to analysing processes
Pareto Analysis	M			M			M	Method for identifying the important issues
Performance Measurement	M	M				M	M	Method of setting performance targets
Process Capability Study	M	M	M	M			M	Statistical method of process evaluation
Process & Document Flow Charts	M	M	M					Process Analysis
Quality Award Schemes	M	M	M					Models for Quality Improvement
Quality Circles	M	M	M	M	M	M	M	Team approach to Quality Improvement
Quality Function Deployment	M	M			M	M		Technique for understanding customer requirements
Quality Planning					M		M	Quality Control
Root Cause Analysis		M	M	M	M			Analysis Technique
Sampling			M					Statistical technique
Scatter Diagrams				M				Statistical method for investigating relationships
Six Sigma	M	M	M	M	M	M	M	Statistically based approach to quality improvement
Statistical Quality Control	M	M	M	M			M	Statistical method for process monitoring
Suggestion Schemes	M					M		Improvement Identification Technique
Value Analysis	M	M						Cost reduction method

Following, some of the more important quality improvement techniques are described in greater detail. A full description of all of the above and more quality improvement techniques is contained in the companion book, Quality Management (Tools & Techniques). Some quality improvement techniques have not been included in the above table. The reason being certain techniques do not fit this pattern (identify improvement, evaluate improvement area, etc.) as they are more of an approach to Total

Quality Management and Quality Improvement rather than a technique. For example Quality Award Schemes.

Brain Storming

Introduction:

The purpose of brain storming is to generate as many ideas as possible that come from many different perspectives. The concept is that teams tend to generate more ideas than individuals. As individuals we may run out of ideas quickly, brain storming in teams is an effective way of obtaining more new ideas. One person's ideas may trigger ideas that others would not have thought of by themselves. It is in this way that the team build on each other's ideas which trigger off an individual's imagination. The technique is also useful in team building and cohesion. There are many ways in which brain storming can be carried out. The following guidelines have been created to help ensure a successful brain storm session.

Guidelines

The team should be sitting in a room away from distraction. Identify the theme or problem that the team wishes to discuss. Sometimes it helps to brainstorm something silly before attempting to brain storm the chosen theme, e.g. *How many uses for a brick?* This can make the team more relaxed. To get the best out of brainstorming there are some simple rules which have been found to work.

Rule 1　Encourage everyone to participate by presenting only one idea per "*turn*." One way is by taking turns to suggest one idea at a time. If an individual cannot think of anything, say "pass."

Rule 2.　There are no silly or bad ideas. So team members should not put each other down by making them feel stupid. Encourage each other to say whatever comes into their heads.

Rule 3　Criticism or judgement is not allowed. Team members should not criticise the ideas of others. The idea is to be open minded and constructive.

Rule 4　Discussion of the ideas should not take place until after the brain storming has finished. Accept everything without comment - it could trigger off new ideas.

Rule 5　Exaggeration and enthusiasm are helpful - there is no such thing as a crazy idea. Very often so-called crazy ideas lead to new ways of thinking and imaginative solutions.

Rule 6　Look for possible combinations of ideas, in this way the team may arrive at new ideas.

Brain Storming

Rule 7   If you run out of ideas try using the six key words - What, When, Where, Why, Who and How.

Rule 8   Build on other people's ideas where possible.

Rule 9   Record all the ideas.

There are different types of brain storming, some are listed below. It can also help to return to the problem at some later date - Incubation.

Table 7

Brain Storming Approaches	
Advantages	Disadvantages
Free Style: The team calling out ideas to be written down (usually on white board or flip chart, by the team leader).	
! Spontaneous ! Can be more creative ! Possible to build on each others ideas	! Strong personalities may dominate the session ! Can be confusing; listing ideas and too many talking at once
Round Robin: Each team member in turn calling out their idea to be written down.	
! Difficult to dominate the session ! Discussion tends to be more focused ! Everyone is encouraged to take part	! Difficult to wait one's turn ! Loss of spontaneity ! Embarrassing if cannot think of any ideas - puts participants under pressure ! Reluctance to pass ! Not as easy to build on others ideas
Notebook Style: Each team member writes on pad or sheet of paper their own ideas, later to be collated by the team leader.	
! Ensures anonymity if sensitive topics are to be discussed ! Can be used with very large groups ! Not necessary to speak	! Not possible to build on ideas of others ! Some ideas may not be legible, understandable ! Difficult to clarify ideas

Exercise: Brain storm
               "Why do improvement teams sometimes fail?"

Cause and Effect Diagrams

Introduction

These diagrams provide a means of logically analysing a problem with a view to tackling the root cause. Generally the construction of a Cause and Effect Diagram is a team exercise. The diagram is to formalise and to keep a record of the team's logical approach to the problem. This provides a method by which the team's thoughts and deliberations can be documented, and provides a catalyst for discussing the problem.

Cause and Effect Guidelines

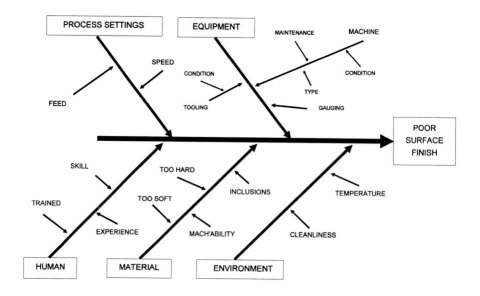

Figure 11 Cause & Effect Diagram

The first stage is to clearly define the problem. This definition may be provided from a Pareto Analysis or from statistical process control data. The diagram **Figure 11** records from a fixed point what the team considers are the main causes of the problem, such as human, material, machines, environment, sequence, procedure, process system, equipment etc. Having determined the major group causes, the team brainstorms the likely sub-causes within the major groups and possibly the further sub-causes.

Having established the team's views on possible suspects or causes of the problem, the team next needs to consider which, in their view, is the most likely culprit. The possible causes can then be ranked in order of most likely and most easy to eliminate from the investigations etc.

Having prioritised the most probable culprits an action plan for investigation can be drawn up and implemented. This plan would detail the most likely causes, the method of evaluation and who is responsible for conducting the investigation. This stage would be repeated until the actual guilty party was discovered, again Pareto Analysis may be put to useful effect. (See section on Pareto Analysis)

In certain cases the problem may be so complex that more sophisticated statistical methods may need to be employed such as Taguchi Techniques; sometimes known as an analysis of variance.

Histograms or bar charts

Introduction

A histogram is a method of representing data in a bar chart format. These diagrams can be used when gathering and analysing data.

This may be discrete categories of data. This could be used to analyse numbers of customer complaints against the reason for the customer complaint or the hours spent on inspection of each operation or product. **Figure 12** opposite shows the number of rejects for each fault type. This type of histogram can be employed when performing a Pareto Analysis, in this case the causes of rejects would be listed in descending order.

Alternatively, the histogram could show data spread over a period of time or over a range of dimensions or sizes. There are

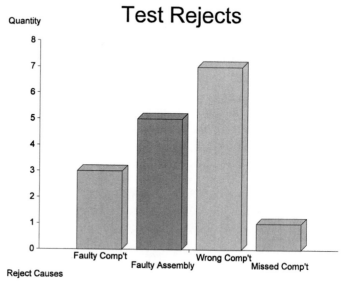

Figure 12 Histogram

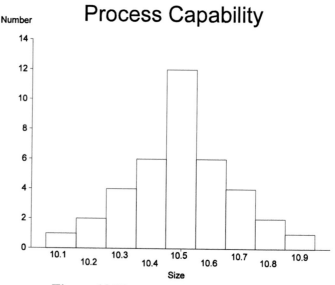

Figure 13 Histogram - Process Capability Study

numerous ways in which histograms can be usefully employed, two examples are:

To analyse the change in the cost of quality of a company by displaying the total cost of quality on a month by month basis over the past year.

Or, as in **Figure 13**, opposite, the number of components manufactured between a particular range of sizes (10.1 to 10.9mm). This type of histogram is particularly useful when performing a process capability study.

Guidelines for Creating Histograms

a. Determine the factors to be analysed and collect the data (possibly by the use of check sheets).

b. Rank the data in ascending or descending order.

c. Establish the appropriate horizontal scale by determining the number of columns required (normal 6 to 8 is adequate) and the width of each column.

$$Width\ of\ each\ column\ = \ \frac{Largest\ Value\ -\ Smallest\ Value}{Number\ of\ Columns}$$

(1)

Establish the vertical scale. The vertical scale is often cost, quantity or frequency of an event.

Pareto Analysis

Introduction

Establishing the factors that together make up all the various causes of rejects invariably means that a considerable number of problems are discovered. To tackle all these problems at one go would require enormous resources and in many cases some of the problems may be trivial and not worth pursuing for the time being.

A technique that is invaluable in singling out those problems which have the greatest influence on the total reject quantity or costs is Pareto Analysis.

Very often when this type of analysis is conducted, the results show that when placed in order of importance out of a given number of causes, only a small percentage, usually around 20%, account for 80% of the total problem. For this reason the concept is often known as the 80 - 20 rule.

Table 8 Scrap Records

Operation	Dept Resp	Scrap Qty	Cause	Value	Total Cost
Saw	105	50	Wrong Size	0.30	15.00
Turn	105	61	Wrong O.D.	0.40	24.40
Mill	103	87	Flat Position	0.50	43.50
Drill & Tap	120	230	Hole Position	0.60	138.00
Heat Treat	110	239	Wrong Case Depth	0.80	191.20
Cyl. Grind	110	320	Wrong O.D.	0.90	288.00
Bore Grind	103	616	Wrong I.D.	1.00	616.00
Hone	103	701	Over Size	1.50	1,051.50
Lap	103	1991	Surface Finish	2.00	3,982.00
Total		4,295			6,349.60

As an example of this technique the reasons for rejects or scrap from a process were recorded over a convenient period of time. This information has been tabulated. **Table 8** above shows the number of scrapped components found by inspection at each operation.

This information can been arranged in order and a graph plotted of the results, see **Figure 14** Graph Pareto Analysis. Examination of this graph reveals that approximately 20% of the causes of reject items are responsible for 80% of the total cost of rejects.

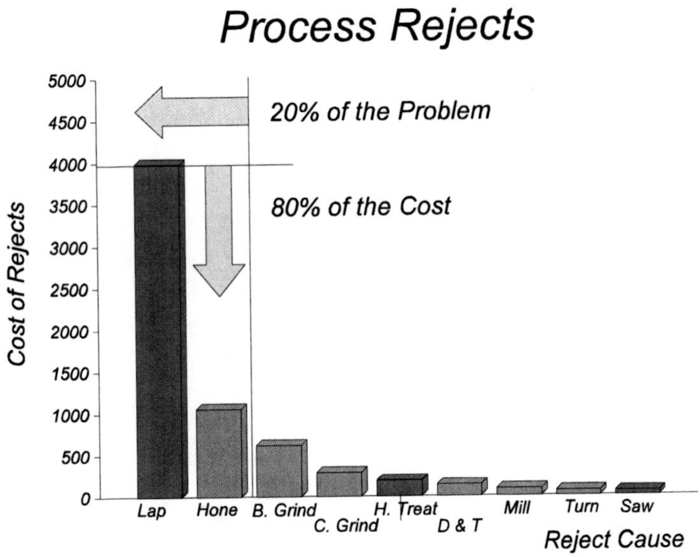

Guidelines for Pareto Analysis

Figure 14 Pareto Analysis Graph

Select the factor to be analysed. Determine how the data is to be collected (possibly by the use of check sheets) and what the duration of data collection will be.

Rank the data in ascending order.

Establish the appropriate horizontal and vertical scale.

Table 9 below shows other criteria which can be analysed using the Pareto technique depending on the nature of the problem.

The object of Pareto Analysis is to identify 'THE IMPORTANT FEW' with a view to avoiding 'THE TRIVIAL MANY'. Thus it is possible to make an 80% improvement by tackling and eliminating only 20% of the problems.

Table 9 Pareto Graph Axis

HORIZONTAL AXIS	VERTICAL AXIS
Part No./Machine No./ Operator or Dept. No.	Cost of defectives
Supplier	Goods inwards inspection rejects
Reasons for warranty returns	Quantity of warranty returns
Reasons for test failures	Quantity of test failures
Reasons for rework	Quantity of rectification work

Process Flow Charting

Introduction

Process Flow Charting and Document Flow Charting are techniques that can be employed to provide a visual representation of a procedure. Flat text can be boring and an uninteresting way of describing a process; the reader is likely to lose interest and concentration. A picture can tell a thousand words - it can convey, in certain circumstances, a better graphical indication of the sequence and methods employed within a process. The flow chart can be used to describe a number of activities, sequence of tasks, the way documents flow around an organisation, a computer program etc. Once the chart has been completed, the Process Flow Charts can be employed to analyse all the activities involved in processes or system. This may be used to explain why a process is done in a particular sequence or why a particular route was taken. The flow chart will also show the suppliers and customers of a particular task or activity. The flow charts can be used to determine the stages that require special quality control activities. With the flow chart being a comprehensive description of the process, identification of value added and non-value added activities, any unnecessary transportation and delays, becomes much easier. Boundaries can be added to the flow chart to denote when a responsibility for a particular set of activities changes from one person to another.

There are a number of different methods and approaches to representing a process using a flow charting method.

N ISO 5807 The specification for data processing flow chart symbols, rules and conventions
N Cross Functional or Swimlane - A charting method that displays the process tasks, indicating the flow of information and materials across different departments. Sometimes known as swimlanes or document flow charting
N IDEF0 - Integration Definition for Function Modelling. A method developed by the US Air Force to graphically represent process activities, showing process activity inputs, outputs, controls and resources. IDEF0 is the Integration Definition for Information Modelling.

When selecting the process charting method there are some considerations. What is being displayed; information, data or material? What will provide the information in a suitable format for the user? What level of detail is required? What is the business type (service, manufacturing, etc.)?

ISO 5807 - Process Flow Charting

There are a number of different standards that can be used for the process flow symbols. ISO5807 contains the most generally accepted symbols.

Process - Identifies the activity or task and contains a brief description of the work performed.
Decision - The point where a decision is made and the flow chart can slip into two paths. The paths are labelled true/false, yes/no etc. depending on the outcome.
Terminator - Identifies the beginning or end of the process.
Document - Where a document is required, used or created then this symbol can be employed.
Flow lines - Used to represent the next step in the process, connecting activities and tasks.
Connector - Used to indicate a connection between flow charts on separate pages.
Visual - When a computer is used to convey information this symbol can be used.

Guidelines for Process Flow Charting

1.   Select the process or system to be examined.

2.   Complete the Process Flow Chart **Table 10** representing each of the activities diagrammatically with the appropriate symbol (see **Figure 15**). The table needs to be completed by discussion with the person most knowledgeable about the process under investigation (the person doing the job?).

Table 10 Process Flow Chart Form

Operation: Department: Name: Date:			
Stage	Symbol	Description	Remarks

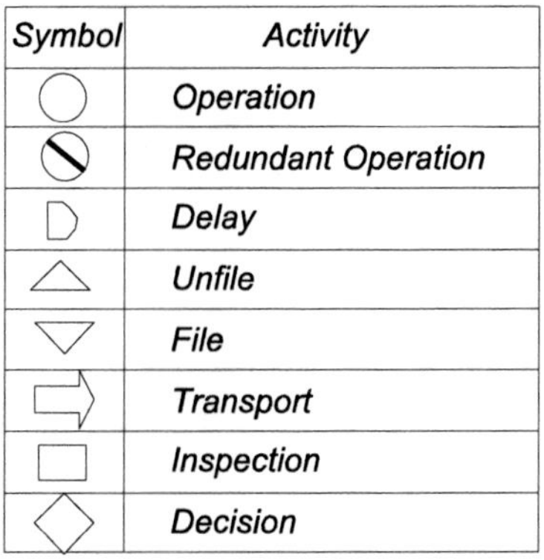

Symbol	Activity
◯	Operation
⦸	Redundant Operation
D	Delay
△	Unfile
▽	File
⇨	Transport
☐	Inspection
◇	Decision

Figure 15 Process Symbols

Table 11 Activity Summary

Activity	No. of Activities	
	Current	Proposed
Operations		
Redundant Operations		
Delays		
Unfile		
Files		
Transports		
Inspections		
Decisions		
Total		

Examples of this type of Process Flow chart can be found in the section on Quality Planning - specifically a Service Quality Plan.

3.   Critically analyse the chart to identify:

     a.   Whether the objectives of the process are being met? (Are there any omissions or duplications?)

     b.   Whether the activities are necessary? (Use the activity summary to show the number of current and proposed activities)

     c.   Whether the process is under control? (Where could the process go wrong and have all the necessary reviews or checks been included and are they being performed?)

     d.   Whether all the resources and information are available to perform the activities?

     e.   Whether there are any redundant operations and unnecessary delays.

     f.   Whether there are any non-value added activities (see section Non-Value Added Activities).

4.   Complete **Table 11** indicating the current proposed number of activities, showing the savings made.

5.   The finally agreed flow chart then needs acceptance and approval by the appropriate authority.

Cross Functional Process Flow Charting

Introduction

This technique is very similar to Process Flow Charting but provides the facility to analyse the process flow of materials or information (paperwork) across different departments. Rather than use the term Cross Functional Flow Charts the shorter term swimlane will be used.

Guidelines for Document Flow Charting

1.   Select the process to be examined.

2.   Complete the Swimlane chart. (**Figure 16** shows a Swimlane chart for information or paperwork).

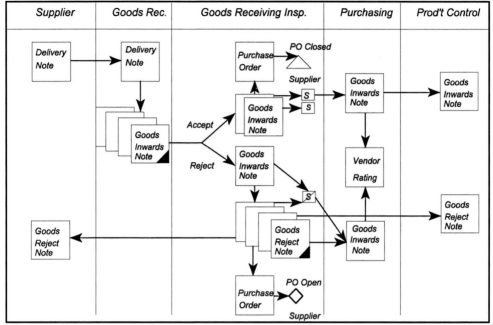

Figure 16 Document Flow Chart

Enter the name of each department, section or operator at the head of each column. Complete the chart by using a symbol to denote each stage and document employed. An arrow is drawn between the stages to indicate the flow of information around the departments. Other examples of Swimlane flow charts can be found in the section on Business Process Analysis.

3.   Analyse the chart to identify:

   a.   Are the objectives of the procedure being met? (Are there any omissions or duplications?)
   b.   Are all the activities/documents necessary?
   c.   Is the procedure under control? (Where could the process go wrong and have all the necessary reviews or checks been included and are they being performed?)
   d.   Are all the resources and information available to perform the activities?
   e.   Are there any redundant operations/documents and unnecessary delays?
   f.   Are there any non-value added activities (see section on Non-Value Added Activities).

IDEF0 or Input/Output Diagrams

IDEF0 means Integration Definition for Function Modelling (level zero). There are other levels but level 0 is the most basic.   It is a Process Flow charting method which is based around defining the process in terms of activity or task, inputs, outputs, controls and resources. These activities are then linked together to form the process and provide a process model.

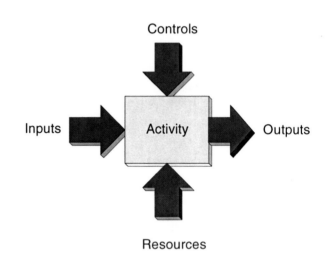

Figure 17 Basic IDEF0 diagram

Figure 17 shows the basic IDEF0 model.

As an example **Figure 18** shows the process of making tea.

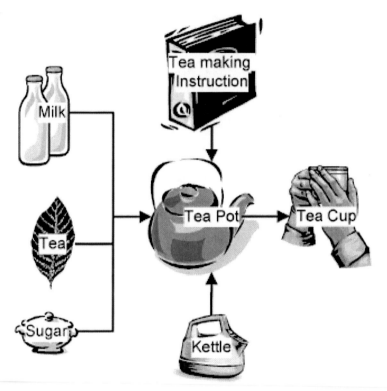

Figure 18 Making Tea

Now using IDEF0 format **Figure 18** would become as show in **Figure 19**.

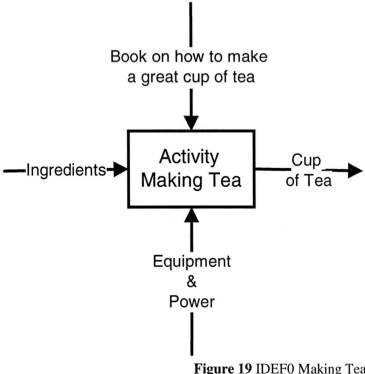

Figure 19 IDEF0 Making Tea

The arrows represent:
Inputs - Items that are used (consumed) in the activity.
Resources - Items that are used or employed in the activity but are not consumed by the activity.
Controls - Items that ensure that the activity is performed correctly for quality.
Output - The product of the activity.

The box represents
Activity - The box that is labelled with task to be performed, using the verb (making) and noun (tea) approach.

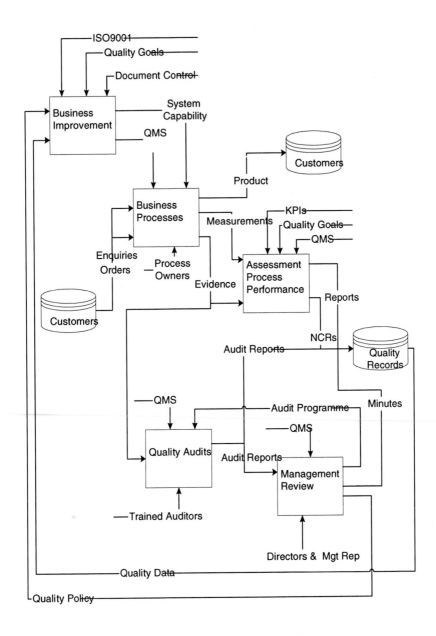

Figure 20 Quality System Model in IDEF0 Format

Figure 20 shows how a Quality System model would look if drawn in IDEF0 format. The diagram uses the same methodology of inputs, outputs, controls, resources and the verb/noun approach to describe the activities. In the bottom right hand corner of each box is the activity reference number. The process activity information can be entered into a database, which together with process performance data can be used to measure process performance. The sort of process data that could be in each record of the process activity database includes:

N Time to complete conforming activities.
N Time to complete any nonconforming activities - See Cost of Quality.
N Activity waiting time.
N Activity queuing time.
N Activity action time - See Business Process Analysis.
N Benchmarking data to compare performance against similar processes.
N Target setting and Key Performance Indicators (KPIs) - See Performance Measurement and Benchmarking.

Next is another example of IDEF0, in this case it is a software process.

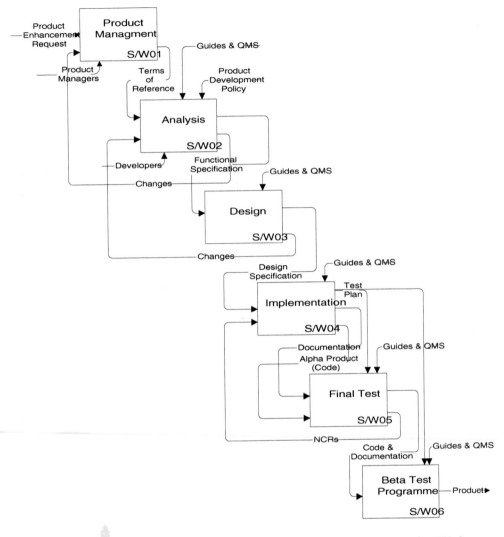

Figure 21 Example of a Software Process in IDEF0 format

In this example an input/output table has been provided below. These tables can be a useful addition to the IDFE0 process flow chart. Where the flow chart can show diagrammatically the process sequence, it is sometimes difficult to show the correct level of detail. In this situation an Input/Output table can be used to further describe the detail of the process. For example, in the input/output table the process users attention is drawn to the availability of certain guides and codes of practice, terms of reference, software coding, etc.

#	Activity Description	Activity Input	Activity Output	Activity Control and/or Resource
SW01	Product Management	Product Enhancement Request	Product Development Policy Product Terms of Reference (ToR)	Guide for ToRs
SW02	Analysis	Product Development Policy Product Terms of Reference	Functional Specification	Guide for a Function Specification
SW03	Design	Functional Specification	Design Specification Documentation synopsis	Guide for Design Specifications
SW04	Implementation	Design Specification Documentation synopsis	Test Plans Preliminary Test results Documentation Code	Guide for Test Plans Documentation Guide Code writing code of practice
SW05	Final Test	Test Plans Code Documentation	Test Results NCRs Accepted code	Testing Code of Practice
SW06	Beta Programme	Accepted code	Product	

Quality Planning

Introduction

Every stage of a process or project is a possible source of poor quality. The objective of a Quality Plan is to anticipate possible sources of poor quality and to arrange for means of identifying such failure and preventing them from occurring.

A Quality Plan tends to be a project or product-specific document which defines the Quality Assurance tasks to ensure meeting specific customer requirements and time scales. It enables the identification of preventive activities to provide early warning of any possible problems occurring or becoming major. It allows anticipation of any project or product risk areas and for the opportunity to take appropriate action to eliminate or mitigate any such difficulties. This differs from a Quality Manual which is project or product independent and a Quality Programme which usually describes the implementation of the Quality Manual.

A Quality Plan identifies any existing and additional procedures or activities that may be necessary. Often Quality Plans are required on large capital cost projects such as construction projects or the launch of a new product or software development etc. - where main contractors need to control the activities of sub-contractors. The Quality Plan can be used as a model or method of describing the Quality Assurance activities so that everyone can comment on, criticise and develop the plan, ensuring their involvement in project achievement.

Normally the project manager or project controller is responsible for the generation of the Quality Plan; the plan would then require approval by the project team and possibly the customer.

The stages involved are:

Defining the process - this can often be established by drawing a flow chart of the process showing each of the key stages and the sequence.

The next stage is to identify which parameters or key stages require control, specifying the criteria for judging conformity, deciding on the means of control, deciding on the means of assessment, preparing the appropriate documentation and monitoring the effectiveness of the plan.

Quality Planning

Guidelines for Quality Planning

How to complete a Quality Control Plan:

a. The sequence to follow in the compilation of a Quality Control Plan is first to select a process, project or operation, e.g. a manufacturing or servicing sequence, processing a customer or purchase order, processing documentation, a project etc.

b. Identify the process or project owner or person responsible for the process. Ensure that there are adequate resources to complete the process satisfactorily in terms of:

> Labour (quantity, skills, ability etc.)
> Facilities (equipment, assets, buildings etc.)
> Time
> Budget
> Materials

c. Draw the chosen process as a flow chart. Include all stages and activities (transfer, store, inspect, test etc.)

d. Transfer the flow chart onto the Quality Control Plan Form.

> i. Number and describe each stage.
> ii. Select the appropriate quality control activities associated with each stage; trials, design reviews, project reviews, tests etc. Determine when in the project sequence such quality control activities should take place.
> iii. *Source of Information*: Describe the source of information for the person performing the task e.g. Quality Manual, Work Instruction Number 1234 etc. The work instruction would need to include: the activity or task description; the sequence; the resources necessary to perform the task i.e. quantity of people; skills; materials; equipment (both process and measuring); the process standard and tolerance to be achieved.
> iv. *Responsibility*: Who is responsible for performing the task?
> v. *Record*: What records (if any) will be maintained showing successful completion of the task?
> vi. *Check by*: Who carries out (if anyone) the check on the task, confirming if successfully completed and what inspection and records will be maintained of this check?

vii.   *Overseen by*: Who oversaw (or audited or reviewed) the check of the task, confirming successful completion and what inspection and records were maintained of this check?

e.   Re-assess the process or project commitments in light of the information gained from the review of the necessary resource availability, the creation of the flow chart and the quality plan. Gain agreement and approval of the overall process or project quality plan from the project team members, key managers and customers.

Following are two examples of a Quality Control Plan Flow Chart, one for a Service Organisation (shown in **Figure 22**) and the other for a Software Process (shown in **Figure 23**). Both the Flow Charts have been developed into Quality Plans. (The Service Organisation is shown in **Table 12**). (The Software Process is shown in **Table 13**).

Quality Planning

Service Quality Plan

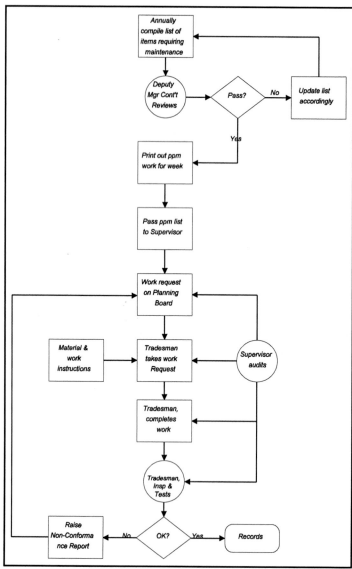

Figure 22 Flow Chart - Service

The numbers in the Quality Plan Flow Chart correspond to the stage numbers in the Quality Plan Table. This Quality Plan is for a Service organisation involved in providing Planned Preventive Maintenance (ppm) on electrical and mechanical equipment and buildings. The Flow Chart represents the initial review of the yearly overall maintenance programme for the facility or organisation. Once the programme has been agreed, the subsequent stages of the Flow Chart show the undertaking of the maintenance programme. This is with the tradesman completing the work as required by the maintenance programme and being responsible for the quality of their own work. The supervisors audit the work completed by the tradesman to ensure the work has been performed in a satisfactory manner. This Flow Chart has been developed into a Quality Plan. Having agreed the activities, stages and sequence of the Flow Chart (no easy task!) the next step is to establish:

"   Where the information (work instructions) will be found to explain how to perform each stage, e.g. Quality Manual, Labour Management System Operation Handbook. For stage 1- the instruction for conducting the review of the annual maintenance programme are to be found in section 3 of the Quality Manual.

"   Who is responsible for completing the stage and meeting the quality standard. For stage 1 the person responsible for holding the review is the Deputy Manager of the organisation.

"   What records need to be maintained, the format of the records and where the records will be kept. For stage 1 the records will be kept on the completed contract review check list. This check list is used as an aide-memoire during the contract review process (see ISO 9001). The check list will be signed by the Deputy Manager indicating satisfactory completion of the contract review stage.

"   The check is performed by the Deputy Manager.

"   In this case there is no need for anyone to oversee that the stage was performed satisfactorily.

Table 12 Quality Plan for a Service Process

#	Description of Stage	Source of Info.	Responsible	Records	Checked by	Over-seen by
1	Contract Review for Planned Preventive Maintenance (ppm)	QM Section 3	Deputy Mgr	Check List	Deputy Mgr	
2	Weekly print of all equipment requiring ppm	Labour Mgt System (LMS)	Clerical Officer	Weekly List		
3	Pass list to supervisor		Supervisor			
4	Pass ppm Instruction to Tradesman	QM Section 8	Supervisor			
5	Tradesman draws material, starts work and updates job card	Ppm & stores Procedure	Tradesman	Job card	Tradesman	Supervisor
6	Tradesman carries out work as per job card	Service Manuals and job card	Tradesman	Signs ppm	Tradesman	Supervisor
7	Final Inspection & Test (sample)	QM Section 9	Supervisor	Completes Audit Form	Deputy Mgr	
8	Raise Instructions for any defects found	QM Section 8	Supervisor	Instructions	Supervisor	
9	Raise Non-Conformance Report	QM Section 12	Supervisor	NCR Report	Supervisor	
10	Ppm instruction to Planners for closing & updating (if necessary)	LMS	Planner	Note on ppm	Deputy Mgr	
11	Modify ppm (if necessary)	QM Section 4	Supervisor	Change Note	Deputy Mgr	
12	Ppm to Planner for computer feedback Statistics	LMS	Planner	Computer Records		Deputy Mgr

#	Description of Stage	Source of Info.	Respo nsible	Record s	Checked by	Over- seen by
13	Records updated on weekly list		Super- visor	Weekly List		

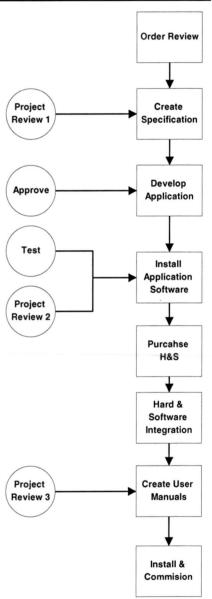

Figure 23 shows a Flow Chart outlining the process of software development. The flow chart starts with a review of the order. Having accepted the order the specification is detailed and the project reviewed. The software application is then developed and approved. On completion of the software development the software is installed and tested - on completion of successfully testing the software the project is again reviewed. The proprietary hardware and software is purchased and the developed software integrated on to the customer system. The user and maintenance manuals are created and a final project review is conducted prior to final installation and commissioning on the customer site.

With the completion of the flow chart, the quality plan can be developed. The following table shows the development of the Flow Chart into a full Quality Plan. The plan includes:

" A detailed description of the various stages.
" Quality criteria and reference documents that contain the procedures to be observed.
" The responsibilities for observing the procedures and the records to be maintained.
" Identification of the responsibilities for approvals.

Figure 23 Flow Chart Software Project

Table 13 An example of a Quality Plan for Software Development

Quality Plan		
Client Name: **Client Order Number:**	**Plan Description:**	**Prepared by:**
		Approved by:
Client Address: **Client Telephone/Fax Number:**	**Plan Number:**	**Date of Issue:** **Rev:**

#	Stage Description	Quality Criteria	Reference Documents	Resp.	Record	Approvals	
						Org	Cust
1.	Order Acceptance	Contract Review	Order review procedure QM Section 3	Project Man-ager	Order File	DR10-0%	
	Project Mobilisation						
2.	Create Contract Specific Project & Quality Plan	Design/ Project Input	Standard Project Plan Format QM Section 4 & 5	Project Man-ager	Project Plan	DR10-0%	
3.	Project Review 1	Design/ Project Verifica-tion	Project Review Min-utes Check List	Project Man-ager	Project Review Minut-es		
	Develop Application Software						
4.	Develop Prototype Ap-plication Specification	Design/ Project Input	Standard Application Specification Format	Project Man-ager	Appli-cation Specifi-cation	DR10-0%	
5.	Create Acceptance Specification	Design/ Project Input	Standard Acceptance Specification Format	Project Man-ager	Accept-ance Spe-cifica-tion	DR10-0%	

#	Stage Description	Quality Criteria	Reference Documents	Resp.	Record	Approvals	
						Org	Cust
6.	Develop Application Software	Design/ Project Process	Codes of Practice Application Development	Progra-mmers	Code	DR(s ample)	
7.	Install Application Soft-ware in house. Records of acceptance will be shown on the Accept-ance Specification docu-ment, copy retained of acceptance in project file	Design/ Project Process	Codes of Practice for Installation	Progra-mmer	Accept ance Spec-ifica-tion	DR10-0%	
8.	Acceptance of Appli-cation Software. Recor-ds of acceptance will be shown on the Acceptance Specification	Design/ Project Verifi-cation		Progra-mmer	Accept ance Spec-ifica-tion	DA(i-nd)	
9.	Project Review 2	Design/ Project Verifica-tion	Project Review Min-utes Check List	Project Man-ager	Project Review Minut-es		
	Hardware & Software Procurement						
10.	Purchase Proprietary Hardware & Software	Purchasing Control	QM Section 6 Hardware & Software Schedules Approved Supplier List	Purch-asing	Purchas e Order	DA	
11.	Hardware & Software delivered	Verifica-tion	QM Section 10	Goods Inward s	Deliv-ery Note	Insp	
12.	Hardware & Software Integration		Hardware & Software Integration Procedure				

#	Stage Description	Quality Criteria	Reference Documents	Resp.	Record	Approvals	
						Org	Cust
13.	Hardware & Developed Software Acceptance	Verification	QM Section 4	Programmer	Check List & Acceptance Specification	DA	Wit
14.	Create User & Maintenance Manuals	Design/ Project Control	Standard Format for User Manuals QM Section 9	Programmer	Standard format	DA	
15.	Dismantle for Shipment		QM Section 9	Tech Services	Check List	Insp	
16.	Project Review 3	Design/ Project Verification	Project Review Minutes Check List	Project Manager	Project Review Minutes		
17.	Site Survey		QM Section 9 Site Survey Procedure	Project Manager	Check List	Visit	Wit
18.	Installation & Commissioning	Verification	QM Section 9 & 10 Installation & Commissioning Procedures	Project Manager	Acceptance Specification	Insp (Full)	Wit
19.	Customer Acceptance/Handover		Handover Certification QM Section 9	Project Manager	Handover Certificate	Insp (Full)	Wit
20.	Software & Documentation Archiving	Records	Archiving QM Section 9	Project Manager	Various		

Quality Management (Principles & Practice)

#	Stage Description	Quality Criteria	Reference Documents	Resp.	Record	Approvals	
						Org	Cust
21.	Final Report	Records	Project Control QM Section 4	Project Manger	Project Summary	DA	

Description of Check		
Key	Explanation	Approved or checked by
Cust.	Customer	
DR100%	100% Examination of documentation for Review & Approval	Peer
DR(sample)	Sample Examination of the documentation for approval	Peer
DA(ind)	Independent approval of document	Project Mgr. & Peer
DA	Approval of document	Peer
Insp	Inspection activity	Peer
Insp(Full)	Full Inspection & Test of System	Project Mgr.
Org.	Organisation	
Visit	Visit Customer & Inspection	Project Mgr.
Wit	Witnessed by customer	Project Mgr. & Customer

Stratification

Introduction

Stratification or sampling is a technique where a small sample is taken from a large sample or batch, usually to determine the quality of the large sample.

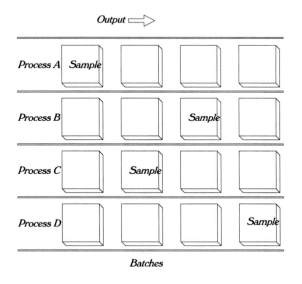

Figure 24 Sampling from Batches

Sampling can be used for attribute data (pass/fail) or variable data (measured). The advantages are that it provides a quick method of determining the state of the batch without having to examine every item. Often, examining every item can result in mistakes, possibly through boredom or inattention of the checker. To determine the correct sample size to use, sampling tables such as BS 6001 can be employed. The diagram **Figure 24** shows how a sample could be randomly taken from four processes.

Guidelines for Stratification

Stratification involves:

Planning to identify the batch to be examined and the sample size to be taken.

Data collection by randomly selecting the sample and examining the selected sample. The diagram shows random selection of samples from a number of processes.

Analysis of the results of sampling.

Scatter Diagram

Introduction

Scatter diagrams are used to examine if there is a relationship between two factors or variables. These diagrams can be employed in gathering and analysing data, problem solving, and testing solutions

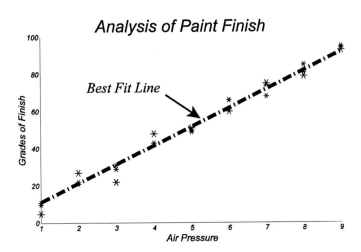

When analysing a problem, it is sometimes necessary to determine if there

Figure 25 Scatter Diagram

is a relationship between two factors. For example, measurements taken by two inspectors, tool life and cutting speed or, as shown in **Figure 25**, air pressure and paint finish.

Guidelines for Scatter Diagrams

To perform this analysis:

Planning to determine the factors to be monitored, possibly using the horizontal axis for the cause and the vertical axis for the effect.

Data collection of approximately 50 or more results.

Analyse the graph and draw the 'best fit' line through the points. (There are statistical techniques which can be employed, i.e. Regression Analysis to determine the best fit line).

It is important to ensure that the relationship is real, remember there are lies, damn lies and statistics. With statistics, it is probably possible to prove a direct relationship between the number of new Methodist Ministers and the number of unmarried mothers.

This relationship is obviously (hopefully) false, but with statistics it may be possible to demonstrate such a relationship, so care needs to be taken when attempting to determine a relationship between two variables. If there is a relationship between the factors then it should be possible to fit a line between the points plotted and consequently make predictions regarding the cause and effect. Using **Figure 25** as an example an experiment was set up to determine if there was any relationship between paint finish and pressure of the spray gun. As can be seen from the graph, the results tend to suggest a relationship. If the variable pressure is increased then there is a corresponding improvement in grade of finish. Presumably there would be a limit to this relationship - continuing to increase pressure would eventually not improve the paint finish. But within the limit of the graph shown above, the paint finish grade does improve. From this data it should be possible to determine the optimum setting for the air pressure.

SECTION 3 - QUALITY MANAGEMENT SYSTEMS

Quality Management Systems

This section covers a description of Quality Management Systems (QMS) and associated standards, e.g. ISO 9001. The ISO 9000 series of standards is examined with particular reference to ISO 9001:2000. In the case of ISO 9001 an interpretation and application of the standard is provided, not only for general application but also applied to specific industrial applications including the service, software, automotive and aerospace industries.

The creation, implementation and monitoring of a QMS is included by describing the structure and content of the quality manual, an implementation programme and auditing.

Other management systems are discussed in the context of an Integrated Management System (IMS) embracing and addressing standards of Health and Safety, Training, Environment and Security.

There is no perfect solution to controlling quality, all the various methods and approaches have their own particular advantages and disadvantages. The QMS approach is no exception to this and the limitations of the QMS approach are outlined at the end of this section - see Limitations of the Management System approach.

A Model for a Quality Management System

A Quality Management System (QMS) standard provides a model that management can employ to give guidance to the selection of appropriate quality controls. It is possible to apply a QMS to most key areas and processes and in most stages of supply of the product or service. This is to ensure that the process of providing the product or service has been fully managed effectively. The aim of a QMS standard is primarily to prevent non-conformity or customer problems and to achieve customer satisfaction by concentrating on the product or service process. The objective of this type of standard is the minimisation of risk and cost and the maximisation of benefits that the organisation can obtain from achieving the required quality requirements.

Table 14 Risk/Cost Benefits

Factor	For the Company	For the Customer
Risk	The risk of an adverse effect on image or reputation, the loss of market, possible liabilities, customer complaints, waste of resources.	Dissatisfaction with the goods or service, availability, general loss of confidence in the product or service.
Cost	The cost of rework, scrap, replacement, lost production, warranty and field repair, cost of change.	Operating costs, maintenance costs, total life costs, down time, repair costs and disposal costs.
Benefit	Increased profit and market share - satisfied customers.	Reduced costs, customer satisfaction, fitness for use and purpose, confidence.

Table 14 shows the risks and costs the organisation can be exposed to if the company does not introduce a QMS. The table also shows the risks and costs the customer is potentially exposed to if the customer buys from a company which does not have a QMS.

What is a QMS?

In order to regulate a process, (whether the process is an aircraft control system, a manufacturing sequence or a design and development process), it is necessary to have some formal method of control and feedback, otherwise the system may become unstable or go out of control.

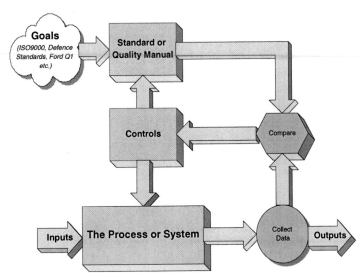

Figure 26 A Control System

A simple control system is described in **Figure 26**. There is an *input* to the system (possibly data or raw materials). The *process* then manipulates the data or material, providing an *output* in terms of an acceptable or unacceptable finished product (the process deliverable). If the process consists of data manipulation, the output could be a report - controls are necessary to avoid the production of an inaccurate report.

There will be a *goal* which could be costs, quantity, delivery targets or the QMS model - ISO 9001. This goal will need interpretation into a *Standard* or possibly the *Quality Manual*.

There will be a feedback mechanism to control the process allowing timely action to be taken to avoid failure to achieve the goal. This could involve *collection of data* regarding the performance of the process and a *comparison* with the goal, possibly by performing an audit. If the comparison indicates an unacceptable trend *controls,* as described in the Quality System or Quality Manual, may need to be updated or improved.

Why do organisations need a QMS?

There are a number of reasons why organisations embark on the implementation of a QMS:

a) The organisation may consider themselves to be leaders in their own particular field and wish to retain and consolidate their position by the introduction and application of a QMS.
b) The organisation will have competitors, these competitors will not be stationary and the competitors may be actively pursuing the introduction of a QMS.
c) Often customers are demanding the introduction of a QMS as part of their purchasing policy or as part of the contractual agreement. (We only buy from firms of assessed capability!).
d) The introduction and application of a QMS saves time and money.

The application of a Quality Management System (QMS) may help to provide a goal for system control and to maintain the achievement of quality at each stage in the process.

At the end of the section, Quality Management Systems, some of the problems associated with the use of QMS have been discussed. See - Limitations of the Management System approach.

History of the ISO 9000 Standard

The most commonly accepted QMS model is the ISO 9000 series.

Historically, ISO 9000 originated with the American Military Standards which arrived from across the Atlantic with NATO to become the Defence Standards 05-21 series. Later these standards evolved into the Allied Quality Assurance Publications (AQAP) series. (See **Figure 27**).

In the meantime civilian organisations considered these standards to be of value and developed their own, namely BS 5750 (1975), which was revised in 1987 and adopted by ISO as an international standard ISO 9000. In 1994 the ISO 9000 was revised and updated. The standard has again been revised and is now ISO 9000:2000.

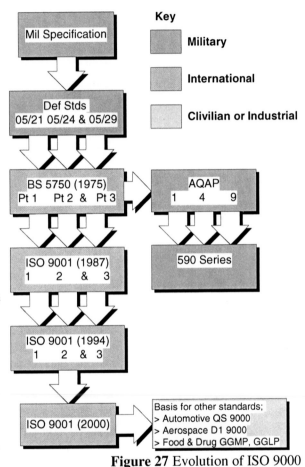

Figure 27 Evolution of ISO 9000

The 1994 structure of ISO 9000 was as shown in **Figure 28**. BS 5750 (mentioned previously) was originally a purchasing standard and possibly because of this there were a number of omissions. For example marketing, motivation, economics, product safety and product liability

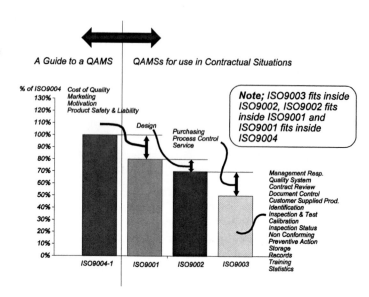

Figure 28 ISO 9000:1994

were not addressed. Subsequently these omissions were addressed with the publication of ISO 9004-1. Although ISO 9001 was originally a model for quality assurance aimed at providing confidence in suppliers, ISO 9001:2000 aims to provide a minimum standard for a quality management system. ISO 9001:2000 is a subset of ISO 9004:2000 which embraces many more requirements and provides a guide to a fully comprehensive quality management system. **Figure 28** shows how ISO 9003 used to fit inside ISO 9002 and how ISO 9002 fitted inside ISO 9001 etc. The list adjacent to ISO 9003 shows the contents of the previous version of ISO 9003. The list above ISO 9003 shows the additional requirement for the standard to be the same as ISO 9002. Similarly the list above ISO 9002 shows the additional requirements for the standard to be the same as ISO 9001.

Some of the major changes to ISO 9000 and specifically ISO 9001 are now explained. For more details regarding the contents of ISO 9001 standard refer to the section on Interpretation of ISO 9001 requirements.

The latest version of ISO 9000 is ISO 9000:2000 - an update on the ISO 9000:1994.

Revisions to ISO 9000

When BS 5750 (the forerunner of ISO 9000) was first introduced it provided a nationally agreed benchmark for quality management systems in the manufacturing sector. A great deal has been learnt in the intervening years with regard to the usefulness and the limitations of the standard. Consequently it is necessary to regularly review and revise the standard, not only to remain relevant but also to provide a lead in continual improvement for all sectors.

The need for revision

The policy is that standards should be revised every five years. However, this tends to slip since the process involves achieving international agreement. Since its first introduction in 1987 there has been one revision in 1994. The aim at that time was intended to be cosmetic and essentially to eliminate anomalies and to present clearer objectives in a more generic form. In the event there were a number of additions over and above this, such as a move towards continuous improvement. For example, quality planning received more focus along with the need for preventive action and the use of statistics for analysis of quality performance. There was also a recognition of the widespread use of IT and the acceptance that quality documentation and records may be stored electronically. In revising standards consideration must also be given to the time needed for industry to assimilate and consolidate the requirements of the standard by the phasing in of revisions. Consequently the 1994 revision was referred to as the phase one revision of the standard with phase two planned for five years later.

The phase two revision was to be more radical and to review not only the content but the architecture of the standard. On reflection, the ISO 9001:1994 standard looks like a patchwork quilt of requirements lacking shape. Elements having a natural affinity are not always found together. For example, Management Review was found in the first requirement, while quality auditing was found at number 17; Product Identification was found at number 8 and product handling, storage etc. were found at number 15; Document Control at number 5 and Quality Records at number 16 and so on. In addition, there has been a proliferation of guides resulting in a total of 11 separate documents making up ISO 9000. The majority of companies are only aware of either ISO 9001 and ISO 9002. An increasing concern with the old ISO 9001:1994 standard is its interpretation for different sectors of industry and commerce. Originally conceived as a standard for manufacturing companies it is now widely applied to all sectors including hardware, software, material processing and service. A creative imagination is required to fit the various elements to non-manufacturing companies.

ISO 9000:2000 Portfolio

So what are these 2000 revision changes? Firstly the overall structure of the ISO 9000 family of standards and guides has been reduced to just three documents: ISO 9000, ISO 9001, ISO 9004, supported by the ISO 10000 series of guides.

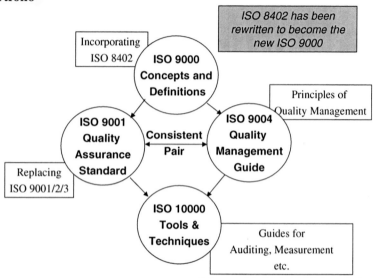

Figure 29 ISO 9000 Portfolio

ISO 9000:2000 is the foundation standard based on a revision of ISO 8402 glossary of terms used in quality assurance. ISO 9000 also contains eight quality management principles which form the basis for organisations wishing to control quality in a systematic and process-based manner. These eight principles are the foundation of the ISO 9000 portfolio and consequently the fundamental guide to the direction and contents of ISO 9001.

1. *Customer focussed organisation* - organisations should exist for their customers and consequently, are required to fully appreciate current and future customer needs and expectations and continually strive to exceed them.
2. *Leadership* - managers should be leaders in establishing unity of purpose and direction. Creating an environment in which all stakeholders can become fully involved in achieving the organisation's objectives.
3. *Involvement of people* - active participation and utilisation of all stakeholders' skills and abilities is fundamental to an organisation wishing to achieve the very highest levels of performance.
4. *Process approach* - defining, owning, supporting, controlling and measuring process behaviour is essential to continually improve performance.
5. *System approach to management* - a systematic means of identifying, understanding and controlling all the organisation's interrelated processes for quality.

6. *Continual improvement* - continual and never ending improvement in quality performance must be a permanent objective of the organisation.
7. *Factual approach to decision making* - for decisions to be effective, suitable and sustainable they must be based on accurate and reliable data.
8. *Mutually beneficial supplier relationships* - organisations performance can be heavily reliant on the quality of their supplies and suppliers. Consequently, development of mutually beneficial relationships with suppliers is a vital element in adding value.

ISO 9001:2000 replaces ISO 9001, ISO 9002 and ISO 9003 as the compliance standard for quality management. ISO 9002 was a subset of ISO 9001 having identical requirements with the exception of design. Similarly, ISO 9003 was a subset of ISO 9002. These three levels of requirements were intended to match the typical extent of various businesses, e.g. 80% of companies are not involved in design. It is now felt that a single standard is sufficient, taking into consideration that a company seeking registration will agree with its certification body as to which elements are applicable and which can be legitimately considered not applicable.

ISO 9004 is a guide for Quality Management. It has been designed to be consistent with ISO 9001 but provides a much wider scope in the direction of total quality management.

The ISO 10000 series is the repository of the guides for tools and techniques which may be applied in isolation or in support of ISO 9001/4.

Quality Management Systems

For example:

N ISO 10005: 1995
Quality
management
guidelines for
quality plans

N ISO 10011:
Guidelines for
quality auditing

N ISO 10012:
Guidelines for
measurement

N ISO 10013: 1995
Guidelines for
developing quality
manuals.

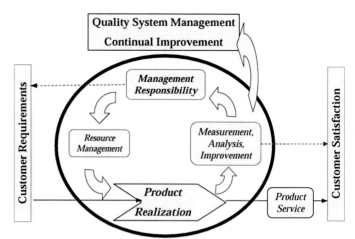

Figure 30 Adapted from Fig 1 ISO 9000:2000

Returning to the structure and content of ISO 9001 and ISO 9004, all the elements of ISO 9001 are included and in many cases clarified and enhanced. However, the structure of the standard is based on what is considered to be a generic process model comprising four principal subsystems:

N Management Responsibility - requirements, policy, planning, management systems and responsibilities, and review.

N Resource Management - requirements, human resources, information, infrastructure and work environment.

N Product and/or service realisation - customer related processes, design and development, purchasing, production and service operations, and control of measuring and monitoring devices.

N Measurement, analysis and improvement - measurement and monitoring of system performance (auditing), customer satisfaction and processes, control of non-conformity, analysis of data and improvement.

Summary of some of the ISO quality standards available

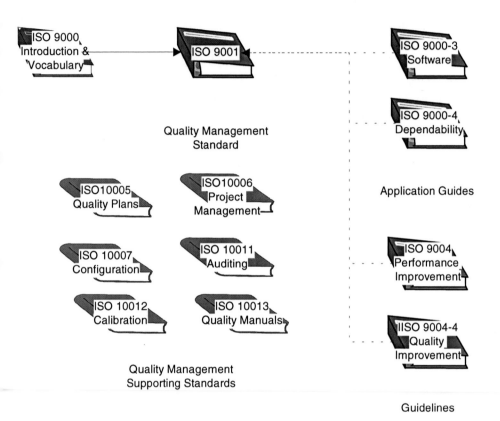

Figure 31 Overview of ISO Quality Standards

Figure 27 shows that ISO 9002: 1994 and ISO 9003:1994 have been incorporated into ISO 9001. It will be necessary for organisations that previously used ISO 9002:1994 and ISO 9003:1994 to limit the scope of application, by specifying which requirements are applicable.

The use of the word *"Assurance"* has been dropped and no longer refers to a Quality *Assurance* Management System but a Quality Management System. This is the start of a reference to an integrated management system (see section on Integrated Management System on page 209). Other terms that have been changed from the previous ISO 9001 standard include *"Supplier"* to *"Organisation"*. This reflects the change in the standards use from a standard used on suppliers to one which is used for internal quality management purposes. Similarly the term *"subcontract"* has been replaced with the term *"supplier"*.

The Defence Standards (AQAPs) have now incorporated ISO 9000 as the basis of the defence QMS standard. The latest defence standards are the 05/90 series that invoke ISO 9000, with the addition of a number of supplements to the ISO 9000 paragraph headings. (The additional requirements include the right to review supplier's systems and have, unusually, extended the requirements for calibration). These NATO military standards are used for contractual requirements for MOD procurement. They specify to prospective suppliers the controls they and their quality management systems must apply. Thus hopefully ensuring that the product or services supplied will, in all respects, meet the customers' requirements.

Other Quality Assurance Publications

Table 15 shows some further details of the International Quality standards shown in **Figure 31** together with some other QMS standards. These additional standards are 2nd party standards (see section on Quality Audit and different levels of audit), used in the purchasing process, to determine the acceptability of suppliers to 2nd Party (Customers) organisations.

Table 15

Issuing Organisation and Identification	Remarks
ISO 9000-3	Quality management and quality assurance standards - Part 3: Guidelines for the application of ISO 9001:1994 to the development, supply, installation and maintenance of computer software
ISO 9001	Quality management systems - Requirements. *A model for quality management system. This is the requirement standard and used for third-party certification.*
ISO TS 16949	Quality systems - Automotive suppliers. *Sector specific guidance to the application of ISO 9001:1994 in the automotive industry.*
Department of Health and Social Security	*Two standards*; Guide to Good Manufacturing Practice and Guide to Good Laboratory Practice; Similar to ISO 9001 but includes issues such as sterility and product recall. labs- ISO 15189
NATO	590 series general reflects the previous version of ISO 9000. 591 (formally AQAP1) ≡ISO 9001(1994), 592 (formally AQAP4) ≡ISO 9002(1994), 593 (formally AQAP9)≡ISO 9003(1994)
QS 9000	An interpretation of ISO 9000 for the Automotive Industry Includes additional requirements such as Quality Control Planning, Failure Mode and Effects Analysis, Statistical Quality Control, Measure System Analysis. (See section Supplier Quality Assurance).
AS 9000	A Quality Management System for the Aerospace industry, containing ISO 9001 and 30 aerospace specific requirements.

Issuing Organisation and Identification	Remarks
Motorola Six Sigma	The use of statistical techniques to reduce variation. Specifically how to improve measuring and controlling these variations. With a view to parameter selection and measurement. Analysis of the results to enable definition of the optimisation method and finally control the process for quality. (See section Statistical Quality Control).

Instead of using one of the above nationally recognised Quality Management Standards an organisation could develop its own QMS - possibly because it felt that the available QMS did not *fit* or was not appropriate for the organisation. However, there are certain problems associated with this approach:

o   Can agreement be reached with all parties concerned as to the content of such a QMS standard?

o   Resources may be devoted to the development of such a QMS standard only to find that it is very similar to an already existing standard.

It is possible to interpret ISO 9001 for most industries. An interpretation of ISO 9001 follows, describing an approach that may be adopted in meeting the requirements of ISO 9001. Where appropriate, at the end of some of the ISO 9001 requirements a typical procedure has been provided. These procedures outline an approach and sequence which has been frequently used successfully, as the basis of various organisations' documented quality systems.

Overview of ISO 9001

ISO 9000 and ISO 9001 are based on eight guiding principles which helped in the development of the standard.

N   Customer focused organisation
N   Leadership
N   Involvement of people
N   Process approach
N   System approach to management
N   Continual improvement
N   Factual approach to decision making
N   Mutually beneficial supplier relationships.

Figure 32 shows that the general structure of ISO 9001 is now based on the process model. For Shewharts PDCA cycle see, W. Edwards Deming. The process model sequence is:

Process Inputs (Customer Requirements) ⟶ *Processing* ⟶ *Process Outputs (Customer Deliverables)*

The central process is supported by the management who identify resources necessary to convert the process inputs into the process outputs. Establishing measurement and analysis methods to ensure targets are met and that improvements are continually made. There are many other processes that could have been chosen, for example the Supply Chain Process; *Supplier* ⟶ *Process* ⟶ *Customer.*

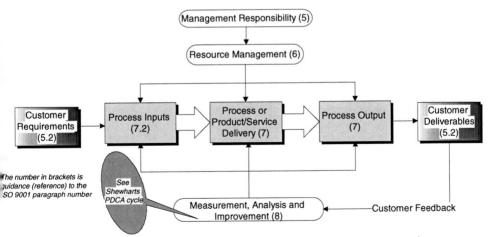

Figure 32 Quality Management System Structure

Quality Management Systems

ISO 9001 can be thought of as a series of requirements that can be sequentially worked through and addressed independently of each requirement. This can be achieved by identifying a department or section and establishing which ISO 9001 requirements are relevant to the department's functions and tasks. See section on Quality Improvement Initiatives & Techniques, specifically Process Flow Charting. The sequential 'requirement by requirement' approach to the interpretation of ISO 9001 has been adopted and can be found in the section - Interpretation of individual ISO 9001 requirements, on page 97. However, it is also important to see the standard not only as a series of independent requirements but that the requirements interrelate. One example of this could be the change management process.

ISO 9001 contains five elements:
- N   Quality management system (ISO 9001 Section 4)
- N   Management responsibility (ISO 9001 Section 5)
- N   Resource management (ISO 9001 Section 6)
- N   Product and Service realisation - process management (ISO 9001 Section 7)
- N   Measurement, Analysis & Improvement (ISO 9001 Section 8) - See the Section Deming for Shewhart PDCA Cycle.

Sections 1 to 3 of ISO 9001 provide information regarding; the scope of the standard, references, definitions and an introduction to the above five key elements.

Interpretation of Individual ISO 9001 Requirements

The interpretation of ISO 9001:2000 is given by an explanation of the requirement and then followed by application of the particular requirement, i.e. the requirement in practice. Here, practical guidance is given in the application of the requirement, by providing examples of procedures, forms, check lists, etc. **Table 15** contains the key requirements of ISO 900 :2000.

Frequent cross references are made in this section to the section on specific Improvement Techniques. This is to avoid mixing and confusing the ISO 9001 requirement with specific (improvement)techniques and to indicate that further information is available, if required. Where reference is made to a specific technique, this does not imply that the techniques is a requirement of ISO 9001 only that the technique may help in addressing the ISO 9001 requirement.

Scope of the QMS

There is only one set of requirements for ISO 9001 as ISO 9002 and ISO 9003 have been removed. Consequently, it will be necessary for organisations to determine and define which ISO 9001 requirements are applicable to their individual set of circumstances. For example, in a software house calibration or 'control of monitoring and measurement devices' it may not be relevant and therefore excluded from the documented QMS. In a Warehousing organisation there will probably be no design activity, therefore the 'design and development' requirement may be excluded.

Table 15

4 Quality management system
    4.1 General requirements
    4.2 Documentation requirements
5 Management responsibility
    5.1 Management commitment
    5.2 Customer focus
    5.3 Quality policy
    5.4 Planning
    5.5 Responsibility, authority and communication
    5.6 Management review
6 Resource management
    6.1 Provision of resources
    6.2 Human resources
    6.3 Infrastructure
    6.4 Work environment
7 Product realisation
    7.1 Planning of product realisation
    7.2 Customer-related processes
    7.3 Design and development
    7.4 Purchasing
    7.5 Production and service provision
    7.6 Control of monitoring and measuring devices
8 Measurement, analysis and improvement
    8.1 General
    8.2 Monitoring and measurement
    8.3 Control of nonconformity
    8.4 Analysis of Data
    8.5 Improvement

This ISO 9001 requirements selection will also need to be consistent with the organisation's stated scope of their QMS. What is the scope of the organisation's QMS? Well, the scope needs to be defined, it may be that the organisation has determined that the QMS will not cover all of their organisation. For example, it may exclude accounts, the restaurant and any other activities or departments that do not have a bearing on the quality of the end product A typical scope could read *"Design, Development, Installation and Support of Network Management Software"*. Having defined the scope of the QMS the next issue is to determine which of the ISO 9001 requirements are applicable to the particular organisation. For example, calibration often has no application in service industries, as no physical measurements are taken.

It may be that the Certification Body has a role to play in reviewing the proposed scope of registration. The organisation's proposed scope of registration should adequately reflect the organisation's normal business, products or deliverables. If the scope does not reflect the organisation's business, then the Certification Body may request changes. These changes would be requested because the organisation may be misleading its customers. These customers may be unaware of the organisation's scope of registration and mistakenly believe all the organisation's product and service processes are covered by the certificated ISO 9001 registration.

The ISO 9001 Requirements

Following each of the five key requirements of ISO 9001 namely section 4 (Quality Management System) through to section 8 (Measurement, Analysis and Improvement) are individually examined and interpreted.

Quality Management System

General Requirement

The organisation will need to establish a Quality Management System (QMS) which reflects all the requirements of the international standard ISO 9001. Not only in documented sense but a comprehensive system, completely implemented and maintained. The system will need to embrace:

N   the determination of which processes are necessary for the complete working of the QMS.

N   detailing these processes and their interrelationships.

N   methods that ensure these detailed processes are effectively implemented, controlled and maintained.

N   the determination of the process dependencies in terms of process; inputs, information, resource, controls, etc.

N   systems which will enable the measurement of the process performance (including output - deliverables) and facilitate continuous improvement.

Clearly organisations need to give careful consideration to the management of these arrangements. However, this does not preclude the controlled outsourcing of this management (see Purchasing on page 133).

Documentation Requirements

Quality Manual

Having determined the need for a Quality Management System then there is a need to document the system. This ensures that all the necessary requirements have been addressed and the QMS is agreed, available and understood by all personnel who have an effect on the quality performance of the organisation.

ISO 9001 standard refers to a Quality Manual and Quality Planning. Where Quality Manuals tend to be organisation specific Quality Plans tend to be project or process specific.

The Quality Manual is a collection of all the policies, organisational structure, responsibilities, procedures, processes and resources for implementing quality. The quality system should only be as comprehensive as needed to meet the quality objectives. See section on The Quality Manual (The Documented Quality Management System, page 204) for further details.

Control of Documents

Documents associated with the quality managment system will change with organisational changes and process improvements. Control of these changes is important to ensure that the procedures correctly describe the processes, are readily available and are up to date.

Document creation, approval and issue (see **Figure 33**) - there are a number types of documents associated with the QMS that may require control, both of their issue and change. These documents may include the Quality Manual, Work Instructions, Forms, etc. Once created documents like these will need to be reviewed and approved by the process owner or user, for their completeness and accuracy prior to being issued. This means that documents which are under the change control system will probably need to carry the following information: document title and number, an author, an approver, its issue date and number, the page number, total number of pages and a circulation list. This information will usually be placed in the header for the document. Having created the document, it will require checking or approving. Typically a document check list could consist of:

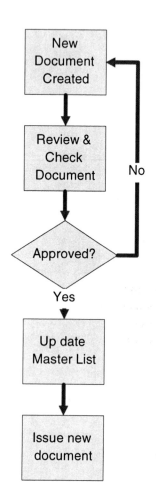

Figure 33 Document Creation

    a.   Is the document accurate?
    b.   Is the document complete?
    c.   Is the document in the correct format?
    d.   Is the document issue status correct?

Typical Document Header

Organisation plc		
QUALITY MANUAL VOLUME 2	**Title & File Name:** Section 8.2 Inspection & Testing	**Issue Number**: 3
Issue Date: 17 May 1999	**Print Date**: 29 July 2002	Page 1 of 6 Pages

Having accepted the document, the document will require registering on the Quality Manual Master List. A typical Quality Master list could comprise, title and file name, document and issue number and circulation list. The new document can then be issued.

If at some later stage the document undergoes changes, procedures may be necessary to control approval of the change, control of the issue and circulation of the new documentation and implementation of the change.

Quality Records

It is necessary to provide recorded evidence of compliance with the QMS. Such records may include: design decisions regarding quality; design reviews; any tests or demonstrations that were performed in design; goods inwards; in process or final inspection records. There is a need to establish where and what records will be kept, their contents, the responsibilities for maintaining the records and for how long they will be maintained.

Below is a typical list of some of the records required by ISO 9001.

Quality Records		
Section	**Subsection**	**Typical record**
Quality Management System	Control of Documents	Records of controlled document creation and change
Management Responsibility	Management Review	Minutes of meetings
Human Resources	Human Resources	Training Records including an individuals; education, skills, experience and appraisals history

Quality Records		
Section	Subsection	Typical record
Product Realisation	Planning of Product realisation	Process records e.g. Control charts, supervisor monitoring, audits and checks, etc.
Customer-Related	Review of customer requirements	Review of the customer quotation or order and any changes to the customers requirements
Design and Development	Inputs	The Product or Service Terms of Reference or scope, regulatory or legal requirements e.g CE Marking, Environmental requirements e.g. Waste or packaging disposal requirements, Project Plans, etc
	Outputs	Drawings, Bills of Materials Test Specifications, User or Maintenance Handbooks, Software code, etc.
	Review	Records of Project or Design review minutes, include actions, responsibilities and dates
	Verification	Approvals and checks of software, calculations, drawings, specifications, etc.
	Validation	Records including actions and follow-up confirming the design out $\equiv$ design input.
	Control of changes	Index/register of controlled documentation, Document approval & changes
Purchasing	General requirements	Approved Supplier Lists, Supplier Performance and approved, Vendor Rating, Purchase orders.
Production and Service Provision	Identification and traceability	(No specific requirement for records) however; Serial No's, Part No's, Material used, Batch No's. Lot No's., Drawing No's.
	Handling, packaging, storage, preservation and delivery	(No specific requirement for records) however; Stock records, Identification, Storage conditions, Shelf life, Delivery Notes

Quality Records		
Section	**Subsection**	**Typical record**
	Validation of processes	Qualification of processes and personnel; Process Approval first offs, Approved Inspectors, Records of control of Inspection stamps
Control of measuring and monitoring devices	Register of measuring equipment	Calibration history, Software validation, Validation certificates, Calibration certificates
Measurement, analysis and improvement	Customer satisfaction	Records of Customer Satisfaction surveys
	Internal Audit	Internal Quality Audit; time table, results, nonconformities and corrective action
	Measurement and monitoring	Records of Inspection and Test Delivery notes (record of receipt inspection), Inspection reports, Final inspection and test Release to production records, Records of progress, Signatories, Condition label, i.e. passed/awaiting inspection quarantine
	Control of Nonconformance	Records of scrap, rework, concessions, regarding, supplier rejects, customer complaints, etc.
	Improvement	Records of corrective and preventive action taken. See *Quality definitions* for the difference between corrective and preventive action.

Management Responsibility

Management Commitment

Senior management needs to
demonstrate their awareness of
and commitment to the QMS.
This can be done through:

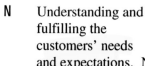

N Understanding and
   fulfilling the
   customers' needs
   and expectations. Not only the stated needs as in the customer order and
   contract review but also the implied needs including such issues as
   reliability, availability, safety and the organisation's legal responsibilities
   to the customer, etc. See Quality Function Deployment
N Determining the organisation's quality policy and objectives
N Holding management reviews
N Ensuring the organisation, and more specifically, the quality tasks and
   activities have adequate resources
N Establishing procedures that ensure adequate levels of communication
   within the organisation
N Ensuring that the organisation's legal obligations are met. Including
   addressing all safety aspects of the organisation's products and services,
   such as legislative and CE marking issues. See QA and the Law.

Customer Focus

See Customer-related Processes (Bidding to Winning) and Customer Satisfaction.

Quality Policy & Objectives

It is essential that management define and document their policy, showing clear
objectives and commitment to quality. In conjunction with this policy it is of obvious
importance that the policy and objectives are understood, planned, implemented and
maintained at all levels within the organisation.

In practice this means writing a Quality Policy Statement (usually half a page) which is signed by the Managing Director or Chief Executive. **Figure 36** is a typical quality policy statement.

Quality Policy Statement

As the leading chilled foods producer our company has built up a reputation with retailers and consumers at home and abroad for high quality products.

To maintain and enhance this reputation, a Quality Management System has been introduced based on the requirements of ISO9001.

The primary aim of our organisations is to satisfy its customer. Fundamental to achieving this aim is our Quality Manual which provides written quality practices for all aspects of managing the business and compliance is mandatory for all employees.

The quality system will be adequately resourced, continually improved and reviewed on a regular basis by the Quality Manager to ensure compliance with ISO9001 and this Quality Assurance Manual. The results of these reviews shall be issued to the Directors of the company.
Signed: Managing Director

Figure 36 Typical Quality Policy Statement

This Policy Statement only shows management commitment but does not demonstrate that this policy has been understood, accepted, planned and implemented. There is a need to back this policy up with action. Namely, the provision of resources to fulfil these aims and objectives, the creation of a Quality Manual and regular training, communicating the Quality Policy and the Quality Manual to all employees. This would also need to be followed by audits and reviews to confirm implementation and acceptance.

Planning and Quality Planning

It is necessary to define and document how the requirements of quality are to be met. This means that the individual functions and levels within the organisation will need to define their quality objectives (goals). For example, the organisation's quality policy may be to satisfy its customers. Interpreting this policy of "Satisfying its Customers" in the marketing and sales department could require a policy on establishing customer needs and expectations, measuring levels of satisfaction, etc. (See Section on Marketing and Sales)

Quality Planning will also need to embrace how the requirements are met and continually improved. This could be achieved through the Quality Manual and audits but the need to continually improve will necessitate the establishment of quality goals and targets. (See section onPerformance Measurement and Benchmarking)

Responsibility, Authority and Communication

This will normally entail establishing an organisation chart (which includes the authority and lines of communication of the quality department) and the written job descriptions containing quality roles and responsibilities.

In the organisation chart below (**Figure 37**) the Quality Manager, although working for the Operations Director, still has a dotted line responsibility (communication) with the Chief Executive Officer indicating the right to appeal and communicate, possibly where clarification is required. It is also of note that no names are provided on the organisation chart - people can move roles quite frequently but changes to the organisation's structure is usually less frequent - thus reducing the number of updates to this chart.

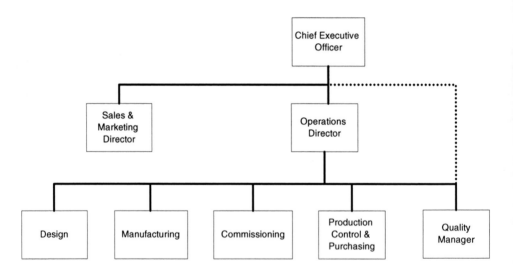

Figure 37 Typical Organisation Chart

Written job descriptions can also be required, following are some examples of the quality responsibilities of certain roles.

Management Representative or Quality Manager

It may be appropriate in certain circumstances to appoint someone with the responsibility and authority to monitor the Quality Control arrangements. In particular, this person would need to have the organisational freedom and the authority to:

N   Ensure that the QMS reflects ISO 9000 and is fully implemented, monitored and any non-conformance is reported.

N   Take action to prevent the occurrence of any quality problems with the product or service.

N   Identify and record any known or possible quality problems with the product or service.

N   Organise solutions to any quality problems.

N   Verify that these solutions have been fully implemented and are effective.

N   Control any further processes, delivery or installation of non-conforming products or services, until the quality deficiency or unsatisfactory condition has been corrected.

N   Engender a customer focus and quality improvement philosophy throughout the organisation.

The appointment of a Quality Manager, with a direct line of responsibility to the Board of Directors, could assist with achieving some of the above objectives. However, this person need not necessarily be a full time Quality Manager, thus there is a need for someone with Executive Responsibility for quality which implies that there is a need to have someone on the Board with responsibility for quality (not necessarily solely). This will not preclude Q-Support schemes where the quality support role is outsourced.

Purchaser or Buyer

Another role within an organisation may be purchasing, typically their quality role and other responsibilities would primarily be:

N   Purchasing in a cost-effective manner, and ensuring that the recommended suppliers deliver within an acceptable time period.

N   Selecting sources of supply which have a sound financial base and the required background etc, and that the suppliers have effective control procedures.

N   Ensuring that every supplier understands that all supplies must be to specification and that deviations may only be permitted after formal agreement.

N   Making certain that the ordering information and specifications issued to suppliers is up to date and that where required modifications to the purchasing specification are issued and implemented in a controlled manner.

N   Developing relationships with the suppliers aimed at reinforcing their application of effective quality control.

Chief Executive Office or Managing Director

Typical the Chief Executive Officer would be responsible for:
- N   Providing advice on all matters relating to the operation of the organisation.
- N   Leading in the preparation of policies, strategies and standards relating to the organisation.
- N   Monitoring the effective execution of the organisation in co-operation with the Managers and leading the effort for quality improvement.

Internal Communication

The methods associated with internal communication need to be established, not only for communicating the quality policy, goals and manual but also the non-conformance results (Customer Feedback, Audits etc.). There are numerous means of establishing good communications but these methods need to be viewed in the light that most managerial problems seem to stem from poor communications. Effective and efficient means of communication can pay huge dividends. Methods available include:
- N   The Management review meeting
- N   The Intranet - See Computer Aided Quality Assurance
- N   Team briefing by managers and supervisor - where managers and supervisors on a regular basis get their teams together to pass on key information and receive feedback from their subordinates.
- N   Quality Newsletters and reports containing the latest information regarding quality performance, changes and general news of some recent "quality" achievements

Management Review

Quality performance should not be static and improvements need to be continually pursued. A review of the current quality performance can give an indication as to what areas require improvement. This review could involve a minuted meeting discussing such topics as: internal audit reports, supplier performance, customer complaints, quality policy and objectives etc. (See section on Measurement, Analysis and Improvement). Although, the management review is described below as one meeting in practice it is more likely to be a number of separate management meetings, e.g. Monday morning management meeting, project management meeting, etc.

Management Review in Practice

On a regular basis the Managing Director holds a Management Review with the Quality Manager and others as appropriate. The frequency of the meetings needs to be determined in accordance with the stability and complexity of the organisation. During this meeting the following items are reviewed:

a.   Results of any audits:
     (1)   Internal Audits
     (2)   Certification 3rd Party Audits
b.   Customer feedback:
     (1)   Results of any Customer 2nd Party Audits
     (2)   Customer complaints (both of customers and from customers)
     (3)   Customer Satisfaction
c.   Quality Performance Indicators as appropriate for each of the key processes:
     (1)   Process Bidding to Winning, e.g. Quotation v Orders, Customer Satisfaction, Order levels and as a consequence, resource needs.
     (2)   Product or Service Delivery, e.g. Scrap, rework, warranty, concessions, in-process and final inspection and test results, concessions, etc.
     (3)   Supplier Development, e.g. Supplier rejects
     (4)   Product or Service Development, e.g. Number of projects on time to budget.
    For each of the above processes: Identification of Key Performance Indicator (KPI) categories; current and historical performance figures; targets for each category; actions associated with improvement (including corrective and preventive) and review of current and future resource needs.
d.   Review of the Quality Management System (including Quality Policy, Responsibilities, Manual, Plan and any changes).

Minutes of the meeting are recorded together with responsibilities, and any agreed corrective and preventive actions taken to avoid recurrence and timescales. The minutes are issued to those in attendance and others as required.

NOTE: The above list is not comprehensive but should be covered as a minimum.

Resources Management

Resourcing the process and individual process tasks is not just about people it also requires the identification and timely provision of materials, equipment, procedures, information and finance. However, the aspects and provision of material, equipment, procedures and finance are covered in the requirements for product or service realisation. The focus here is on the people and the information needs of the process and task.

Human Resources

This is the most important of all resources. The Quality Management System with its quality manuals and audits tends to concentrate on the system and structure aspects of quality. This requirement (Human Resources) balances this by emphasising the importance of; motivation for quality, culture and attitudes. (See sections on Quality Philosophy and Quality Improvement for more details on quality motivation).

Demonstration of the correct people resource could be limited to the provision of training records. These records could include; who requires training, what tasks require training, the training that should be given, the responsibility for performing the training and what training records need to be maintained. This is interpreting the requirement too narrowly. A broader view of resource management is necessary, embracing personal performance, the staff contribution to the "quality" pot, information dissemination, etc.

Resource Management in Practice

The answer to "who requires training?" must be everyone in the organisation but they will need training in different things.

Everyone requires induction training and training in their own specific responsibilities within the documented QMS. Everyone should be trained with regard to basic quality awareness. Why quality? What is quality? What is the company's position with regard to quality? What is the company's approach to addressing the needs of its customers? What are the needs of its customers? These issues can often be included within the new starters induction training.

The Auditors will also require training, whether they are performing external (supplier) or internal auditing.

Typical Competence, Awareness and Training Procedure:

All staff on joining an organisation should attend the induction training course covering such topics as health and safety, fire precautions, etc.

Included within the induction training is an overview of each Division and the range of services provided. At this stage the new employees are made familiar with general organisational procedures and are made fully aware of the Quality and Integrated Management procedures.

Typical Induction Check List

Task	Understood
Introduced to all staff individually	
Shown the Fire Exits & Fire Extinguishers	
Advised of Evacuation Procedures	
Introduced to First Aiders	
Accepts and understands the Health & Safety policy and manual	
Shown how to use all office equipment, i.e. fax machines, photocopiers, etc	
Shown how to access Quality Manual	
Accepts and understands their role and responsibilities in connection with the Quality policy and manual	
Shown staff memo file	
Allocated a computer password	
Computer training given by appropriate person	
The new employee should spend 2-3 hours with each department to help them understand the function carried out by that department. This is to be arranged when convenient for both parties (preferably during first six months). Departments/Processes: ! Order Processing ! Operations ! Commercial ! Finance ! Support	
Each day, if possible a different person to go to lunch with the new employee to show the local facilities, i.e. banks, sandwich shops, etc.	

It would be normal for the organisation to engage staff fully qualified to do a specific job with a high degree of competence. Usually it would then be left to the Managers in conjunction with Personnel to decide upon any specialised training which may be required and to make arrangements accordingly.

As an ongoing activity (possibly part of the appraisal process) staff training needs can be discussed between the individual and the Manager in order to ascertain any specific requirements which may be necessary.

Resource (including training) requirements can then be reviewed during the Management Reviews (See Management Review). However, individual Process Managers and Supervisors would be required to review :

On an *individual needs* basis:
- i)   What tasks require training?
- ii)   What individuals require training and what should they be trained in?
- iii)   How frequently do they need to be trained?
- iv)   What will the training programme be and what is its content?
- v)   What will be the test of individuals' competence?
- vi)   What records of training will be retained?

On a *process or individual task* basis:
- i)   Are the workspace and associated facilities adequate (including issues of health & safety, working methods and general working conditions)?
- ii)   Are the equipment, hardware and software requirements identified?
- iii)   Have suitable maintenance arrangements been made?
- iv)   What supporting services are required?
- v)   What information is required to adequately control and ensure conformity to specified requirements?

The above would be reviewed on a regular basis by the Process owner or Manager, specifically addressing each of these process issues. These process issues are also covered in the section on Product or Service realisation.

The review of the *"Individual needs"* can be achieved during the annual appraisal, where the individual with their Supervisor or Manager identifies their training needs. The Supervisor then agrees this information and may advise or identify where training is needed. Records of these appraisals can be included on the training record.

Training Records

The training record can contain information on the training received both internally on the job and externally, including copies of certificates CVs, etc. All members of the organisation would be included in the master records maintained by the Personnel, Departmental or Process Manager. The records could also detail any training received, either in-house, external courses attended or 'on the job' training. The Departmental Manager may also maintain an inventory detailing who in their Department has special skills or has had training or experience on a particular process or equipment. The training records are reviewed during the management review confirming, among other things, that the annual staff appraisals have been satisfactorily completed.

A typical example of a training record

Organisation plc - Training Schedule & Record

Name:			Job Title:	
Division:			Responsible/Head:	
Training Scheduled			**Training Received**	
Type of Training Proposed	Training Date	Action Date	Description of Training Received	Rec. Date
			Induction: Products/Services Organisation	
			Quality Assurance: Quality Manual Quality Responsibilities	
			Health & Safety	
			Appraisal	

Training Matrix

Records of Technical Support training can be augmented by a Training Matrix which shows the training status of the technician. These matrices are reviewed by the Department Manager during Training Appraisal and when appropriate further or new training is given to the Technicians. Records of this training is shown on a training matrix, an example of which is shown below.

Technician Name / Product or Process Name	Tech A	Tech B	Tech C	Tech N
Process A	A	B	C	D
Process B	D	C	B	A
Process C	A	A	A	A
Process N	B	B	B	B

Key
A   Can teach the operation/process - how to support and maintain
B   Can provide support to Level One within the standard response time
C   Limited experience
D   Very limited or no experience

Product or Service Realisation - Process Management

Product Realisation, Process Management or Work Flow can be usually broken down into the an organisation's key processes; Bidding to Winning, Product or Service Improvement, Supplier

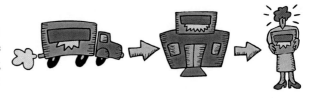

Development, Product or Service Delivery and Product or Service Support (See Section on Quality Improvement Initiatives & Techniques, specifically Business Process Analysis). In the case of ISO 9001 these key business processes have been identified as shown in **Figure 40**. The figure also indicates the probable sequence for each stage in a work flow process.

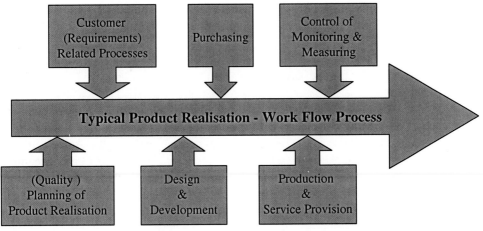

Figure 40 Process Management

Planning for Product Realisation

It is necessary to define and document *what* the quality requirements are and *how* they are to be met.

What the requirement for quality are can simply mean defining the features and specifications (tolerances) for particular products. Alternatively, for a service organisation, department or function the quality requirements or objectives may be defined as "to satisfy its customers". Interpreting this objective in the Marketing and Sales department could require a policy on establishing customer needs and expectations, measuring levels of satisfaction, etc. (See section on Marketing and Sales)

How the requirements for quality can be achieved can easily be described in a Quality Plan. A Quality Plan aims to describe each key process, with the desired results and how the results will be achieved and verified. (See sections on Process Flow Charting, IDF0 and Quality Plan).

- o A description of the Process scope and stages including their inputs and outputs.
- o Procedures or Work Instructions describing how each task is performed and verified.

Quality Planning can also embrace confirmation that the requirements are met and continually improved. This could be achieved through the internal quality audits but the need to continually improve will necessitate the establishment of quality goals and targets (See section on Performance Measurement and Benchmarking).

Customer-Related Processes (Bidding to Winning)

This was more commonly known as contract review but contract review gave the impression of only being concerned with the contract or customer order when there is a need to quality control the whole process. From marketing through enquiry (bidding to gain the order) to order receipt (winning the order or contract) to finally accepting the order, it is necessary to examine the tender[4], contract and order (customer requirements) to ensure that the customer's needs and expectations can be fully met and that any quality requirements have not been overlooked. A review of the contract may provide adequate information regarding the customer requirements. Often understanding of the customer requirements needs to start at a much earlier stage, probably at the enquiry or tender stage.

Marketing and Sales

Quality Assurance of Sales could include such issues as:
- o Setting and monitoring of sales targets for each of the salespersons

---

[4] With the inclusion of tenders, procedures may need to be extended to include control of tender generation.

- o   Conducting appraisals on salespersons performance to determine areas of weakness (ability to identify a customer need, presentation and listening skills etc.)
- o   Determining an appropriate Sales Strategy for the products - advertising, mail drops etc.

As an early warning of any quality problems in the field, procedures or systems may need to be established for reporting where product failures or shortcomings become apparent. This is particularly important with newly introduced products, where there may not be a sufficiently accurate database describing any possible quality failures or shortcomings.

Another area that may be worthy of consideration is the Marketing department's role and responsibilities with regard to:

Customer Needs: How is the marketing brief established and communicated with other departments to gain agreement to the organisation's ability to fulfil the customer requirements? Possibly in terms of price, quantity, quality and delivery. The use of Quality Function Deployment (QFD) may be appropriate (see section on Quality Improvement Initiatives & Techniques, specifically Quality Function Deployment). QFD can also be usefully employed in conducting Benchmarking or competition analysis to compare the advantages and shortcomings of the organisation's product or service over its competitors. There is a need to create an image of a quality organisation for the customer (quality sells). Third party certification may partly help in creating the impression of a quality organisation with the customer.

Customer Satisfaction: There are a number of ways of determining the level of customer satisfaction; marketing or customer satisfaction surveys (see section on Customer Satisfaction), customer complaints analysis etc. The customer complaints may require the creation of a customer complaint log and customer complaint escalation procedure. Where customer problems cannot be immediately dealt with the problem is escalated throughout the organisation.

Marketing Trends: What are the implications of market trends, new technology and legislation? One of the key quality issues can be the accuracy and reliability of any marketing predictions - can the market information be relied upon to make future investment plans?

Marketing Literature: How is the accuracy of the information approved?

Legal requirements (Product Safety and Liability): All safety aspects of the product or service need to be identified. The overall objective is to enhance the product's safety and minimise any product liability problems. Steps should be taken which limit the risk of product liability and minimise the number of cases of potentially dangerous situations.

These steps may include:

- o   Identification of any safety standards that need to be applied to the design of the product or service.
- o   Carrying out evaluation and prototype testing, confirming the safety of the products (see Failure Mode and Effects Analysis).
- o   Maintenance of records of the results of the evaluation and testing.
- o   Carrying out analysis of the instructions or warnings that need to be given to the user, together with the design of the maintenance and labelling on promotional material to ensure that no misunderstandings occur.
- o   The development of means of traceability to facilitate any product recall or

the creation of outline hazard or advisory notices should any adverse health or safety features be discovered after the product has been introduced into the market place.

See section on CE Marking.

The enquiry to Customer Process:

Figure 41 shows a typical sequence that may be followed when controlling the process *"Bidding to Winning."* The process starts with the customer's requirements and ends with an accepted order. Included in the diagram are the use of standard formats for tenders and quotations. The diagram shows the typical reviews or approvals that may be appropriate at each stage.

The review could take the form of completion of a check list, which ensures that all key aspects of the customer requirements have been identified and

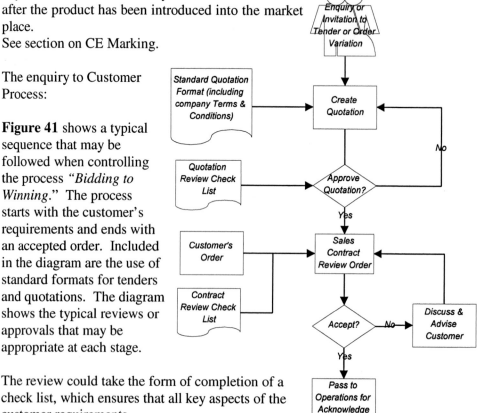

Figure 41 Customer-Related Processes (Contract Review)

addressed. Contained in the following procedure for Customer Requirements Review is a typical series of customer requirements review questions. Due to the importance of this activity it is critical that records of customer requirements reviews are maintained. It is worth noting that customer requirements review also applies to orders, even when not written.

Guidelines for general and customer requirements review

Note, "general" to cover legislation and other constraints not necessarily specified or known by the customer.

Review of customer enquiries/specifications, quotations and orders

a. Review of customer enquiries/specifications
   On receipt of a customer enquiry or specification: when the enquiry is special (e.g. away from the standard price list) the Salesperson concerned completes an enquiry form/check list detailing the customer's requirements. (See Appendix A on Page 121).

   On completion of the enquiry, the form is signed by the (technical) reviewer and where appropriate submitted to a relevant Manager for approval. If the enquiry is acceptable to the supplier and the customer's requirements are understood, a quotation is raised on the basis of the information contained within the enquiry form.

b. Approval of quotations
   On raising a written quotation, the Salesperson, Technical Administrator or other appropriate person concerned reviews the quotation against an appropriate relevant check list (see Appendix A). The quotation is then provided to the customer.

c. Approval of orders
   On receipt of a customer order - the order is then reviewed against the relevant check list (See Appendix A) by the salesperson and the listed technical advisors. On completion of the review, which may involve drawing up an initial project plan (in the case of large orders), the order is then stamped and signed *"Customer requirements review - accepted"*. The order is then entered into the computer system via a series of screen prompts.

   If rejected the customer is advised.

NOTE: All these actions require checks for Quality Assurance requirements and may require frequent and lengthy discussions with the customer in order to establish that both parties are satisfied with regard to what is to be supplied.

d. Should there be any subsequent amendments to the customer requirements the above procedure will be repeated and the contract updated accordingly.

Appendix A

General Check list for reviewing customers enquiries, quotations and orders[5]

Customer (Requirements) Order - Check List						
Customer Number	Order Number		Date			
Customer Name	Customer Address					
Responsibilities for approval shown thus "X"		Sales	Finance & Legal	Technical	Procurement	Production
Product/Services Defined?		X		X	X	
Installation, Commissioning, Training and Support Defined?				X		
Customer Contractual Requirements Defined?		X	X	X	X	
Unspecified Customer Requirements identified? I.e. Issues which will effect the products or services fitness for purpose but not specified by the customer. E.g. Product or Service Health & Safety.		X		X		
Prices Correct?		X				
Delivery Times Acceptance?				X	X	X
Customer Financial Health Acceptable?			X			
Supplier's Terms & Conditions accepted by Client?			X			
Customer Terms & Conditions acceptable?			X			
Legal or Regulatory consideration acceptable?				X		
Any special Quality Assurance requirements (e.g. special customer tests)?		X		X		
Signatures and dates						

---

[5] It is unlikely that this check list would be completed, it is for reference purposes when conducting a Customer Requirements Review.

Note 1. This form would only be used for significant or large orders.

Note 2. With this form different groups have different responsibilities. Ownership of each different aspect of the contract is shown by the X for responsibility, and ownership by the signature at the end of the form. This clearly shows who has taken responsibility for on time delivery, price, meeting customer requirements, etc. The downside is obtaining the signatures and the delay in progressing (starting) the customer's order. Organisations have chosen not to follow this approach because of the delays involved. This can be counter productive - as when the project or product does not meet specification or is delivered late - who is at fault? Sales for accepting the order? Technical or Procurement for not completing their tasks quickly enough?

Note 3. The quality department is conspicuous by their absence from this form. Does the quality department have a role to play? Yes, but only to ensure that the forms are processed and signed correctly. Quality Department personnel signing the form will only re-enforce the belief that it is they who are responsible for the quality of the product or service, when quite the reverse is needed.

Note 4. The above approach to understanding customer requirements is very formal and proceduralised. There are other less formal approaches to establishing customer requirements together with discussing the advantages and disadvantages of tight and lose specifications. See section on Customer Satisfaction and the exercise at the end of this section.

Design and development: (Product or Service development or enhancement process)

Controlling the design of any product or service is fundamental in ensuring that all quality requirements and considerations have been adequately addressed. It is worth considering that no amount of control in manufacture or installation will correct a design which is inherently wrong. At best all the manufacturer can achieve is to make something which is perfectly wrong, (meets the drawing but fails to meet the customer requirements). (See section on Project Quality Assurance).

So having gained a complete understanding of the customer requirements and specification, the next stage is to

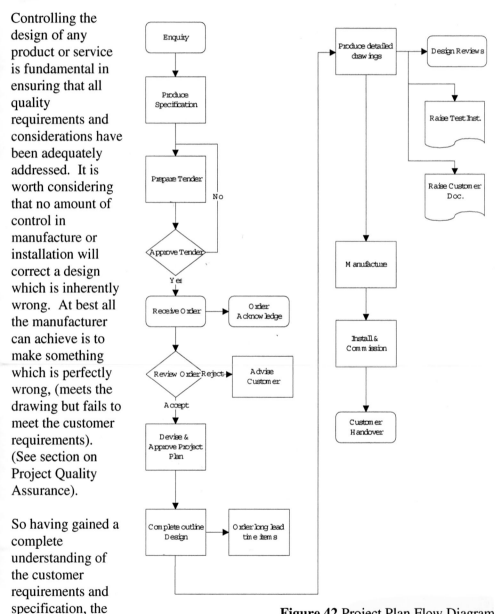

Figure 42 Project Plan Flow Diagram

ensure that the designed solution will fulfil the customer expectations. Note, the design specification is not only useful for design purposes, it can also be easily rewritten into a test specification.

Design and development planning - To ensure that the responsibilities and tasks for each development activity have been identified, plans can be compiled (sometimes known as PERT charts) which describe events and indicate time scales for the various activities. These plans can include identification of personnel responsible for particular quality tasks in the design and development programme, such as design and safety reviews, trials and tests and project audits (see section on Quality Auditing). **Figure 42** shows a typical project plan flow diagram from receipt of the Invitation To Tender (ITT) or enquiry through to handover. It is worth noting that **Figure 42** displays some of the weaknesses in showing activities and tasks in this serial manner. Concurrent manufacture suggests that manufacturing should start when the first drawings are produced and before the final design review is completed. The final design review may only take place before despatch, although for some organisations after commissioning (or never at all). Personally, I would not accept final design review taking place after despatch or test without extremely good reasons.

The stages can include:

Understanding of customer requirements - Possibly by the creation of a product's specification. It is often the case that the customer does not know exactly what he wants and it may be necessary for the supplier to draw up their own specification for approval by the customer. However, prior to the release of this specification to the customer an internal review may be necessary to check the proposals and quotation. See section on Customer Satisfaction.

Acceptance of the order - Necessitates an investigation similar to the stages described in the section on Customer requirements review.

Design Input - At the beginning of any project it is essential that all the relevant information is agreed, available and understood. The type of information required could include:

Design and Development Plans, Functional Specifications, Customer, Contractual, Statutory and Safety Requirements, budgets and costings. It may be appropriate to review these design inputs to confirm the information is complete, accurate and adequate to safeguard the customer and user of the product or service.

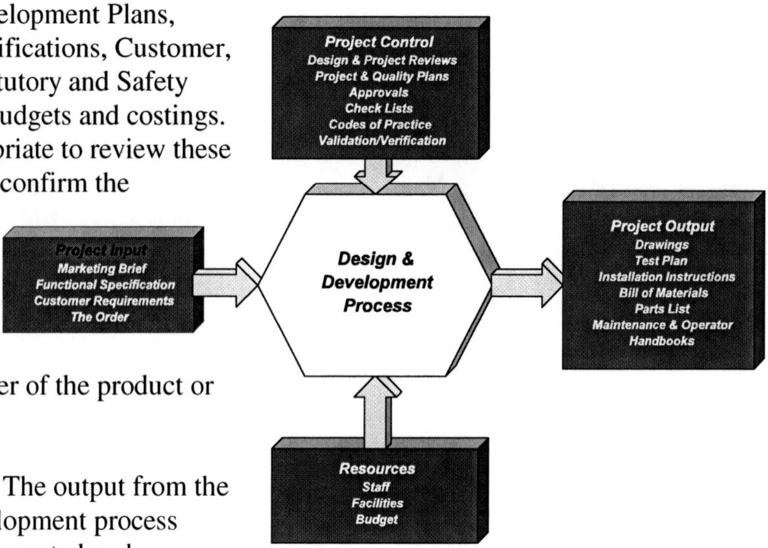

Figure 43 Design & Development Control

Design Output - The output from the design and development process needs to be documented and reviewed. This review is to confirm that the design output meets all the expectations of the customer. These expectations would have been detailed during the design input. The review identifies those characteristics of the design which are crucial to the safe and correct use and function of the product. The design output ought to define the checks and tests that need to be carried out during manufacture, installation, commissioning, and possibly at regular intervals throughout the life of the product. The Design Output could include: reports, results of tests, trials and analysis (e.g. safety analysis), drawings, bills of materials, costs, process instructions, test instructions, operation and maintenance manuals etc.

Design Validation & Verification

Definitions:

Word	**Dictionary definition**	**ISO 9001:2000**
Verification	Establishment of truth or correctness	Conformation, through the provision of objective evidence, that the specified requirements have been fulfilled.
Validation	Ratification or confirmation	Conformation, through the provision of objective evidence, that the requirements for a specific intended use or application have been fulfilled

The design output (drawings, test results, trials etc.) needs to be checked, validated and verified to confirm that the design output is not only accurate and reliable but also fulfils the criteria for the design input, namely it meets original specifications. This may be achieved in a number of ways; holding design reviews (see **Table 16**), undertaking tests or demonstrations, proving, verifying and validating the appropriateness of the design. Verification may be performed by completing alternative calculations (doing the calculations in a different way) and having all key documentation, design decisions, calculations etc. checked and approved by competent personnel. **Figure 43** shows typically what may be included in design input, design output and design verification.

Table 16 Typical Agenda for a Design Review Meeting

Design/Project Review Minutes		
Project Name:	**Project Number:**	**Project Manager:**
Distribution:		**Date:**
Items		**Remarks**
1 Specification: 1.1 Mechanical Specification 1.2 Electrical Specification 1.3 Services & Support Specification (Training, Technical etc.) 1.4 Any amendments to specification? 1.5 Will performance still be as defined?		
2 Target dates: What is the status of the following (are they still on target)? 2.1 Design 2.2 Purchasing 2.3 Release for production 2.4 Installation & Commissioning		
3 Design/Project review: 3.1 Safety factors/requirements (FMEA) 3.2 Drawing; GA, Detail 3.3 Calculations		
4 Status of documentation: 4.1 Inspection & Test Instructions 4.2 Project & Quality Plan completed 4.3 Installation & Commissioning Instructions 4.4 Operating, service and maintenance manuals (Spares List)		
5 Approvals: 5.1 Customer Approval 5.2 Third Party Approval		
6 Commercial aspects: 6.1 Is the project within budget, if not what are proposed actions? 6.2 Is the project within time scale, if not what are proposed actions? 6.3 Invoice & Payment Received		
7 Any other business?:		

Although reference is made to documents, approval is required for other types of data and information. The table below shows various activities that may require approval and the nominated persons that can perform the creation and approval function.

The first two columns show the typical activities that will require verification. Adjacent to each activity are **named** individuals who can create the documentation and an independent person who can approve or check the output.

Table 17 Verification Activities

VERIFICATION			
Activity	Remarks	Author	Approver
Calculations	Evidence of any calculation checking is recorded on the calculation sheet showing who performed the check and the date. (See Calculation Check List).	Draughtsman	Chief Engineer
Drawings	Detail drawings show the date, the originator, title, drawing number and are then independently checked.	Draughtsman	Design Engineer
Specifications	Specifications written by the Designer are checked and approved.	Draughtsman	Design Engineer
Operating Manuals	Operating Manuals written by the Designer are approved. Manuals written or obtained from the manufacturers or other external sources are approved by the Designer or Design Manager. (See document Check List).	Draughtsman	Design Engineer
Subcontractors	Designs produced at subcontractors or by contractors are reviewed and approved.	Subcontractors	Design Engineer

This next table shows a typical checklist that can be used to help in the checking process. See section software Quality Assurance, specifically Document Inspection.

Table 18 Typical Calculation Check List

Calculation Check List	
Description	Response
Check for document control purposes e.g. title, number, issue number and date, originator etc.	
Calculation objectives stated.	
Methodology correct e.g. formulae or sequence etc. *Reference to text book solutions may be appropriate.*	
Definition of terms available and correct.	
Statement of constants and variables e.g. P=pressure (variable) g=9.81 m/s^2.	
Data accurate and correctly entered.	
Arithmetic correct e.g. 2+1=3.	
Units constant e.g. Imperial/metric.	

Note 1: The questions are meant as a guide and in certain circumstances may not be applicable. Completion of this check would not absolve the author of the responsibility for the quality of the calculations.

Note 2: This form would not normally be completed. However, the facility to record the approver's response is provided.

Note 3: Use of this calculation check list in no way removes the responsibility for the accuracy of the calculation from the author. Accuracy of the calculation (as always) remains firmly with the author of the calculation.

Installation & Commissioning - This stage can include the compilation of installation and commissioning plans and instructions. These instructions can include (but are not limited to): all the various checks and tests that will need to be performed; the expected or target figure and tolerances; the records of tests that will need to be retained and the handover certificate that is to be provided.

Design & Development Changes

Document Approval and Issue - It is often the case with projects of any size that a certain amount of documentation will be generated. Many documents require to be controlled with respect to issue and change (sometimes known as configuration control). Examples of such documents include: the original specification, drawings, test specifications, software, forms, procedures, manuals etc. Note, the words *software* and *drawing* are interchangeable with the word *document*. Documents such as these will need to be reviewed and approved for their completeness and accuracy prior to being issued. This means that the following information will need to be kept for documents which are under the change control system: document title and number; an author; an approver; the issue date and number; page of pages and a circulation list. **Figure 44** shows the sequence from document creation to document issue. Having created the document, it will require checking or approving. Typically a document check list could consist of:

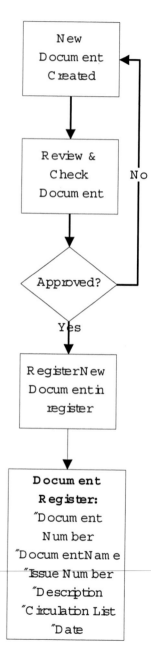

a. Is the document accurate?
b. Is the document complete?
c. Is the document in the correct format?
d. Is the document issue status correct?

It is very important to remember at this stage that checking or approving documentation does not shift responsibility for the quality of document from the author to the checker. This responsibility still remains firmly with the author. The checker is only assisting the owner of the document.

Having accepted the document, the document will require registering. **Table 19** shows a typical drawing or document register. The left-hand column would contain the drawing numbers and as new issues were created the columns to the right would be completed by

Figure 44 Drawing Creation Control

adding the issue level and circulation date, i.e. Issue A, Issue B etc.

At the bottom of the table is space to list names or titles of people on the circulation list and to the right of the name, the date of transmittal of the drawing.

Table 19 Typical Drawing Register

Drawing Number	Issue Number							
	A	B	C	D	E	F	G	H
Circulation List								

If at some later stage the document undergoes change, procedures may be necessary that control approval of the change, control of the issue and circulation of the new documentation and implementation of the change.

A typical drawing or document control sequence from creation to issue and subsequently change control (should the drawing require updating) is detailed in **Figure 44** and **Figure 45**. The first stage is to raise a document change note; this note is necessary to detail the content of the change and to record the reasons for change control. It may also be necessary to detail the effects of change on fit and function and the implication of change on such items as stores stock, work in the field, service, maintenance manuals etc. In the case of software the analysis of the effects and implications of change is important, as a small change to the software in one place could have significant effect on the performance of the software elsewhere. Having agreed and completed the modification, the modification itself requires approval to confirm that the change meets the original objectives. The register can now be updated and the document circulated.

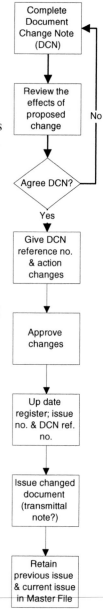

Figure 45
Control of
Drawing
Changes

Purchasing

In industry today it is unlikely that any organisation will process raw material into a completed finished product. It is more likely that purchased items or sub-assemblies will be obtained for re-processing or assembly into the finished item. These sub-assemblies or purchased items need to be controlled as they can have a significant effect on the finished product's ability to meet the quality requirements.

Assessment of Suppliers - It is important that the selection of suppliers is on the basis of the supplier's ability to meet the quality requirements. For this reason suppliers may be assessed to confirm their ability to meet the customer requirements. Assessment could take the form of a formal external audit (see section on Audit). Alternatively, the assessment could take the form of reviewing and accepting a satisfactorily completed quality assurance questionnaire from the supplier. Another method of assessment is confirming that the supplier has a quality assurance system of assessed capability (by a recognised assessment body). Records could be maintained for the supplier's performance in the form of an approved suppliers list and Vendor Rating. (See section on Supplier Quality Assurance).

Purchasing Information - Purchasing documents need to accurately describe the product or service to be ordered and include identification of any key requirements which, if not met, could have an adverse effect on quality. The purchasing information could also include instructions regarding certificates of conformity or any tests or inspections the supplier must perform. A review of the Purchasing Information must be obtained prior to issue. This review usually takes the form of an authorising signature on the purchasing document.

Guidelines for Purchasing Control

1.   General Procedures

A supplier is defined as *an organisation that provides a product* (ISO 9000:2000). Suppliers also include any manufacturer or stockist of proprietary equipment or products.

Suppliers must be evaluated for their ability to satisfy the purchaser's requirements. This may include considerations such as having a sound financial base, the required background, capacity and capability. Suppliers should be chosen from an approved suppliers list, wherever possible. Exceptions to using preferred suppliers may be made subject to the following conditions:

○ The product to be purchased does not significantly affect the quality standard required by the organisation.
○ The Quality Manager, or nominated deputy, approves the supplier.

2. Supplier Assessment & Evaluation

Suppliers should have established and effective quality control procedures based on ISO 9000 or other appropriate standards. Not withstanding this, the organisation should reserve the right to carry out its own assessment of the supplier's Quality management system which may be by the use of the supplier questionnaire or by an assessment visit to the supplier. An example of such a questionnaire can be found at the end of this section on Purchasing Control.

New Supplier Selection

If a new supplier is to be selected or used, i.e. a supplier not on the approved supplier list, then the new supplier can be added to the approved list provided that the new supplier:

i. Has established and implemented effective quality control procedures based on ISO 9000 or other appropriate standards. If possible confirmed by an independent body.

or

ii. Can satisfactorily complete the supplier's questionnaire.

or

iii. The supplier is found to be satisfactory when assessed.

On satisfactory completion of one or more of the above the new supplier is added to the approved list at the provisional level.

3. Purchasing Information

The suppliers must be provided with complete and comprehensive documentation which details the standards to be achieved. Any modifications to the Purchase Order are agreed with the supplier and the documentation amended as appropriate.

The Buyer must also develop and foster relationships with the supplier aimed at reinforcing their appreciation of the need for effective Quality Assurance. Purchase orders would typically contain the following information:

a. Supplier's name and address
b. Order number
c. Date

d.   Some reference to standard terms and conditions
e.   Any Quality Management System requirements of the supplier
f.   The appropriate inspection level
g.   Delivery address
h.   Invoice address
i.   Description of product to be supplied
j.   Quantity
k.   Delivery date required
l.   Actual/estimated cost (on organisation's copy)

NOTE: Purchase orders may refer to the inspection level. For example:

Inspection Level 1 -	Normal inspection by Goods Inwards staff as per the Goods Receiving Instruction in Section 10 of the Quality Manual
Inspection Level 2 -	As Inspection Level 1 but supplied with a Certificate of Conformity
Inspection Level 3 -	Inspection as Level 2 but with full electrical and other safety tests (or checks as specified by the Purchase Order originator)

The authorised Buyer then reviews the order for the above and signs to provide evidence that the buyer has authorised the order.

2.   Verification of the Purchased Product

The suppliers must understand that all supplies must be to the specified standards and that any deviation from the standard can only be permitted after formal agreement with the purchasing organisation. Where it is a requirement of the contract or order, reasonable access shall be provided for the Customer to verify compliance of the product at source.

3.   Supplier Performance Evaluation

A record of acceptable suppliers and their products or services may be maintained by the Quality Manager and held by the Buyer and Accounts. This record will be supplemented by notes of the results of any supplier appraisal gained by questionnaires and/or assessment visits, delivery monitoring and any customer feedback.

The suppliers' performance shall be monitored during the Management Review by examination of the reject and concession notes. The goods inwards checking person annotates the delivery note with any problems found with the delivered goods, such as damaged packaging, damaged goods, incorrect goods etc. A reject note is raised on the basis of this information. (See sections "Inspection and Test" and "Control of Substandard Product and Work"). Depending on the frequency and category of rejection and concession, the suppliers shall either remain on the approved list or be removed.

Removal or addition of suppliers to these lists is discussed during the Management Review and the lists updated accordingly and re-issued.

Table 20 Typical example for Approved Suppliers List

Approved Suppliers List			
Name	Address	Product or Service	Vendor Rating

Typical Example of a Supplier Assessment Questionnaire[6]

Supplier's Name and Address

#	Question	YES/NO/DETAILS
1	Is the Supplier's quality system of assessed capability by a recognised body? If yes please give details and ignore questions 3 to 17.	
2	Does the Supplier have: I) A person with written responsibility for Quality Assurance? If yes please give details ii) A person with responsibility for inspection? If yes please give details	Name: Title: Name: Title:
3	Does the Supplier have a Quality Manual?	
4	Does the Supplier review the Purchase Orders for completeness, accuracy and viability?	
5	Does the Supplier further subcontract the organisation's work?	
6	Does the Supplier identify work throughout the process?	
7	Does the Supplier identify the inspection status of work throughout the process?	
8	Does the Supplier provide any written instructions describing how the work is to be performed? Please give details.	
9	Does the Supplier inspect incoming material?	
10	Does the Supplier perform any in-process and final test and inspection of completed work? If so what form does this take?	

---

[6]   Although very popular these questionnaires are of limited value.

Quality Management Systems

#	Question	YES/NO/DETAILS
11	Does the Supplier calibrate measuring and test equipment?	
12	Does the Supplier perform any Quality Audits? If so, what type?	
13	Does the Supplier keep records of the results of: Receipt inspection and test? In-process inspection and test? Final inspection and test? Quality Audits (Product/System)? Calibration?	
14	Does the Supplier train any personnel performing an inspection activity?	
15	Does the Supplier have scrap or reject labels?	
16	Does the Supplier have a written procedure for dealing with remedial action that may be necessary as a result of supplies being rejected by the organisation?	
17	Does the Supplier arrange for goods sent to the organisation to be packaged?	
18	Is there any additional information that may be relevant? If so please provide details below:	
Signed:	Position in Company:	Date:

Production and service provision (Process Control)

Control of Production and Service provision

Controls need to be applied to the processes or tasks to ensure that all the methods are clearly specified and procedures followed. Such controls may include a documented work instruction, this work instruction will usually define:

- The process stages and the sequence.
- The features that need to be controlled.
- How the controls are going to be maintained.
- What the specified requirements are, i.e. the tolerances or standards to be achieved.
- The records that will be maintained, indicating successful completion of the process.
- The equipment (including measurement) that will be used and what environmental conditions are necessary.
- Descriptions regarding the process preventive maintenance arrangements.
- Any other Work Instructions, special standards or codes of practice. These may include any other criteria for workmanship by objective or subjective standards.
- The means of verification and monitoring prior to release.

A typical format for a process planning sheet that can be used for describing the process control procedures is shown in the table below.

Table 21 A Process Planning Sheet

Stage	Process Description	Work Instruction or Codes of Practice	Specification	Equipment	Records

See sections; Process Flow Charting and Quality Manual

Other processes which may require control include service and after sales support:

o   Servicing

If products are not properly serviced this can have a detrimental effect on the quality performance of the product. For this reason procedures need to be established which describe the proper maintenance and servicing arrangements for the product or service. For service organisations this may include call escalation procedures.

o   After Sales Servicing and Support

Procedures may need to be established which describe the correct installation and commissioning of any equipment to ensure that it will perform adequately for quality. The installation and commissioning instructions may include specific inspections and tests that may need to be performed. Records on the satisfactory conclusion of the inspection and test may also be required. After sales support may also include help desk or technical support.

A typical process associated with technical support is shown in **Figure 46**.
See BS 15000 *Specification for IT Service Management*, but applicable to most support services.

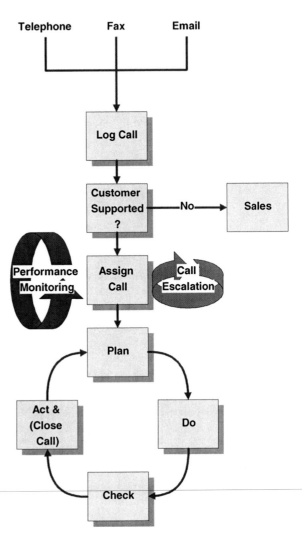

Figure 46 After Sales Support

140

Validation of Processes

With some processes it is impossible or sometimes economially unjustifiable to determine whether the resulting process output meets specification. In these circumstances the process itself has to be validated rather than the process output or deliverable. For example "Making an omelette" economically - it is not very sound to check that the output is correct, far better to control (validate) the process and its inputs (eggs, heat, etc.). Similarly in the manufacture of ordinance or bombs.

To that extent, controls need to be applied to qualification of the equipment, materials, method and people before running the process. Records should be made, providing evidence that during the running of the process, the key measurable features have been satisfactorily controlled. Also after a suitable period of time the process parameters are re-validated.

Identification and Traceability

Material requires identification so that the wrong material is not used or the wrong part processed. This identification may need to extend throughout the process. It is important to identify work in such a manner to show whether the work is awaiting inspection or test. Once the work has been inspected it is necessary to indicate whether the work is acceptable or not.

Traceability: The extent to which traceability is required is largely based on; the industry sector (medical, food etc.), the customer requirements (aerospace industry JAR145) or a statutory requirement. The requirement for traceable material may, on occasion, extend to purchasing material which has undergone certain tests and inspections to ensure its suitability (e.g. Cast Certificates for raw material).

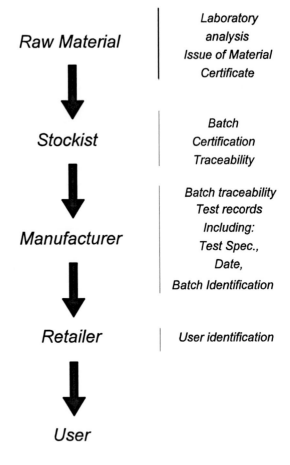

Figure 47 Traceability

In these cases it may also be appropriate to identify this material throughout the process to ensure traceability is maintained. **Figure 47** shows traceability of an item from the raw material production and laboratory tests (certification), through to manufacture and test (final test certificate). It may be necessary to extend this traceability into the field, particularly for items which are safety critical and may be recalled (medical industry). The level of identification could include test specification number, date of test, batch identification etc. The records may include the eventual destination of the item.

Customer Property (Customer Supplied Product)

It may be that on occasions the customer supplies material or products which need to be processed and then returned to the purchaser (Free Issue Material - FIM). Procedures need to be established and maintained to ensure that any FIM is controlled and looked after in the same manner as the organisation's own material. In the security industry this takes on a more important aspect as there will be a need to properly safeguard and secure data and information (including electronic) supplied by the customer. This data may be of a commercially sensitive nature or pose a security (defence) risk.

Preservation of Product

The preservation of product embraces the handling, packaging, storage, protection and delivery process. If product preservation is not properly controlled it can affect the quality of the product.

Handling - Procedures need to be established describing the correct and safe methods of handling the product that prevents any damage or deterioration, e.g. static precautions for electronic devices.

Packaging - Controls of the packaging, preservation and marking of the product may be necessary to avoid any problems in transportation which could adversely affect the quality of the product. This may be particularly important with sterilisation processes.

Storage - Control of the stores area is important to ensure that no damage or deterioration of the product pending its use or delivery, can take place. These controls may need to extend to first in and first out procedures (FIFO), stock control, issue and receipt etc.

Protection - There is a need to identify where the product is at risk from the environment and take steps to ensure that the product is maintained in a satisfactory condition. Controls such as shelf life, date coding and reviews of condition of stock can be employed.

Control of Measuring and Monitoring Devices (Calibration)

When tests are performed, it is essential that the measuring or test equipment used is accurate, otherwise inaccurate results and wrong judgements can be made, e.g. faulty work could be inadvertently passed. The following list describes the key requirements of a calibration system.

Table 22 Calibration Labelling

i) Identify all measuring equipment with a unique identification, e.g. serial number and its calibration status. See **Table 22**.

ii) Establish the frequency with which the measuring equipment needs to be checked, e.g. for a set of weighing scales this could be every 6 months.

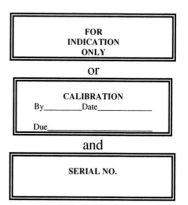

iii) Define procedures that describe the calibration system (measuring equipment recall procedure etc.). This can be a card file; one card for each piece of measuring equipment. The cards are then filed in next calibration date order, so at the beginning of each month the equipment that requires calibration is identified and located.

iv) Detail the individual calibration procedures for each type of measuring equipment. For weighing scales this could be having some calibrated weights placed on the scales and checking the readings correspond with the calibrated weights.

v) Ensure that the inspection and test equipment has the necessary accuracy and precision. For the weighing scales example the accuracy of the calibrated weights could be 10% of the accuracy of the scales.

vi) Define the procedures that describe the activities necessary if the results of calibration highlight equipment error. If the weighing scales were found to be in error when calibrated and used for weighing drugs, then it may be necessary to take corrective action, possibly to recall the drugs.

vii) Establish calibration history records showing the previous calibration results. **Table 23** shows a typical calibration history sheet.

Table 23 A Typical Calibration History Sheet

CALIBRATION HISTORY RECORD SHEET					
Equipment Type:			Model No.:		
Serial No.:			Size:		
Calibration Frequency:			Procedure No.:		
DATE OF LAST CALIBRA-TION	DATE OF NEXT CALI-BRATION	DATE OUT/IN	LOCATION	RESULT OF CALIBRA-TION	REMARKS

viii) Determine the necessary environmental conditions suitable for accurate calibration.

ix) Detail appropriate handling, preservation and storage procedures.

x) Ensure that equipment is sealed to avoid any possibility of adjustments that could invalidate the calibration setting. For the weighing scales any adjustment screws would need to be sealed to prevent tampering.

Calibration and Automatic Test Equipment (ATE)

ATE equipment is automatic (usually computer controlled) test equipment. Frequently used for the testing of assemblies and sub-assemblies. Typically these types of machines have either an 'in circuit' or a 'functional' test capability (or a combination of both).

'In circuit' testing confirms that a circuit board has been manufactured correctly (i.e. finds short circuits, open circuits and components that are outside tolerance limits). The in circuit tester usually interfaces with the unit under test (UUT) via a bed of nails fixture that has one pin for every electrical node. This allows measuring of characteristics between any electrical connections (e.g. across each component).

Figure 48 shows a typical ATE set up. 'Functional' testing interfaces to the UUT either via a few pins in a bed of nails fixture (e.g. maybe one pin per 100 connections) or by way of flying leads. This means of testing could be used for a printed circuit board or a whole assembly. A 'good' functional test will find any manufacturing defects plus any parameters that are not within design specifications.

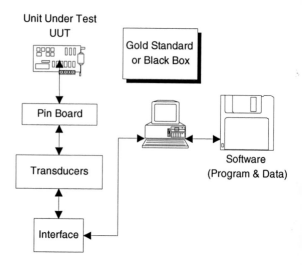

Figure 48 Typical Automatic Test Equipment

Functional testing is quick to highlight a failure whereas in circuit testing is quicker to pin point where the failure lies, (i.e. identifies the fault location down to component level). A typical use for ATE is in medium to high volume production or for high level technology, such as the space industry.

The use of automatic testing ensures that all the assemblies are tested to within predefined tolerances. The testing becomes objective as opposed to subjective. The QA personnel would need to ensure that the preselected tolerances are correct. Once proven this method of testing provides a very high degree of repeatability, plus the availability of automatically logged test results for use in SQC and real time fault analysis (RTFA).

Calibration of the equipment, i.e. transducers and connection between the equipment under test and the computer: The transducer and connection between the computer and the pin board can be tested, although not completely, by the use of a "Gold Standard" or "Black Box." This "Gold Standard" could be a specially selected unit that is a known standard or quality. This "Gold Standard" would be regularly retested by the ATE to confirm that the hardware is working satisfactorily.

Validation and verification of the test software program and data - the software for ATE could consist of:

- the program to drive the ATE
- the sequencer which runs the sequence and determines which test to perform
- the test data (both target value and tolerance)

The program and sequencer will need to be validated and verified. The test data will need to be checked.

Measurement, Analysis and Improvement

Without measurement it is impossible to determine if any improvements have been made. Three key areas where measurement, analysis and improvement is of importance are QMS performance, Process Performance and Product or Service Performance.

It may be also appropriate or necessary to establish statistical techniques which ensure that the processes are of acceptable capability, initially and consistently throughout the process cycle. (See section on Statistical Quality Control).

Customer Satisfaction
Levels of customer satisfaction cannot be measured by the number of customer complaints. Customer complaints are a measure of customer dissatisfaction not satisfaction. There are various means of measuring levels of customer satisfaction, many of these are described in the section on Customer Satisfaction.

Internal Audit
With any QMS it is essential that regular checks are made to ensure that the procedures are effectively implemented. For this reason arrangements need to be made to conduct regular audits. These arrangements need to include the frequency and procedures describing the conduct of such audits. (See section on Quality Audit).

Monitoring and Measurement of Processes

The measurement of process performance depends on the processes under analysis. The table below includes the key processes described in ISO 9001 with some typically associated performance measures (see section on Cost of Quality).

Table 24 Some typical process performance measures

Process	Performance Measure
Customer Related Processes (Bidding to Winning, Order processing, Contract review, etc.)	Number of enquiries turned into order Number of customer complaints Order levels (both numbers and value) Lost customers New customers Number errors per quotation
(Product or Service) Design & Development Process	Project on time Project to budget Project meeting customer requirements
Purchasing or Procurement Process	Number of supplier rejects Number of on time deliveries Shortages
Product or Service Operation or Delivery	Product or service availability and reliability Levels of scrap, rework, concessions, etc.
Service Support	Average response time Average down time

Measurement and monitoring of products - (Inspection and Testing)

In terms of the product or service process this can be broken down into control of the process inputs (Goods Receiving Inspection), control of the process activities and tasks (In-process Inspection and Test) and process output control (Final Inspection and Test).

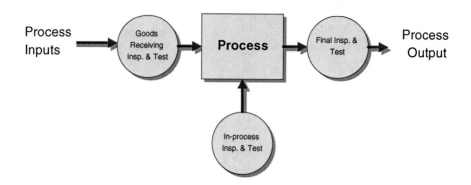

Figure 50 Process Control (Measurement & Monitoring)

Measurement and monitoring of products or services performance in practice.

o *Process Input Inspection & Test*

Process Inputs are all of the material, data, resources, etc. (i.e. materiel[7]) needed before the process can start. Goods Receiving Inspection & Test is confirming that all materiel is available in the right quantity and of the quality. These inspection and tests may be performed by the process operator or more importantly by the process supplier. See section on Supplier Quality Assurance.

Receiving Inspection and Testing - All organisations, to some degree, perform Goods Receiving Inspection (GRI). It may be a full dimensional and physical assessment of the delivered materials ability to meet the purchasing specification or check on quantity, correct identification, condition or damage and documentation. Some decision by the organisation is needed to determine the necessary level of GRI. (See section on Supplier Quality Assurance and Statistical Quality Control, specifically Process Capability Studies).

---

[7]   Materiel as apposed to material is all the items a process requires to start. Including; machines, equipment, people, money, facilities, data, material, etc.

o *In-process Inspection & Test*

It can be more efficient to ensure compliance in the intermediate stages of the process rather than waiting until the service or product has been completed. (See Section Statistical Quality Control).

o *Final Inspection and Test*

Having completed the product or service, checks need to be performed to confirm the compliance.

A typical format of an Inspection and Test Plan for Final Inspection of a cereal packet is shown in **Table 25**.

Table 25 Typical Inspection and Test Plan

#	Inspection or Test Description	Inspection Instructions	Feature	Performance Criteria	Measuring Equipment	Recording Method
1	Printing	Description on how the test will be performed; method, sequence, responsibilities etc.	Clarity, Colours	Visual Visual	Description of the gauges, measuring equipment, fixtures, machines etc.	Attribute Charts
2	Outer package		Peel strength Material Sizes Strength, Thickness Durability Hygiene and sterility	5N ± 0.1N Chemical mm ± mm 5N ± 0.1N mm±mm 5N ± 0.1N Bug count		Variable Charts Attribute Chart Variable Chart Variable Chart Variable Chart Variable Chart Attribute Chart
3	Inner package		Peel strength Material Sizes Strength, Thickness Durability Hygiene and sterility	5N ± 0.1N Chemical mm ± mm 5N ± 0.1N mm±mm 5N ± 0.1N Bug count		Variable Charts Attribute Chart Variable Chart Variable Chart Variable Chart Variable Chart Attribute Chart
It could be that this table also includes checks on the package contents						

Control of Non-Conformity

Where items or products have been found not to comply with the necessary quality standards procedures need to be established and implemented that identify, and if appropriate segregate, the non-conforming material or product until such time as a decision can be made as to the action necessary. I.e. concession, rework, scrap, regrade etc.

Evaluation of Suspect Material: If suspect material is found an approach that can be adopted in determining possible action is detailed in **Figure 51**.

Quality Management (Principles & Practice)

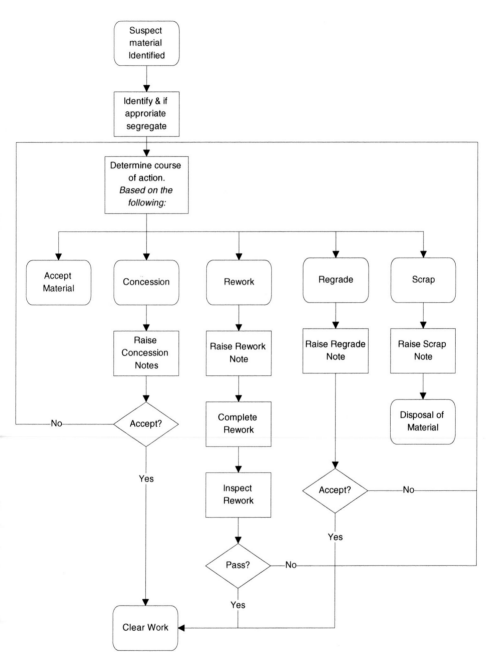

Figure 51 Flow Diagram for Non-Conforming Material

Note 1:   *Suspect material does not necessarily mean faulty.*
Note 2:   *The forms employed could be a combined non-conformance form which could also encompass Audit reports, customer complaints etc.*
Note 3:   ***Figure 51** only covers the action taken to resolve the immediate problem (non-conforming material) and does not include the action taken to prevent recurrence - see section n Corrective & Preventive Action.*

In the case of safety critical products e.g. food manufacturing, electrical goods etc. it may be appropriate to establish procedures in the event of a product recall being necessary. Not only is this good preplanning (hopefully unnecessary) but also because it can possibly lead to a reduction in the insurance premium.

A guide to such a product recall procedure could be:

i)   Circulate a note to key members of the company, including the Managing Director, indicating the situation and proposing the following action.

ii)   Establish the seriousness of the problem, where possible the likely effect on health and safety, fit and function, aesthetics etc.

iii)   Establish the extent of the problem, how many items are affected and how the items affected are to be identified (date of manufacture, serial number etc.).

iv)   Determine the most appropriate corrective action; recall, rectification, check etc.

v)   Determine the most appropriate method for notifying customers or users of the suspect items and the action they should take (e.g. return item to factory for replacement). Hazard or advisory notice to all customers either by letter or in the form of a press release.

vi)   Determine the most appropriate method of monitoring the effectiveness of the corrective action. Also the success with which the customers affected have been contacted and items affected have been located.

Analysis of Data

Having recorded nonconformance events (scrap, concession, customer complaint, etc.), then some form of data analysis may be suitable to establish trends and determine whether corrective action is effective.

Customer Complaints

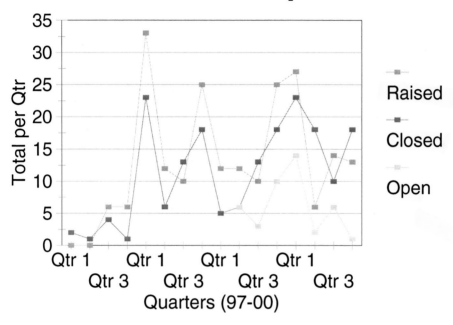

Figure 52 Customer Complaint Performance

Figure 52 represents an organisation's customer complaint performance over a period of three years. The graph shows the numbers of customer complaints raised, closed (resolved) and open (not resolved) each month. This enables the manager to quickly determine any trends and determine current performance. Is there any thing missing from the graph[8]?

---

[8] There does not appear to have been any targets set.

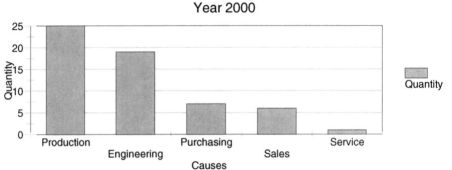

Figure 53 Pareto Analysis of Customer Complaint Causes

Figure 53 represents departments which have been the source the customer complaint.

Improvement

Corrective Action

It is essential that any non-conformance such as a faulty product is quickly detected and quarantined, thus stopping any faulty or dangerous items or products reaching the customer. This is also applicable to service organisations. For example in the medical profession, where the identification of poor service takes on great importance in terms of mis-diagnosis and incorrect operations or procedures, causing injury or in some cases premature death. The preference is that faulty work or service is not provided in the first place. For this reason it may be appropriate to establish, document and maintain procedures that investigate any causes of non-conformance to determine appropriate action to prevent the same non-conformance problem happening again. *Avoiding making the same mistake twice.* Particular attention needs to be paid to any non-conformance of a dangerous nature. **Table 26** indicates some areas that may require corrective action.

Table 26 Corrective Action List

Some sources that may require corrective action could include:

- Goods Inwards Rejects - Supplier reject notes, See Purchasing and Vendor Rating .
- Bug Reporting - Bug Report notes. The Project Controller could review the reports as appropriate.
- Test Rejects and Concessions - test and inspection sheets, Concession forms. The Project Controller could review these as and when they arise to ensure that corrective action is carried out and that the problem can be solved to avoid recurrence.
- Customer Complaints - Customer Complaints form See customer satisfaction section.
- Audit Reports - Audit Report form. Audits can be used to confirm that corrective action was effective.
- Installation Reports - Possibly the Service Manager could regularly review to determine where corrective action is necessary.
- Calibration - Quality Manager could review the results and calibration periods when found to be outside specification.
- Service Reports - The Service Manager could review the Service Reports and issues a report to the Management Review Meeting.

Control of Non-Conforming Products is to do with detection - Corrective Action is to do with remedial acts. **Figure 54** shows how the various systems; change control; non-conforming material; corrective action and improvement team groups; may need to interact with each other.

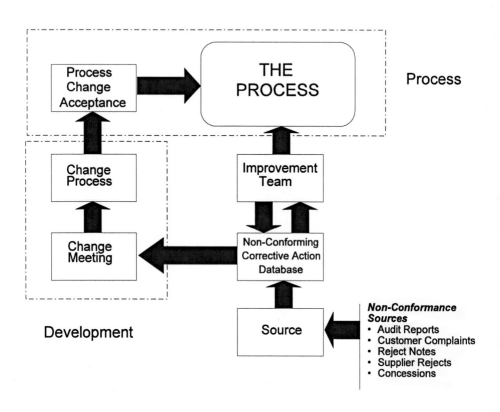

Figure 54 Corrective Action Control

Information regarding the Quality Problem data requires collation, possibly by using a database. This database can be analysed to separate the signal from the noise (the key issues from the trivial issues). This information can then be acted on possibly by introducing a change to either a procedure or design. While what changes to make might be clear, making the changes can be quite sophisticated and involve careful management of change through the change control procedure. The effect on work in progress, stores, stock, equipment in the field etc. will need to be considered. Alternatively the solution or change may not be so clear and require the involvement of the quality improvement team to investigate the problem and to determine an appropriate course of action.

A general approach to corrective and preventive action can be:

N   Monitoring to determine whether corrective action is required.
N   Analysis of results to determine what corrective action to take.
N   Programme, plan and initiate corrective action.
N   Monitor the effectiveness of the corrective action. (See Root Cause Analysis)

It is the responsibility of each Manager or section head to ensure that reports are made regarding Quality problems so that any adverse trends and/or major contributory factors causing rework can be identified and acted on.

The corrective action taken in the key areas above will be reviewed at the Management Review Meeting to ensure that it has been effective in solving the immediate problem and will avoid recurrence at a later date.

Where corrective action was necessary in specific departments, confirmation that the corrective action was completed and was effective will be obtained during the regular Quality Audits.

Preventive Action

Corrective action refers to the steps taken to avoid the same mistake being made twice and monitoring trends to take timely action. Preventive action refers to the steps taken to predict or identify possible causes of failure that have not yet occurred. On the face of it this is an impossible task, however, there are numerous techniques available which can help identify possible causes of failure. See section on Quality Improvement Initiatives & Techniques, specifically Failure Mode and Effects Analysis and Quality Planning.

The previous section described a general interpretation and application of ISO 9001. However, certain industries have evolved their own particular quality needs and expectations. These needs and expectations require further clarification that is not contained in the basic ISO 9001 standard. For example, greater emphasis on statistics and statistical process control in the mass production and automotive industries; parts traceability in the aerospace industry; organisation of adequate resource in the service industries, etc. - these are sometimes known as sector schemes. Some of the available sector schemes include Software - ISO 9000-3 (TickIT); Aerospace - AS 9000, Automotive - QS 9000, Service - ISO 9004-2. The next section provides an interpretation and application of ISO 9001 in these and other specified industrial or organisational settings.

ISO 9000 for Service Industries

One of the principle criticisms of ISO 9000 as a Quality Management System (QMS) is that it is readily applicable to manufacturing industries but when applied to service industries (banks, hospitals, maintenance, financial, scientific etc.) then the standard is not suitable - it is not applicable. This is a fair criticism as the background to ISO 9000 is very much based in the manufacturing industries. The interpretation provided in the previous section is intended to be a fairly general guide to applying a QMS. In an attempt to answer this criticism of non-applicability to the service industry, and to help interpretation, the next section has been compiled. The section describes a strategy and approach to applying and interpreting a QMS (ISO 9000) to first, a service industry and then the software industry. The description includes the basic Quality Control elements of the Quality Assurance system that would expect to be found on how ISO 9000 can be applied to these industries. The service industry can encompass Banks, Financial Institutions, Hospitals, Communication, Health, Maintenance, Utilities (Cleaning, waste etc.), Trading, Financial, Professional, Administration, Technical (Consultancy, Test Labs etc.) Scientific (Research, development etc.), Food (Processing and Catering). There are too many service industries to cover in this book, so two particular types have been selected, namely, a Service and Repair Organisation and a Bank. The Service and Repair organisation has been used to describe an overall approach to controlling quality of service. A Bank has been used as an example on how to interpret ISO 9001 for the Service Industry.

Quality of Service

Quality Objectives

1.   Identification, evaluation and definition of customer requirements. This could be established by conducting Market Research or by the customer providing a specification.

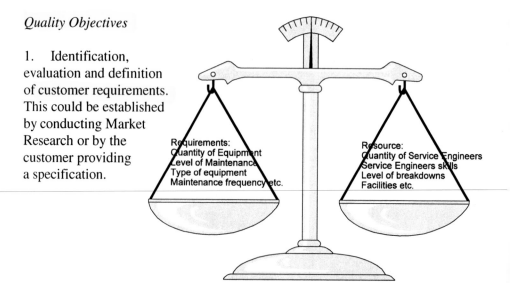

Figure 55 Balance Between Requirement and Resource

For example in the case of a servicing organisation (say maintaining equipment and buildings in a hospital), the list could include: determining the number of types of equipment that can be serviced; the quantity or number of pieces of equipment to be serviced; the type of equipment that can be supported; job description of the service   work content - time allowed; the maintenance periods/frequency/priority (based on past experience); the current level of break downs. *Note this is only the maintenance or service element and does not include any repair aspects.*

2.   Organisation of adequate resources that will be able to provide the service to the required specification.   Thus avoiding the provision of inadequate or non-conforming services.

For the servicing organisation this could include: the number of Service Engineers and their skills; the facilities in terms of equipment, technology, infrastructure, documentation etc.

Figure 55 shows the balance that needs to be drawn between the requirements for maintenance support and the facilities that are available.   It is very easy to have "eyes bigger than your stomach", i.e. the maintenance support requirement desired far outstrips the available labour resource.

3.   Establishment of the system to control the relevant key factors which can significantly affect quality performance.

For our service example these controls could include:

"   *Control of work acceptance;* Ensuring complete and correct information regarding the work to be performed is obtained (scope, time, cost etc.) and that these service requirements can and will be fulfilled (availability of people, material, equipment etc.)

"   *Control of Service delivery;* Ensuring that the Service Engineers understand they are responsible for the quality of work provided.

Each Service Engineer is responsible for completing the service or repair and conducting any final inspection and test.   This inspection and test could include the following:
a) Check that safety test has been performed
b) Check that all previous stages have been performed and signed off and records maintained of tests performed
c) Check that the work request is signed off

The secondary overcheck on the Service Engineer's work could be provided by the formalising of the supervisors audits. (It may be considered that good Supervisors do audits as a matter of course - the requirement is that good Supervisors now formalise their audits). The formalisation could include checking that the Service Engineer has completed the work satisfactorily. **Table 27** details a typical Supervisor's Audit Check List.

Table 27 Supervisor's Audit Check List - Service Engineers

Is the work request available?
Is the work identified?
Are the correct tools and materials being used?
Are the correct procedures/work instruction available and being used?
Is the correct test equipment available and being used?
Has the Service Engineer been adequately trained?
Is the Service Engineer aware of the critical features?
Is the area clean and tidy?
Are all the checks adequately detailed and have they been performed?
Is the customer satisfied?
Are Service logs being completed (if required)?
Have safe working procedures and practices been observed?

4. Establish effective measurement and analysis of service quality provided in relation to satisfying customer needs and expectations.

    For the Service example such measurements could include average response and down time, number of breakdowns, numbers of service "failures". This information can be collated to establish the overall cost of quality.

    It may also be worth considering the use of a customer satisfaction survey (See Customer Satisfaction).

5. Evaluation on enhancement of the quality and range of services.

6. Creation of a positive attitude of each person in the organisation towards satisfying both the customer and organisation, possibly by the introduction of a Total Quality Management programme.

A Guide to ISO 9001 for Financial Institutions e.g. Banks

Quality Management System

Quality System (No real change from the standard approach); It really states that there is a programme and documentation for quality.

Document Control; Some key documents that are issued require agreement or approval that the content of the documents are accurate. Occasionally these documents may get changed and there is a need for a system that controls the change of this documentation and its impact on any reference information or documentation.

Quality Records; Quality records need to be maintained to demonstrate that the system is working effectively, comprehensive enough to trigger corrective action in any of the departments.

Management Responsibility

Quality Policy; The organisation needs to clearly define its commitment to quality. This commitment should be from the highest level of the organisation right through to the lowest.

Management Responsibility (No real change from the standard approach)

Organisation; Effective management for quality with all the responsibilities clearly defined in writing. Management with authority - responsibility and ability to resolve problems - and an understanding of where the quality manager fits within the organisation. There must be an "owner" of the QMS designated by the Management Representative.

Management Review; If quality systems are not reviewed they tend to stagnate and not develop, a quality assurance system that provides never ending improvements in quality assurance.

Resource Management

Training and Appraisal; (No real change from the standard approach) To perform the tasks satisfactorily and completely the correct techniques and methods must be shown. It is essential to provide the opportunity to acquire the necessary skills to accomplish the task. Where appropriate, this training should be regularly provided and records maintained, identifying the training needs, together with confirmation that training has been given.

Product Realisation

Customer Requirements Review (No real change from the standard approach)
Design Control; Bank and financial institutions design, develop and provide new products. These new products are often not fundamentally new but variations on a previous theme such as new investment and pension schemes that are offered to their customers. These products must be fully validated and verified. They must be not only internally controlled but also externally controlled, by various financial, regulatory and governmental monitoring bodies.
Purchasing (No real change from the standard approach); This is quite a lengthy requirement which means that we should buy products and also services from the right companies. These are companies that have shown good control of their quality, be that a product or a service. We need to monitor their facilities and to satisfy ourselves that they are up to our standards, it may be that we need to go to the extent of assessing the sub-contractors or supplier's ability to meet our requirements. This could include requirements for security, specifically with regard to cheque and credit card suppliers and for controls on banking systems suppliers in terms of the reliability, robustness, maintainability etc. of the computer equipment and software supplied. We also place orders on these sub-contractors and it is necessary to ensure that the order describes precisely what our requirements are.
Process Control; There are numerous processes taking place within financial institutions; some can be very complex. Almost all of these processes will require clear written instructions on the activities and controls that need to be applied. Such controls may include: defining each activity, the sequence, work instruction for each activity, what records will be maintained etc. It may be that special checks, instructions or training is required.

Validation of processes

Receiving Inspection & Testing; This is checking the quality of the services or materiel supplied, checking that all the resources are available for the operator to fulfil the service that is being provided, e.g. Computer systems and the need to verify and validate any purchased software to ensure it actually fulfils its intended purpose.
In-process Inspection and Testing; There would be a need to validate and verify; data entry (e.g. entering numbers into a computer), also that the procedures as described in the quality manual are being observed. Such verification may be completed by the supervisor or possibly by the application of techniques or methods that validate data entry.
Final Inspection & Testing; There would need to be inspection of any documentation prior to issue, including papers despatched to a customer. Also it would be important to keep records of any inspection or tests carried out.

Product Identification & Traceability; When appropriate it is important that there are procedures which identify documents - files accounts - locations - source - etc.

Inspection & Test Status; If documentation is produced, the inspection status of this documentation would need to be identified, i.e. that the documentation has been or is awaiting checking.

Customer Supplied Product; In financial terms this must mean looking after the financial resources provided by the customer or client, ensuring the best return on investment and that financial resources are safe and secure.

Handling, Storage, Package, Preservation & Delivery; This requirement could relate to:

" handling of money or financial resources
" the storage of financial resources
" the security of financial resources
" the location of financial resources; type, owner etc.
" electronic data backup and storage
" loading of Automatic Cash Dispensers
" delivery of statements
" transportation of securities
" electronic transmittal records
" security of delivery, e.g. cash & cheques

Calibration; Any measuring equipment that is used, such as, balances would need to be calibrated to ensure its accuracy and consistency.

Measurement, Analysis and Improvement

Monitoring and Measurement; Consideration could be given to the inclusion of hard and soft standards. Hard Standards would be very specific, for example:

" cleanliness of the office
" percentage of debt write off
" average response time to a telephone call
" average response time to a client
" average length of queues

These are very specific standards that must be achieved. Soft Standards would be non-measurable (not quantifiable) requirements but still nevertheless requirements, for example:

" a warm personal style
" efficient service
" managing the problem, e.g. reasons for the delays
" a realisation that the customer may be upset and want to be told or reassured that you will do something about their problem
" a general air of professionalism

Internal Quality Audits (No real change from the standard approach); All of the systems and procedure requirements explained so far would count for nothing if they were just installed and left at that. The systems must be audited from time to time. Are the systems still compatible - pertinent - do they allow for changes - are we as good as we think we are?

Control of Non-Conforming Materiel; Even in the best Quality Management System things can go wrong - on these occasions the suspect materiel needs to be identified for example:

" identification of any wrong data that is entered
" identification of any damaged materiel
" identification of any bad debts

It is unproductive to identify solely the non-conforming materiel or quality problems if no steps are taken to prevent the recurrence, i.e. corrective action - see the next requirement.

Corrective & Preventive Action; This involves identifying the factors or performance indicators that give a measure of the organisation's quality achievement. Having identified the organisation's or department's performance indicators, these factors require monitoring and the establishment of a corrective action plan. Examples of performance indicators could include:

" customer complaints
" number of bad debts etc.

Improvement; Statistical methods can help in most aspects of data collection application, these can be used to appreciate more clearly the customer's needs and forecasting or measuring to assist in making better judgements or decisions.

Software Quality Assurance

Introduction

Like most things software development is a process. This process comprises of a sequence of events culminating in the production of a piece of software. The manner in which this software is developed and controlled can have a large bearing on its suitability and reliability.

Although there are numerous examples of good software, there are also examples of software which does not achieve its intended function.

An example of bad software may be an Air Traffic Control System (ATCS) where software has been written to control the position and direction of aircraft. The software has been written, tested and appears to work satisfactorily. Ninety-eight aircraft are being controlled and every thing is OK, ninety-nine aircraft are now on the system and everything is still OK. The one hundredth aircraft appears on the system and suddenly all the ATCS computer screens go blank. Why? - because the software can only cope with up to ninety-nine aircraft and with the arrival of the hundredth aircraft the ATCS computer crashed.

The need to control software development is becoming more and more important, especially when considering not only the previous example but also other examples of software use, e.g. Controlling aircraft such as in the fly by wire commercial aircraft now being developed, where aircraft control can be performed by the computer. Finite element analysis or simulation where civil, marine and many other structures are analysed for design purposes. This is to enable design decisions to be made regarding the sizes and strength requirements of the supporting structure. Mistakes in the programme could result in a catastrophic failure.

One other key issue, when considering, the need for software quality assurance, is the cost of quality (See **Figure 56**). The figure represents the life cycle of software development; conception, design, development, integration, installation and

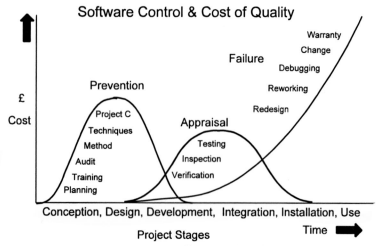

Figure 56 Software Quality Costs

use. The vertical axis shows the cost expenditure associated with each stage, broken down into the typical cost of quality elements; prevention, appraisal and failure (see Cost of Quality section). The prevention cost should be spent at the front end of a project and may consist of: project planning, methodology etc. The appraisal cost will be spent in the middle section of the project on: testing, approval, verification and validation. The final cost of quality expenditure is the failure cost which can grow exponentially. This failure cost can encompass any redesign where the original chosen methodology or system design was not appropriate; the cost of debugging because of failures when testing the system software; and customer complaints or correction of any faults during the warranty period. One way to address the issue of warranty failures is by offering to correct, at no cost, any bugs or system failings discovered during the first (say) three months. Any further software bugs discovered after this first three-month period at half cost and after that at the user's cost. In this way the software developer is not forever responsible for the maintenance of the software system.

Guidelines for Software Quality Assurance

When determining an approach to software QA there are a number of issues to consider:

" The acceptable level of risk. Risk is a concept which is very difficult to define. It can include the financial, programme, performance, safety and quality risks.

" The level of Quality Control required. ISO 9000-3 (TickIT[9]) provides guidance for software QA but does not define the level to be employed. Three possible levels which could be used are:

Level 1 - Associated with safety critical or high integrity systems.

Level 2 - Software to be supplied to the customer which could result in financial or reputation loss to the supplying organisation.

Level 3 - Software with minimal risk to the software developer, possibly small programmes which may not be used on a long term basis.

Figure 57 represents a detailed software sequence overlaid with the controls which may be expected for the situation described in level 2. Although, even within this level 2, software development can be extremely varied. It can range from development of a database using an application database package, to process control software using a computer processor's own machine code language, or number crunching on a high speed computer simulating for example, to ground water flow.

Each of these applications will have their own special needs, problems and approaches to software validation and verification. Consequently, the diagram can only be a general description of software development and control.

---

[9] TickIT is the software accreditation scheme associated with the Software standard based on ISO 9001

Software Quality Assurance

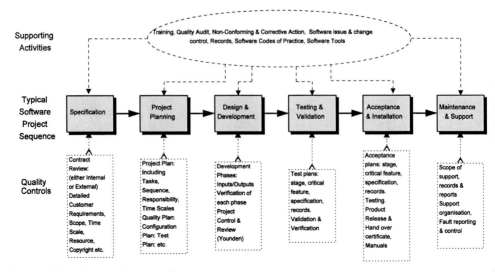

Figure 57 Software Project Sequence

Figure 57 is broken down vertically into three sections:

a.   The central section shows the *Software Project Sequence.*
b.   The bottom section shows the *Quality Controls* that can be applied to each stage.
c.   The top section shows the software development *Supporting Activities.*

Each of these sections will now be explained.

Software Project Sequence and Quality Controls

Although these stages are described as a series of tasks or events it is more likely that many of these tasks will occur in parallel.

Specification: Specification development is possibly the most important element and yet it is often afforded the least amount of time and effort. Studies have shown that up to 60% of quality problems stem from not understanding the client's requirements. To avoid such problems the following action could be taken. An agreed format, content and shape of a standard specification could be completed (with examples). An agreed method of approving and accepting this specification could be provided (agreement and acceptance both internally and externally with the client). See Customer requirements

Review. The specifications that may need to be produced initially are the software, hardware (including hardware configuration) and support specifications. The support specification may include training, maintenance and assistance requirements. These initial specifications may be adequate for quotation stages but once the order or the authority to proceed with the project is given, then detailed additional specifications may be required. These additional specifications may include the functional specification and test specification.

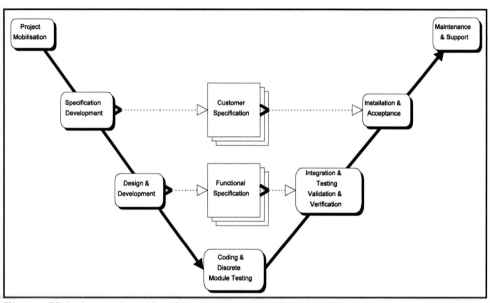

Figure 58 Software Specifications

Figure 58 shows how the specifications can be used in the latter stages of the project. The Customer Specification can be modified without a great deal of work into the Final Installation & Commissioning Test Specification and Plan. By the addition of some acceptance criteria and a column for test results the specification can become the Test Record sheet. This record sheet could be the instruction for the Software Test Engineer and completed during the Final Test Stages. This sheet would show the tests performed, the test data used, the outcome of the test and the name of the tester.

Similarly the Functional Specification produced at the Design & Development Stage can be modified into the Software Integration & Test Specification. Using this approach means that it is much less likely to overlook any key functional or user requirements. It also avoids *reinventing the wheel* in the sense of having to rewrite the test schedule from scratch - simple modification or reinterpretation of existing documentation can produce the required test plans and instructions.

Project Planning: Quality assurance and project management can include (but is not restricted to): Quality Planning (See section Quality Improvement Initiatives & Techniques, specifically Quality Planning) and Project Control (which could be based, in part, on the draft British Standards for Software development and BS 7000 Managing Product Design). See section on Project Quality Assurance. The project plan needs to include:

       o   Identification of the project owner or leader
       o   Project phases and team organisation
       o   Project reporting and analysis
       o   Project, design and development reviews
       o   Specific coding and design practice to be employed
       o   Task assignment or responsibilities

The development methodology of the software needs to be determined (the way in which the software is designed). There are many approaches to establishing the design methodology, from simple flow diagrams to more complex approaches as described in:

       o   Yourdon & Hatley methodologies and requirements analysis
       o   Jackson and Constantine structure charts
       o   Integration of methodologies into the documentation structure.

Software Testing and Validation (Test Plans): As previously mentioned, the approach to verifying and validating software is very dependant on the type of software being produced. Often the approach to software creation is by development of software modules which are later integrated (see **Figure 59**). The approach to software testing in this case can be to test the individual modules to ensure satisfactory performance against a predetermined test plan. Then integrate each module, retesting after each module integration (Records of the success or otherwise of the testing at each stage need to be maintained). This approach (testing each module) is fine if the software development is to be completed in

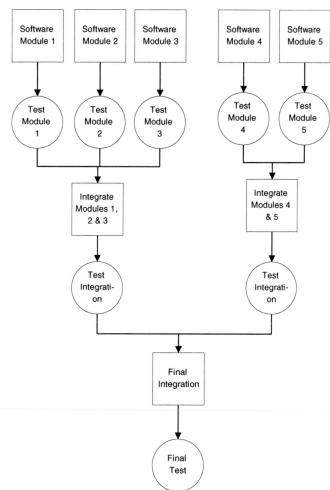

Figure 59 Software Integration & Test

module elements. The problem is that not all software is developed and produced in this way, so alternative testing methods may need to be found, e.g. flat code, database software etc.).

Some of the activities associated with integration and test can include:
" Test plan development and implementation
" Test scheduling and recording (records of individual tests - showing pass or fail and the action taken in the case of failure; rewrite, concession etc.)

"   Contents of Test Plans and estimating their coverage. Typically, a well documented Test Plan will contain (including document control issues) the following;

- Compatibility Testing with other software.
- Functionality Testing against the functional specification.
- Database Testing - often software contain some form of database.
- Stress and Load Testing e.g. number of users.
- Performance Testing against the Terms of Reference and Design specification.
- Content Testing against the Terms of Reference and Documentation.
- Scalability Testing on various operating systems and equipment.

"   Installation, commissioning and acceptance plans

"   Integration methods

"   Bug reporting; setting up of the bug report data base, including bugs open (still outstanding) and bugs closed (actioned, corrected and cleared)

One method that can be employed to check specific pieces of software code is detailed in the section on Document Inspection. This method or approach is not only applicable to software code but also to any documentation (specifications, reports etc.) that requires inspection, verification and validation. See Document Inspection at the end of this Section.

Maintenance & Support: This can include the technical support for both hardware and software - provision of advice and assistance. It can also be as comprehensive as the compilation and provision of training plans and courses. Hardware maintenance - providing a preventive maintenance and repair service. This may entail the creation of an equipment and customer database and a maintenance plan. Software maintenance - resolution of bugs and software inadequacies (e.g. within the customer specification but still causes customer complaints or concerns). Again this may entail the creation of a customer software database; listing customer, software supplied and its issue status.

The technical support and the hardware and software maintenance probably requires the creation of a call logging and escalation system. This is similar to the bug reporting system where customer calls or queries are logged on to the call logging database. The call is actioned and eventually becomes either a call open (still outstanding) or a call closed (actioned, corrected and cleared). In the case of a call remaining open for a predetermined time (say two days) the call is escalated up the management hierarchy, possibly until it reaches the Managing Director. Some of the activities associated with maintenance and support can include:

" Support organisation
" Types of maintenance activities to be provided
" Training plan and course content
" Recording method and reports
" Software updates release procedures.

Support Activities

Documentation: There can be a considerable amount of documentation produced in the course of a software project e.g. user manuals, maintenance manuals, specifications, test plans etc. BS5515 provides some guidance on documentation for computer-based systems.

This documentation and software may require some of the following to be completed:
" Documentation and software issue and configuration control
" Documentation structure in relation to project type
" Documentation contents, use and format
" Documentation standards

Configuration control: These previously mentioned documents and software are very often subject to change (see section on Change Control).

These change activities will probably require the following systems to be established:
" Configuration management
" Configuration activities; plan identification and traceability, change control.

Software metrics and estimating: During planning, development, installation and use of software some method of establishing project performance indicators may be appropriate. These can include:
" Assessing project objectives, critical aspects and timescales
" Preparing proposals and consideration of contractual conditions
" Evaluating development performance and utilising the results
" Number of bugs, Field failures and customer complaints.

Software Quality Assurance

Reliability Measurement: Software is not necessarily as reliable or robust as expected and tests need to be determined to examine these issues - reliability models.

Auditing Software: See section on Quality Auditing. As with most processes and activities confirmation that the procedures are being followed and records are maintained is necessary. Consequently, the following tasks will need to be established and completed: Audit plan, conduct the audit and audit corrective action.

Document Inspection

Introduction

This inspection technique was developed by Michael Fagan of IBM to ensure that all types of project documentation were clear, accurate, and consistent with any agreed standards, e.g. documentation format standards. This inspection technique is equally viable when applied to both software and documentation and can encompass specifications, documents, reports, source code etc. It is a logical, structured, formalised quality control procedure which, when used early in the project development cycle, has shown real benefits. Specifically, faster system development and better system quality.

The rules are strict and the initial reaction can be to see the approach as a bureaucratic imposition. However, the technique has shown that benefits are proportional to the extent that the rules are followed.

The Benefits

Performing this inspection should provide:

- Earlier delivery
- Reduced development costs
- Shorter development time
- Lower maintenance costs
- Fewer non-conformities
- Improvement in testing time

The reasons for these benefits are that:

- Many software bugs can occur in software before the code is written, due to the specifications (functional, design, etc.) being wrong or misinterpreted.
- Subjective examination of documentation is not as effective as using formal inspection methods.
- Statistics have shown that inspection is more effective in identifying non-conformances than testing.

Approach to Inspection Sessions

Codes of Practice
for Inspection
Sessions

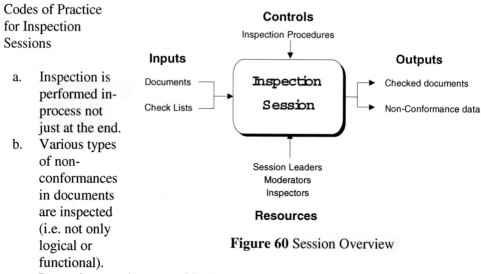

Figure 60 Session Overview

a. Inspection is performed in-process not just at the end.
b. Various types of non-conformances in documents are inspected (i.e. not only logical or functional).
c. Inspection meetings are of limited duration (e.g. two hours).
d. The inspection sessions have a leader.
e. Inspectors are assigned specific roles.
f. Material is inspected at a rate that is found most effective.
g. Statistics are kept on the process to aid fine tuning.

Roles:

Project Leader - Owner of the total project
Session Leader - Coordinator of the inspection session
Inspector - Session participant
Author[10] - Owner of the document

---

[10] The Project Leader's, Session Leader's and Inspector's responsibility is only to assist the author. The author has and retains (post the inspection session) ownership of the document or software. Responsibility for the quality of the document or software remains firmly with the author.

Typically, an inspection session will require 2-5 inspectors including the leader. The project leader will usually assign the inspectors and session leader.

Planning of inspection sessions is essential if the inspection session is to be successful. The Session Leader needs to divide the work carried out into manageable sections and identify the person responsible for each section inspection. This could be up to thirty pages for a document such as a specification or about three thousand lines of code.

The document author (owner) should:

" Print a copy of their work for each inspector. (If inspecting software, then the source code files need to be printed with line numbers).

" Ensure that all inspectors have access to the appropriate higher level specifications or objective and purpose of the document.

" The inspector needs to have access to the standard or code of practice (if there is one) for document formats.

" If source code is being inspected, produce a sorted function listing for each inspector.

All documents and source files being inspected should be uniquely identified and issue numbered under the document/software change control system before commencing the inspection process. (If there isn't a change control system then one will need to be created before starting!)

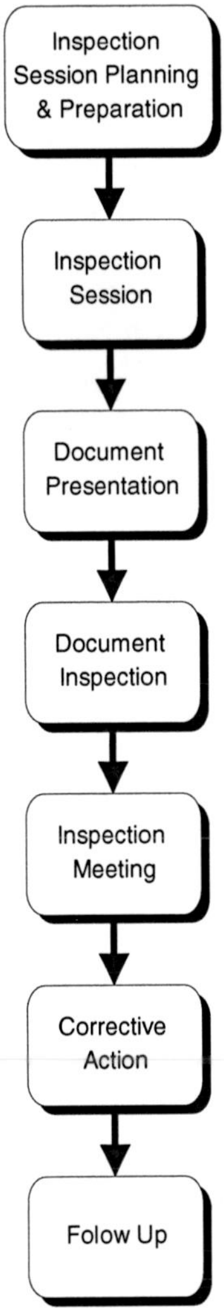

Prior to starting inspection the document owner or Session Leader should explain or present an overview of the project and the purpose or objective of the documentation.

The inspectors should then work independently familiarising themselves with the documentation and identifying any possible non-conformances in the documentation (approximately two to three hours)[11]. These non-

Figure 61
Inspection
Sequence

---

[11] It is possible to allow longer but the effectiveness of the sessions drops dramatically.

conformances will be presented by each inspector at the inspection meeting. Each inspector may have different roles, e.g. checking legal aspects, financial implication etc.

The inspection meeting is attended by all the inspectors but it is not necessary that the document author is there (otherwise there is a danger of becoming defensive).

The role of the inspectors is to identify simply non-conformances in the document not to look for solutions or improvements. During the session the Leader should record the non-conformances found on a standard form. The summaries of these forms can then be fed into a database after the session.

Each non-conformance is graded with two classifications:

    N   Severity Classification - Major/Significant/Minor[12]
    N   Quality Classification - Omitted/Wrong/Superfluous/Unintelligible[13]

Once the inspection has finished, the Leader should provide a copy of the report to the original author and file another copy in the non-conforming record database.

After the session the Leader needs to ensure that corrective action on the non-conformances is taken. The non-conformance forms/reports can be used for this purpose.

---

[12]   Class A - Major Discrepancy -One that would effect Health & Safety
    Class B - Significant Discrepancy - One that would result in financial loss
    Class C - Minor Discrepancy -A problem that warrants attention

[13]   Omitted   Missing or not available
    Wrong   Incorrect material or information
    Superfluous   Additional material which is unnecessary
    Unintelligible   Incomprehensible, incoherent or meaningless

Inspection Non-Conformance Report Log

This Inspection Non-Conformance Log would be completed by the inspectors detailing the document control information and identifying any non-conformances found.

Inspection Non-Conformance Report Log									
Document Number:						Document Number, Issue Number & Date:			
Document Author/Owner:						Session Leader:			
Inspector:						Date:			
#	Location of Non-Conformance	Severity Classification			Quality Classification				Non-Conformance Description	Corrective Action	OK
		A	B	C	O	W	S	U			

Corrective Action

Next to each non-conformance description in the inspection report, there is space for the author to suggest the corrective action to be taken. Once this corrective action has been successfully completed, the tick box can be signed. Note, any corrective action needs to take due account of any document change control necessary. If the author decides that the non-conformance is invalid and no work is necessary then a comment is made in the corrective action column.

Once all valid corrective actions have been fixed then the author should advise th
Session Leader. If all corrective actions have been completed then the Summary Shee
will require updating.

Inspection Check Lists

Inspectors should be given check lists to help in identification of errors and to increase the effectiveness of the inspections. The lists can be created from several sources; previous common faults (experience), specialists[14], document format standards, etc. The general check list below, is as its name implies a check list which can be employed for various types of documents such as the quality manual or procedures. Some of the following check lists are more specialised.

#	Question
General Procedural Document Check List	
1.	Does the document follow the approved standard for documents?
2.	Have the documents followed the necessary document control requirements? (Author, Number, Issue Level etc.)
3.	Is the document accurate? Cross references correct e.g., other documents, equipment or form numbers Does the document reflect current working practices? Does the document have any omissions?
4.	Is the document adequate to complete the task?
5.	Has the document adequate depth or detail? Would it be possible to complete the task directly from the document or would further assistance be necessary? I.e. training.
6.	Is the document clear and understandable?
7.	Are there any omissions that could adversely affect quality?
8.	Does the document include the monitoring and control activities necessary to ensure the process is carried out satisfactorily?
9.	Does the document include the control settings?
10.	Does the document state the approvals necessary before the process runs and once the process is running?
11.	Are the workmanship criteria clearly stated?

---

[14]   Used when looking for particular requirements, e.g. legal or specific stages in a project; specification, integration, test etc.

This Test Plan check list is for use when checking test or inspection instructions. This type of check list could be employed where test or inspection failure could result in major financial or safety losses.

#	Test Plan Check List
	Question
1	Does the Test Plan follow the approved standard for Test Plans?
2	Is the Test Plan issue controlled?
3	Is there a test covering each individual customer and functional requirement?
4	Does the Test Plan encompass the User and Maintenance documentation needs?
5	Does each test specify the test method?
6	Does the Test Plan specify specific test responsibilities?
7	Does each test make reference to accept and reject criteria?
8	Does the Test Plan show the steps to take in case of rejection?
9	Does the Test Plan specify what records are to be held?
10	Does the Test Plan specify responsibilities for retaining test results and the retention duration?

This is a check list for Purchase Orders and Purchase Specifications. It may be that this check list would only be used for Purchase Orders of a significant size, although even getting the smallest Purchase Order wrong can have a catastrophic effect. The responsibilities for employing this check list could be divided into the three aspects: Document control, general and technical.

#	Question
	**Inspection Check List for the review of Purchase Orders & Specifications**

#	Question
1	**Purchase Order - Document Control** Is the Purchase Order approval available and correct person and level? Does the Purchase Order follow the style guide for Purchase Orders? Is the relationship with other documents specified? Is the Purchase Order distribution detailed and correct? Has the Purchase Order classification level been established?
2	**General** Is the order correctly identified? Does the order contain a description and appropriate technical (drawing specification etc.) information? Does the order contain any Inspection and Test criteria (including certification) or Quality Standards to be applied? Does the order contain delivery instructions? I.e. Is the addresses specified (Payment, Invoice & delivery)? Are the contact points specified? Has the Purchase Order been spell and grammar checked? Is the Purchase Order in sufficient depth or detail? I.e. Is the order pitched at the correct level of understanding for the intended recipient? Does the Purchase Order use too much jargon? Are abbreviations, specialist terms, titles etc. defined? E.g. Is a glossary required? Are units consistent and correct? Is the Purchase Order presentation quality satisfactory? (Including drawings, diagrams etc.) Have responsibilities been identified i.e. specific sections attributed to individual personnel? Have the original Purchase Requirements been clearly stated and been fully addressed? Are references to other documents sufficiently comprehensive and adequate?

Inspection Check List for the review of Purchase Orders & Specifications	
#	**Question**
3	Technical Are all Legal issues adequately addressed? Is the scope of requirements specified? Does the Purchase Order specify a period for validity? Are the Terms & Conditions appropriate, adequate and current? Is it clear that prices are specified for duration of the contract? Is the date of issue of the contract clear? Does the contract specify who has the right to change the contract? Has the original source material been specified? Are the risk areas identified?

Note 1: Use of this inspection check list in no way removes the responsibility of the quality of any Purchase Order from the author. Quality of the Purchase Order (as always) remains firmly with the author of the Purchase Order.

Note 2: The Inspection Check List is broken down into three sections. The first section covers Purchase Order Change Control. The second section covers general questions that could be applied to most types of Purchase Order. Section three is more of a technical nature and is intended to be more sensitive to the needs of Purchasing.

This is a check list for technical (mainly) research reports. It may be appropriate to split the responsibilities for employing this check list into the three aspects: document control, general and technical. The document control elements are there to ensure the specific organisations document approval and issue procedures are observed. The general questions can be used by a non-technical person to ensure the report is up to standard. The technical questions are for use by an inspector with a more technical experience or background.

#	Question
	Inspection Check List for the review of Research Technical Reports
1	Document Control Is the Document approval available and correct person and level? Does the document follow the style guide for technical reports? Is the relationship with other documents specified? Is the document distribution detailed and correct? Has the document classification level been established?
2	General Has the document been spell checked? Has the document been grammar checked? Is the report in sufficient depth or detail? I.e. Is the report pitched at the correct level of understanding for the intended audience? Does the report use too much jargon? Does the report over estimate the level of intellect of the reader? Are abbreviations, specialist terms, titles etc. defined? For example, is a glossary required? Are units consistent and correct? Is the report presentation quality satisfactory? (Including diagrams) Have responsibilities been identified i.e. specific sections attributed to individual personnel? Have the original customers' requirements been clearly stated and been fully addressed? Have the report objectives been clearly stated and fully addressed? Have any future work areas been specified? Are references to other documents sufficiently comprehensive and adequate? Is there an adequate method of obtaining and recording customer reaction or feedback regarding the report? Have the Intellectual Property rights been established?

Inspection Check List for the review of Research Technical Reports	
#	Question
3	**Technical** Has the original source material (data, customer specifications, tasking brief etc.) been specified? Have the approach, methodology and any calculations been verified (correctness) and validated (confirmed)? Has any measuring equipment been specified? (Number, calibration status etc.) Have any assumptions made been specified? Are the risk areas in the report identified? (Novel ideas may need to be stated and risks quantified) Is the report up to date and in line with current scientific thinking? Are the results believable? Are the limits over which the results apply specified? Are the data sources defined, complete and validated? Are the conclusions and recommendations clear and specific? Is there sufficient objective evidence to support the conclusions and recommendations? Is there too much information? Does (should) the report address failures as well as successes? Is the report focussed on the customer needs? Do the conclusions and recommendations address and respond to each customer requirement? Have there been any external changes that may invalidate the report or data?

Note 1: Use of this inspection check list in no way removes the responsibility of the quality of any documentation from the author. Quality of the documentation (a. always) remains firmly with the author of the document.

Note 2: The Inspection Check List is broken down into three sections. The first section covers Document Change Control. The second section covers general questions that could be applied to most types of report. Section three is more of a technical nature and is intended to be more sensitive to the needs of research.

Inspection Report Summary

The Inspection Report is a summary of the inspection activities and results. The report shows the quality statistics for a particular set of documents (such as all the manuals, software or specifications associated with a project). The top part of the form details all the documents examined (including issue control information). The bottom half features the overall quality performance indicators of the documentation examined. This form could be completed once all the inspection activities have been completed.

Inspection Report Summary Sheet			
Project Name:		Project Number:	
Document Names:	Document Numbers, Issue Number & Date	Document Owners:	Inspectors
Session Leader:		Date:	
Non-Conformance Type	Total	Percentage of total	Estimated Rework Time
Severity Classification			
Major			
Significant			
Minor			
Total			
Quality Classification			
Omitted			
Wrong			
Superfluous			
Unintelligible			
Total			

Problems with Document Inspection

Document Inspection may be seen as an expensive exercise in that if the job had been completed correctly in the first place it would not be necessary. This is true but not everyone's perfect and some authors are better than others, this technique gives the opportunity to help the weak authors.

Authors may not do such a good job if they know the errors will be picked up by the inspectors.

The responsibility for the quality of the documentation will always be the author's. This does not change before or after inspection.

This approach may be seen as common sense - and just an extension of the existing reviews and approval. Yes this is quite true, all the technique does is to formalise this procedure.

Structure of the Quality Manual

The shape of the Quality Manual could be broken down into three levels or tiers, Volumes 1, 2 & 3. See **Figure 69**. The object of these sections could be:

Volume 1: of the Quality Manual is introductory. It provides an overview of the Organisation's Quality System and the Organisation's policy and management commitment to a Quality

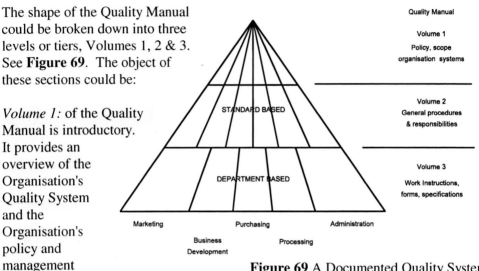

Figure 69 A Documented Quality System

Management System and ISO 9000 (or other QMSs). A description of the scope of product or services offered and covered by the QMS may also be included. (See section - Scope of the QMS). The Quality Manual Volume One can be used by the organisation to introduce themselves to any outside organisation as deemed necessary. The remaining levels of documentation are confidential to the operation of the Company and may only be disclosed to third parties with the agreement of the Organisation. This volume one may be change controlled but not issue controlled as it may be on free issue to all existing and potential customers and employees to indicate the organisation's commitment to Quality.

Volume 2: Describes the general procedures and responsibilities for operating the Quality Assurance System.

Volume 3: Contains the detailed procedures which may relate to task specific activities such as work instructions, test specifications, forms, calibration instruction etc.

Also see Computer Aided Quality Control - specifically Intranetting the QMS.

Generally, the contents of the Quality Manual can either follow the order of the most appropriate Quality Management Standard (QMS) or alternatively, be in the sequence best suited to the organisation. Organising the Quality Manual in the sequence of the requirements of the standard (ISO 9001) makes it easier for auditing purposes but may make the manual more difficult to follow for those people not familiar with the QMS clause titles. It should be noted that the structure of the Quality Manual documentation described above is just one example and there are many other ways to structure such documentation.

The Quality Manual should contain the following:

o *Quality Policy:* A general statement of intent. The policy should include the management's commitment to quality and that the QMS is based on or meets a defined quality standard. Finally, the policy statement should indicate that the procedures included in the quality manual are mandatory for all employees. All of these elements need to be confirmed and authorised by the signature of the Head of the organisation. If the Head of the organisation cannot sign such a document, then this clearly indicates that the organisation is not sure that a documented QMS is the right approach for the organisation. This is a positive not a negative position, as the introduction of a QMS when unsure is almost guaranteed to fail. If by not signing it has exposed this uncertainty, then the QMS programme can be delayed or abandoned until full commitment by the Organisation Head and management can be obtained, thus avoiding any unnecessary and potentially damaging work.

o *Approval:* Approval and authorisation (possibly by the Quality Manager) of the issue of the quality manual.

o *Amendment record:* A record of the issue status of the quality manual indicating for example issue date, section number, page number, approval etc. See Interpretation of ISO 9001 - Document Control.

o *Distribution:* Distribution list of the manual showing holders of controlled copies of the quality manual.

o *Contents:* Contents list of the quality manual. The sections of the quality manual could be based either on the organisation's process cycle or in the order of the chosen quality standard.

o *Definitions and terms:* Explanation or description of some more commonly used terms or abbreviations.

o *Organisation:* An organisation chart, showing the relationship of the quality department with other departments. A brief description of the organisation's background and business could also be included.

o *Procedures:* The procedures and activities affecting quality should be described or made reference to if the procedures are maintained in a separate document (the company operating procedures). It may also be appropriate to provide a look up table showing where each of the quality standards requirements are encompassed. The general format of each procedure could be:

Introduction to the procedure describing its objective, aim or purposes, the scope and topics covered and the applicability of the procedure.

Responsibilities for performing the procedures.

Reference documents that may be required such as forms or work instructions. The input documents (documents required to successfully complete the procedure) and output documents (documents produced as a result of completing the procedure).

Procedure or methods that describe what tasks are to be performed and how to perform the tasks.

The aspects covered can be (See Section Quality Improvement Initiatives & Techniques, specifically Process Flow Charting):

The inputs to the process, e.g. raw material, documents, information, etc.

The output from the process, i.e. what the process turns the input into, e.g. material.

The controls, e.g. instructions, drawings, audit, monitoring method, inspection, validation, verification, etc.

The resources, e.g. people, skills, knowledge, facilities, equipment (measuring and process), consumables, money etc.

Issue control data to describe the title, title number, issue number, author, approver, circulation etc.

One of the most difficult aspects in preparing work instructions is deciding the level of detail. In principle there is a need to strike the correct balance between instruction and training.

As a general rule, for unskilled workers, it may be necessary to break down the tasks or steps. The content of the instruction should be sufficiently detailed for the person to satisfactorily complete the task. The instruction should include the process or task inputs, the process resources, the process controls and the process output.

Skilled people may only require general training on what is to be achieved. The work instruction then may only describe the task objectives and not on how these objectives are to be achieved. For example, a Researcher may only be requested to examine a particular phenomena, not on how to undertake the research. However, a Laboratory Technician may require instruction on how to use a piece of equipment to provide experimental results. See **Figure 70**.

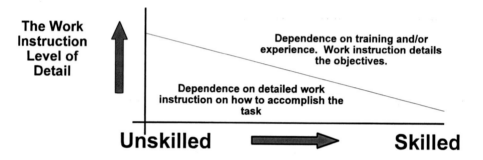

Figure 70 Procedure Detail

An Integrated Management System

Introduction

Quality, the environment and safety, both at work and with the product are issues which receive considerable attention. This attention is manifested in the proliferation of regulations, standards and guides to do with quality, environment and safety. Ignoring or neglecting any of these requirements can have disastrous consequences for the organisation or society; from at best - customer dissatisfaction, or far more serious - injury, death or being put out of business. Apart from those regulations or standards which detail specific requirements or objectives, for example the Health & Safety at Work Act and the Consumer Protection Act, there are also management standards such as ISO 9001 (Quality), BS 8800 (Safety) and ISO 14000 (Environmental). This can lead to duplication of management systems and effort, such as multiple audits and assessments.

There is a need to understand all of these standards and requirements, and to determine and coordinate an approach to addressing each one.

Fortunately, there is a certain commonality between these various standards. Not necessarily in terms of the content of the standards but certainly in terms of the requisite management systems and an approach to addressing them.

What are these various standards?

There are various standards which may be considered for inclusion in the Integrated Management System; Quality, Environment & Health Safety, Security, etc. These are not the only standards or management systems which could be considered. Others include; Information Technology, Training (Investors in People), the Company Operating Procedures, etc. are subjects worthy of consideration.

Table 30 shows some of the current various associated management standards although there are many more.

Table 30 Other Management Standards

Standard	Description
ISO 9001	Quality
BS 8800 & OHSAS 18001	Health & Safety
	Other Health & Safety Regulations Management of Health & Safety at Work Regulations 1992. Provision & Use of Work Equipment Regulations 1992. Manual Handling Operations Regulations 1992. Workplace (Health, Safety & Welfare) Regulations 1992. Provision of Protective Equipment The HSE guide Control of Substances Hazardous to Health (CoSHH)
ISO 14001	Environmental Standard
BS 7799	Security Services
IIP	Investors in People (Training)

The BS 8800 Health & Safety Management System Standard

The general structure of the Safety Standard BS 8800 includes; Policy, Organisation Planning, Control, Monitor and Review.

Policy; Setting the organisation's policy regarding Health & Safety and documenting the senior management's commitment to Health & Safety.

Organisation; Ensuring that adequate resource is provided for the health & safety needs - people, skills, etc.

Planning; The assessment of risk - identifying the potential hazards, possibly completing a Failure Mode Effects, Fault Tree or Hazard & Operability Analysis.

Control; Control of the risks for particular industries such as Hotels, Oil etc.

Monitor; Confirmation of the policy in action - Audit. Records of measurements, incidents and accidents. Measuring the performance of the Health & Safety Management System (HSMS).

Review; Review of the above arrangements in light of audit reports, records, safety bulletins, New Technology etc.

ISO 14000 Environmental Standard

ISO 14000 is a standard for a system for managing environmental effects. By comparison, ISO 9001 is concerned with managing the quality of products or services, whereas ISO 14000 is concerned with controlling the discharges, emissions, waste, undesirable by-products and other environmental effects such as noise, nuisance and pollution.

The general structure of the Environmental Standard ISO14000 includes;

Part 1 provides an introduction to the concepts, elements and applications of the standard.

Part 2 is specification for the Development, Implementation and Maintenance of an Environmental Management System. It contains a number of requirements which includes:

I.	Management responsibility
II.	Environmental management system
III.	Environmental policy
IV.	Environmental effects
V.	Environmental objectives and targets
VI.	Environmental management programme
VII.	Environmental management manual and documentation
VIII.	Environmental operational controls
IX.	Environmental management records

X.   Environmental audits
XI.   Environmental reviews (control, verification, measurement and testing)

Part 3 provides a guide for implementors and assessors

BS 7799 Information Security Management

This standard has been specifically developed to help organisations identify, minimise and manage a range of potential threats to an organisation's data and information. There are ten sections to the standard covering policy to compliance. To gain an appreciation of the style and contents of the standard, below is an example of an audit performed against the requirements of BS7799 to determine the organisation's ability to meet the standard.

#	Area of Concern	Ability to meet the Code of Practice	Level of Perceived Risk
1	Policy and Program Is there a written Information Security Management (ISM) policy in place that management is visibly, actively participating in? Is there a ISM programme in place, implemented and monitored?	1/10 - No policy or programme	10/10 - because no policy or programme or perceived awareness
2	Assets Have Assets (Information, Software, Hardware, Services) been assessed (classified) for security risk and action taken?	4/10 - Asset register but no assessment of risk	5/10 - This is the first assessment
3	People Is Personnel screening actively carried out? Are confidentiality agreements procedures are consistently observed? Is personnel awareness is high of ISM risks?	2/10 - Little documentary evidence of compliance	10/10 - because little awareness
4	Buildings Security of the premises and facilities	4/10 - Building security implemented	2/10 - Building security

#	Area of Concern	Ability to meet the Code of Practice	Level of Perceived Risk
5	Security Operational Management Procedures, viruses, back-up, network controls, communications (e-mails)	6/10 - Most procedures in place	6/10 - Although awareness could be improved
6	Network Access, user, privilege, passwords, monitoring of use, etc.	6/10- Most procedures in place	6/10 - Although awareness could be improved
7	Business applications & In company developed applications. Security of, validation, encryption, signatures,	2/10 - Little documentary evidence of compliance	4/10 - Not seen as high risk area
8	Disaster recovery Continuity plans, testing, contingency, etc.	4/10 - As no testing carried out	10/10 - High Risk area
9	Compliance Monitoring, assessment, etc.	2/10 - Little (if any) documentary evidence of compliance	10/10 - High Risk area

All these standards (Security, Investors in People, Safety and Environmental) are not too dissimilar to ISO 9001 in context and shape (although, very different in content). Consequently the approach to implementation and maintenance could possibly be similar and in this lies the heart of an Integrated management System.

How can these various Standards be applied?

Figure 26 on page 83, shows diagrammatically, that in order to regulate a process, it is necessary to have some formal method of control and feedback, otherwise the system may become unstable or go out of control. In the simple control system described in **Figure 26**, there is an *input* to the system (possibly data or raw materials). The *process* or organisation can then manipulate the data or material, providing an *output* in terms of the deliverable, possibly acceptable or unacceptable finished product. If the process consists of data manipulation the output could be a report - controls are necessary to avoid the production of an inaccurate report. There will be a *goal* which could be the environmental Standard ISO 14000 or the Health & Safety Standard OHSAS 18001.

There will be a feedback mechanism to control the process allowing timely action to be taken to avoid failure in achieving the goal. This could involve *collection of data* regarding the performance of the process and a *comparison* with the standard (the Quality, Environmental & Safety Manual). This data collection could be achieved by performing an audit. If the comparison or audit indicates unacceptable practices or actions contrary to those described in the documented management system manual then the process may need to be modified and brought back into line.

audits → corrective actions - time lines . close out.

This approach necessitates the introduction of an audit system which may already be in place via the Quality Management System. In the case of the audit system being already in place then the scope of the audit will need to be extended to include the additional environmental and safety (both work and product) issues.

The approach presented here has often been used successfully in the application of ISO 9001. It should therefore be possible to follow a similar style for the other standards, leading also to successful operation (see **Figure 71**).

Management Commitment; Clear indication by management of their intention to introduce a management system.

Policy & Programme; The policy statement and programme of events that leads up to implementation of the management system.

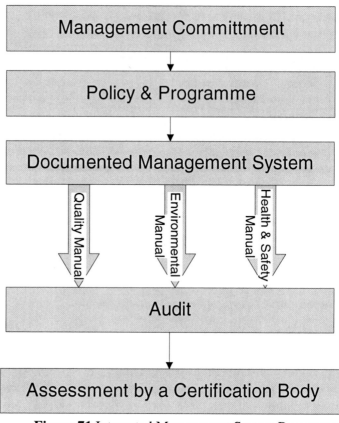

Figure 71 Integrated Management System Programme

Documentation & Procedures; This can comprise the management system's manuals and documented procedures and instructions. Note: The management system manuals could be either a combination of each of these requirements (quality, environmental & safety - a company operating manual) or three separate documents and structures.

A proposed model for a documented Management System

To ensure that all personnel understand their role and responsibilities within the overall system it will be necessary to document the quality, environmental & safety management system. The purpose of this is to demonstrate the organisation's ability to meet the specified and statutory requirements. It may be that this documented management system manual could reflect each of the standard's and regulation's requirements.

When compiling the documented management system arrangements it may be worth considering some of the following activities:

1. Organisation to demonstrate the effective implementation of such a documented management system. In special circumstances this may require preparation of specific management system plans which reflect the needs of particular products and/or processes.
2. Establishment of any specific controls of processes or tasks.
3. The updating and approval of any such management system plans.

Organising the Documented Quality System in the sequence of the requirements of the standard (e.g. ISO 9001) makes it easier for auditing purposes but it may make the manual more difficult to follow for those people not familiar with the QMS clause titles. It should be noted that the structure of the Quality Manual documentation described above is just one example and there are many other ways to structure such documentation.

Audits

A Systems audit can either follow the order of the appropriate Management System Standard. This would be a horizontal audit carried out by trailing a requirement through the organisation. Alternatively, the audit may be vertically structured to fit the organisation's functions, i.e. Design Department, Planning Department, Production etc.

Audits should be carried out by trained personnel, independent of the area being audited.

Audits should be planned to ensure that the whole system is audited at least once a year. There should be auditing procedures which define the method of auditing, reporting and correcting non-compliancies found.

Quality Management (Principles & Practice)

Limitations of the Management System approach and Integrated Management System in particular

Bureaucratic and dictatorial

The standard is bureaucratic in its approach, it does not allow for flare and creativity - it is too dictatorial. This is correct, the management system style means that it directs people to work in a particular way. It is not necessary to defend this. This is exactly what is meant to be achieved. If it forces creative designers to produce project plans so be it - the system dictates that plans are necessary for any number of reasons. Although, if the implemented management system does crush flare and discourages creativity, then change it.

Too much paperwork

Often the way in which the management system has been interpreted has meant the imposition of paperwork and records. Although when examined the actual number of forms and records required by ISO 9001 and the management system is actually quite small. A frequent review of the list of forms may result in a reduction.

Also, the documented quality management system may already be considered too large and unwieldy. Adding safety and environmental documentation and procedures may exacerbate this situation still further. However, this does not negate the need for a Safety and Environmental management system, it just means that the construction of such systems needs careful consideration. See section on Intraneting the Management Systems.

Auditing is expensive in resource and not very accurate

While it is possible to combine quality, safety and environmental audits there are limitations to this approach (not only from the point of view of the necessary, but never-the-less additional work involved). If the audit combines these areas, the auditor may loose focus or concentration. There may be too many targets to aim for at the same time. An alternative approach may be to stagger the audits, providing the auditor time to readjust to the various needs of the different standards.

Auditors, like everyone else, have *"comfort zones"*, things they find easy and enjoy and things they find difficult and hate. When auditing ISO 9001 there is a temptation for auditors to closely audit calibration. This is because it is easy to audit, but there are very few quality problems associated with calibration and yet the auditor will spend considerable time on calibration. Design is often considered a difficult audit area and studies have shown the majority of quality problems stem from this function. Yet, often the auditor does not devote the same amount of energy or time to the design function as they do to calibration - comfort zones! Similarly, safety may be considered an easier audit than quality or the environment and consequently is given greater

217

emphasis as a result. Careful review of the time allocation allowed for each area (quality, environment, safety) should overcome this problem.

Safety may, because of its nature get, a higher priority than quality or the environment. Again the time allocation approach should resolve this problem.

Management Systems do not improve quality performance!
The jury is out on this one, studies have shown this to be both true and false. Although, perhaps the biggest argument that ISO 9001 must work is that Total Quality Management Initiatives have a track record of 60 to 70% failure. Whereas ISO 9001 has a track record of 99% success. Failure and success being measured by the approaches longlivity. Only about 1% of organisations which have been approved by a Certification Body have dropped the ISO 9001 certificate (including bankruptcies). Whereas about 60 to 70% of Quality Improvement initiatives fail to last - *"flavour of the month"* - the latest quality fad?

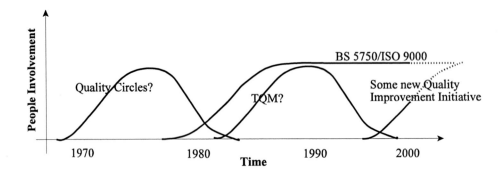

Figure 72 Flavour of the Month

The diagram represents people involvement with time in and on various quality initiatives. In the 70s and early 80s Quality Circles were considered to provide the "correct" approach, then along came TQM. Although Quality Circles popularity has waned it is still in use and has had some major successes. Whereas ISO 9000 which started in 1979 is still running. Do not misunderstand the diagram, it is not suggesting Quality Improvement Initiatives are a waste of time and do not work - only that they have a history of failure, so beware! Quality Improvement Initiatives have a vital role to play and still should be an integral part of any organisation's "quality push". Consequently, it is essential that organisation address both issues of Quality Management Systems (structure) and Quality Improvement (motivation). However, the approach to implementing and maintaining the QMS and QI programmes are not necessarily the same.

Exercise:

Exercise A   Gaining benefit from ISO 9000 after Approval

Introduction: Gaining ISO 9000 approval for an organisation will probably be a major project involving almost all departments (some more than others). The project often starts with the best of intentions - not just to gain approval but to improve the overall performance of the organisation. Unfortunately, as the deadline for certification gets nearer then the emphasis can often change to doing just enough to gain approval. This is because the implication of failure for the organisation and individuals within that organisation has become more important than improving the effectiveness and efficiency of the organisation. Not surprisingly jobs and reputation can be on the line and failure could be very embarrassing. Failure to gain approval could be disastrous for the organisation concerned.

Of course just doing the things that are necessary to gain approval should improve the performance of the organisation. However, all too often these things are done solely to satisfy the assessor. The ISO 9000 project often takes one to two years to complete and the conclusion - hopefully gaining approval, can be something of an anti-climax. People look round and ask "what changed, what has been achieved?" This is asked not because there has been no change but because these changes have been gradual. It is not always apparent that the improvements have been made as personnel have become used to working to the new (possibly improved) system.

There is a danger for managers to see gaining ISO 9000 approval as an end in itself. The programme of introducing and implementing ISO 9000 has necessitated a considerable amount of change and motivation. Having gained approval then the need to change and motivate has reduced. If managers see this approval as an end in itself then a great opportunity is lost. One consequence of conducting the ISO 9000 programme is that people have become used to change and implementing change. Now is the time to start a new quality initiative, rather than just conducting the audit programme or surveillance programme to ensure continued registration. This is a great opportunity to make further improvements in the performance of the various systems and processes running through the organisation. Some particular examples of this could be in Design and Development Department. Rather than just blindly following the procedures for Customer requirements and design review (without gaining real benefit) the procedures could be used to minimise design problems and avoid costly mistakes. Another example, in the Marketing Department which, having gathered data regarding customer complaints, take no real action on understanding the customer's fundamental problems with the product or service.

There is also a danger for Quality Managers to see gaining approval as an end to their role in Quality improvement. Following approval, maintenance of the audit system and programme fully occupies the Quality Manager's time. This leaves no resource or time to consider new initiatives or improvements to the Quality Management System (QMS).

One key complaint in operating an ISO 9000 system is that it becomes a bureaucratic imposition of producing forms and documentation. Will anyone actually read the Quality Manual anyway? Possibly, all the Quality Manual achieved was to document the current ways of completing tasks and processes. Cementing (in writing) all the bad habits and working practices that have been followed religiously over the life of the process.

Questions that now need to be asked are:

" Has the QMS become a bureaucratic imposition?

" Do the procedures reflect on how tasks *are* completed or ***should be*** completed? Does the procedure integrate the process or do people work as individuals?

" Have people within the organisation noticed an improvement in the organisation as a whole?

" Is there a sense of ownership of the QMS - or is the QMS owned by the quality department? Examples of this can be: The inability of obtaining any corrective action for the audit discrepancies; the non-updating of superseded procedures and the mad panic when the surveillance visit comes around.

" Have the customers noticed an improvement in performance of the organisation's product or service?

" Finally, the bottom line, has ISO 9000 saved money?

To help identify the issues raised by these questions, the following section has been written. The section is intended to be used to improve and build on the existing system, grasping the opportunity that registration has brought and reinforcing positively the controls of ISO 9000. This is because the basic concept and the reasons for implementing ISO 9000 still hold good. It is the practical implementation of ISO 9000 that needs continual improvement.

Identification of the improvement area. As in most things, if the reasons and objectives for a task are clearly and properly explained, then people are motivated and more likely to take on responsibility for that task. It is now necessary to evaluate the degree to which ISO 9000 and the QMS have been applied and the benefits (if any) that approval has brought.

The following checklist is intended to be used to help evaluate managers' perceptions about the performance of the quality management system. The statements need to be rated according to whether they are true or false - with reference to the current status of the organisation. If the question is completely false then score one, if completely true score ten. However, the statement may be partly true, e.g. that the quality assurance system has made some contribution to the performance of the organisation. Here a score of five may be appropriate. Guidance notes, shown in italics, are provided to help interpret the questions.

The general intention is not only to obtain a score but to promote discussion and stimulate action.

1. Application of the quality assurance system can make a positive contribution to the overall performance of the organisation?

	False									True
Scale	1	2	3	4	5	6	7	8	9	10
Mark										

ISO 9000? - This question is about whether we truly believe ISO 9000 approval can make a positive contribution to overall performance of the organisation. If managers can't truly buy into this, then there is a need to go back to basics and review the need for this style of quality management system.

2. There are clear, positive measures and data available that demonstrate the quality management system is improving the overall performance of the business?

	False									True
Scale	1	2	3	4	5	6	7	8	9	10
Mark										

Quality Performance - Here the question is about the management information systems regarding quality management systems. Is it effective enough? Is it giving sufficient feedback to determine that the quality management system is working as effectively and efficiently as it possibly can?

3. We know clearly where the quality management system has shown positive benefit?

	False									True
Scale	1	2	3	4	5	6	7	8	9	10
Mark										

Quality Manual - This question is attempting to review and identify those areas within the organisation that have improved because of ISO 9000, the areas that haven't benefited and the areas that could be improved with proper application of ISO 9000.

a. List the areas where the quality management system is weakest and needs to be stronger.

b. List the areas where the quality management system is strongest and the organisation has gained the most benefit.

4. Quality Auditing is an invaluable management tool?

	False									True
Scale	1	2	3	4	5	6	7	8	9	10
Mark										

Auditing can be seen as the method of retaining approval rather than a management tool. Auditing may provide management with important information regarding the compliance of the process and personnel to accepted working practices. Managers may not take notice of the results of audit and not take appropriate or prompt corrective action. This may be due to the managers' workload, the standard of the audit being poor or the results of the audits being trivial.

5. The quality management system fully reflects the way in which the organisation works?

	False									True
Scale	1	2	3	4	5	6	7	8	9	10
Mark										

Ownership - All employees have a role and responsibility for quality. Their contribution and compliance with the quality management system is essential if the system is to succeed. The quality manual may not be used - gathering dust on a shelf. This could be because personnel understand the contents and have no need to refer to the manual. It may be that the manual is difficult to read and understand. Could (or even should) the quality manual be put to greater use? There may be a need to change the quality manual to reflect current working practices.

6. The standard (ISO 9000) has made a positive contribution towards customer satisfaction and the standard of our product and service?

	False									True
Scale	1	2	3	4	5	6	7	8	9	10
Mark										

Has the product or service measurably improved since the implementation of ISO 9000? Has the number of customer complaints reduced?

7. The standard is active in helping to improve the performance of our processes?

	False									True
Scale	1	2	3	4	5	6	7	8	9	10
Mark										

Process Improvement - There are numerous processes running through an organisation e.g. buying, training, development etc. Proper use of the quality manual may help to improve the task or activity and, consequently, the process performance. It may be that there are better ways of achieving the objective of improving process performance.

Note, a process is different from a procedure. A process is a sequence of parallel or serial activities that have an input and output. A procedure is the instruction that describes the way in which an activity is to be performed.

8. Maintaining a quality management system is a cost-effective exercise?

	False									True
Scale	1	2	3	4	5	6	7	8	9	10
Mark										

Improving the profitability of an organisation can be achieved by improving the efficiency of the processes and consequently reducing costs and waste.

The QMS should work on both levels:
" *Improving process efficiency by describing the most efficient and effective way of completing various tasks.*
" *Reducing waste and costs by the analysis of failures and waste and taking preventive action.*

Calculation of your ISO 9000 score

Add up the score from each question and evaluate the organisation's score against the following assessment criteria.

0 - 40 ISO 9000 doesn't seem to be working within your organisation and real benefits are obviously not being obtained. It may be appropriate to conduct a complete evaluation of the organisation's strategy towards ISO 9000.

40 - 60 Obtaining benefits from the ISO 9000 Quality Management System but possibly greater benefit could be derived. An analysis of the answers to the questions should reveal and possibly identify some areas that could benefit from review and evaluation.

60 - 80 Tangible benefits are being derived from the application of ISO 9000. Effort could be focused towards maintaining and enhancing the gains and advantages already derived.

Exercise B

In the section "Guidelines for Customer requirements review", there is a Check List for reviewing customer orders - Appendix A.
Discuss:

N   Are the quality responsibilities correct for Production?
N   Should the Quality Department sign the Customer requirement form?

Notes:

N   *Is the Production Department only responsible for delivery on time? How can they accept "can make to specification" if they have no specification (drawings) available to review?*

N   *What does the quality department know of the customers requirements or the products or services ability to meet them? On this basis what does or can the quality department signature mean?*

Exercise C: Discuss - Should the quality department raise concessions?
Notes: Who requires the concession? - the quality department wishes the product to meet specification.

Exercise D: Discuss - Who is responsible for the quality of a document or report, the author or approver?
Notes: Ownership - does the responsibility for the quality of the document pass to the reviewer after approval - I think not! It remains with the author.

Exercise E: Document Inspection

Create a check list for one the following situations:

    a.   An Applied Research report
    b.   A piece of Software Code (written in C)
    c.   A functional specification

Obtain a suitable document and complete the document inspection process (including completion of the report and summary sheet).

[handwritten notes:]
document control
general - applied to most type research
Technical - ment tied to needs of
research or function

ISO TS 16949 & QS 9000

ISO TS 16949 - A quality system for automotive suppliers identifying the particular requirements for the application of ISO 9001:1994. (Note ISO 9001:1994)

Introduction

In 1999, the technical specification ISO TS 16949 was published. The ISO Technical Specification was developed by the International Automotive Task Force (IATF) incorporating the requirements of the French automotive standard EAQF, the German standard, VDA 6.1, the Italian standard AVSQ, and the current automotive standard QS 9000. ISO TS 16949 standard is aimed at the automotive suppliers who need a single quality system that is recognised by the international automobile manufacturers. It is recommended by Ford, GM and Daimler Chrysler as the next step in the certification process. The standard ISO TS 16949 was developed by the International Automotive Task Force (IATF) in collaboration with the ISO Technical Committee 176. The IATF is an international group of vehicle manufactures that consists of Ford, GM, Daimler Chrysler, as well as various automotive trade associations such as AIAG (America), VDA/QMC (Germany), SMMT (UK), ANFIA (Italy), CCFA and FIEV (France). See **Figure 73.**

ISO TS 16949 may go on to replace some of the current automotive standards such as QS 9000 and VDA 6.1. Also work has begun to restructure ISO TS 16949 to ISO 9001:2000, with publication expected early in 2002 and this can easily be seen in the focus on continual improvement and customer satisfaction that occurs within the standard. Therefore, although ISO TS 16949 does not yet replace existing individual automotive standards, it is set to become the Quality System Requirement for the automotive supply chain globally. Indeed it is accepted by most of the leading vehicle manufacturers such as Ford, General Motors, Daimler Chrysler, BMW, Fiat, PSA Peugeot-Citroen, Renault SA and Volkswagen.

Some of the benefits of ISO TS 16949 are that providers of automotive products to international markets will have the option of maintaining one quality system registration to meet multiple customer quality requirements. This should simplify the management of the quality system as it avoids multiple audits. ISO TS 16949 has also been designed to improve product and process quality while increasing efficiency and reducing variation. There is not yet a single standard that is universally recognised as the definitive statement on quality management, but the emergence of ISO TS 16949 is the first step.

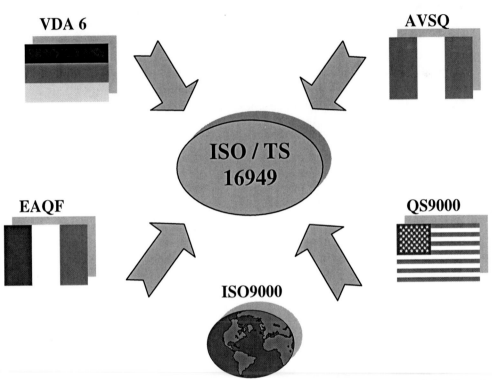

Figure 73 The new TS 16949 standard incorporates the requirements of the French EAQF, the Italian AVSQ, the German VDA 6.1 and the American QS 9000.

ISO TS 16949 combines the requirements of ISO 9000:1994 with those from the individual vehicle manufacturers standards previously mentioned, thus making it demanding, but at the same time securing its almost universal acceptance since it covers all of their requirements. Instead of concentrating on compliance to procedures and ensuring systems to correct problems that have occurred, ISO TS 16949 focuses upon the effectiveness and efficiency of processes. This is a proactive rather than reactive approach to problem resolution with the use of company data to drive continual improvement. This is similar to the revised focus within the new ISO 9001:2000 standard and reflects the new approach to quality systems.

Considerable emphasis is also placed upon Management Responsibility. This section now includes requirements that look at the way in which, and how often, customer satisfaction (including internal customers) is determined, validated and documented.

Also now included are continuous improvement tools and techniques, such as control charts (variables, attributes, CUSUM); design of experiments; theory of constraints; overall equipment effectiveness, parts per million analysis to achieve zero defects; value analysis; benchmarking; analysis of motion / ergonomics and mistake proofing. The standard also covers the impact created on society by minimising risks to customers, employees and the environment, and the way in which company data at all levels is used, including how it measures and demonstrates progress to overall business objectives. Elsewhere, as would be expected, the standard places great emphasis upon the requirements of individual customers. A total quality approach is encouraged by the demand for multi disciplinary approaches to product realisation, problem prevention and solution.

Another important enhancement over previous standards is the requirement to evaluate known or suspect problems against products of similar design and implement appropriate corrective actions.

The development and use of a structured system and the control of its documentation to ensure all relevant information is available whenever and wherever it is needed in the process is paramount. Thus a typical ISO TS 16949 system would be constructed as shown in **Figure 74**.

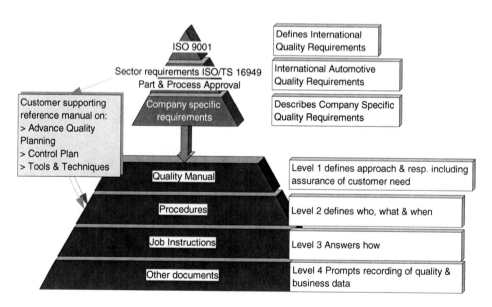

Figure 74 Typical ISO TS 16949 System Structure

Figure 74 shows the traditional pyramid quality manual structure which is also described in other sections of this book, however, the above model has significant customer additions that focus on the planning, approval, control and development of product and processes throughout their life cycles. Quality management planning, processes for production part approval, control plans, plant and facility layout, the identification and control of special characteristics, and mistake proofing figure prominently in the new standard.

As with any quality system, audit provides one of the key measures of performance and conformance and here also there are important additional requirements. System, process and product audits are all compulsory along with the use of specific checklists and the adjustment of audit frequency, dependant upon internal and external non-conformity and customer complaint. Specific customer requirements with regards to auditor qualifications must be followed with the objective of a higher auditor skill level ensuring a more efficient implementation of the management system.

Advantages of conformance to ISO TS 16949 (excluding issues of quality improvement) are possibly the retention of existing, and securing of new business. Gone are the days when orders continue to roll in because that is what has always happened in the past and ISO 9000, even in its 2000 guise, is being increasingly seen as the "entry level" minimum requirement for automotive quality management. Demands are increasingly towards independently verifiable proof of capability against stringent requirements that are becoming more and more customer specific, with demonstrable evidence to prove effective introduction being readily available. The economy of scale that is evident by conformance to one rather than multiple standards is obvious, particularly if it is one that can drive true efficiency and productivity improvements. And of course now is the opportunity to demonstrate commitment by becoming amongst the first to gain certification.

This is not going to go away, indeed the standard itself requires that companies gaining certification in turn develop their suppliers to ISO TS 16949, so be prepared for it to be driven down throughout the supply chain. This means that wherever you are in the supply chain for the automotive industry, sooner or later you will have to work towards this standard.

Clearly, things will not stop here and like any standard, ISO TS 16949 will itself evolve. Work is underway to align it against the process based ISO 9000 : 2000 that also looks at business excellence models such as EFQM (European Foundation for Quality Management) or the American Malcolm Baldridge Award. Moreover, in a world becoming more environmentally conscious, exacting demands around those aspects can also be envisaged, and indeed beyond the 2000 version, the next re-write of ISO 9000 is expected to include joint quality and environmental management system requirements.

In the UK, the Society of Motor Manufacturers and Traders (SMMT) has been appointed by the IATF to manage the launch and maintenance of the registration scheme for ISO TS 16949. It is also responsible for the qualification of certification bodies and certification body auditors, against very stringent requirements laid down by the IATF.

QS 9000

Where as ISO TS 16949 is a TS - a Technical Specification accepted by ISO, QS 9000 is not. It is a sector specific (automotive industry) set of quality requirements, accepted by a specific group of automotive manufacturers - it is their purchasing specification. Although widely accepted, it has not been adopted by all automotive manufacturers. The key elements of a Supplier Quality Assurance System are often based on the interpretation of ISO 9000 for a particular industrial sector, together with some additional customer specific requirements. QS 9000 is no exception to this. There are three elements. The first is based on ISO 9000, the second Sector or Industry Specific requirements and the third, Specific Individual Customer requirements.

These key elements can form part of an approach to ensuring supplier quality, even to the extent that the standard is made part of the contractual conditions contained in the Purchase Order.

One of the main criticisms of ISO 9000 is that the standard is not sufficiently product or process specific, i.e. ISO 9000 is too general and does not describe specific quality controls to the product or service that are needed to guarantee satisfactory supplies. The application of the following approach should ensure the identification and implementation of very specific quality control actions. This approach may be seen as augmenting ISO 9000 as the chosen Quality Assurance Management System of the organisation.

An overview of QS 9000

ISO 9000 Based Requirements

The interpretation of ISO 9000 for the automotive industry, is very similar to the original document, with the following main additions:

Management Responsibility
   Business Planning
   Customer Satisfaction
Quality System
   Quality Planning
   Failure Mode and Effects Analysis

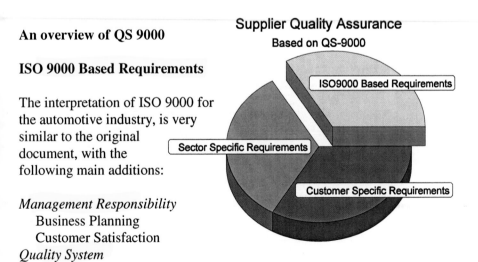

Figure 75 ISO 9001 Based Requirements

Design Control
  Quality Function Deployment
  Value Engineering
  Design of Experiments (Taguchi)
  Design for Production
  Reliability Engineering
Purchasing Control
  100% on time delivery
Process Control
  Safety & Environment Regulations
  Planned Preventive Maintenance
  Process Capability Studies
Statistical Techniques
  Application of fundamental statistical process control

Most of the above requirements can be found by reference to the relevant section of this book. The main theme behind these additions is prevention and quality improvement. In fact these themes are enlarged still further with the next element - Sector Specific Requirements.

Sector Specific Requirements

The Sector Specific Element of QS 9000 covers such issues as:

Product Approval: This usually involves the submission of product approval data and results. These results can be obtained either by self-assessment or from some recognised third party (possibly a test house, see NAMAS). These results could include process capability data from preproduction trials. This data should confirm the processes ability to reliably and consistently produce the

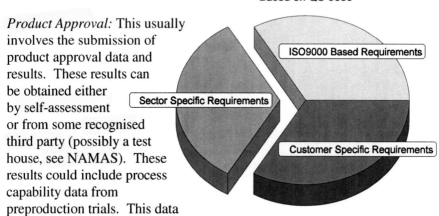

Supplier Quality Assurance
Based on QS-9000

ISO9000 Based Requirements

Sector Specific Requirements

Customer Specific Requirements

Figure 76 Sector Specific Requirements

product to specification, usually within ±four standard deviations of the product specification.

Continuous Improvement: Having demonstrated the processes' ability to consistently produce to specification, the next stage is to improve the processes' quality performance and reduce variation. Techniques such as Just in Time and Process Cost Modelling are suitable methods to be employed to improve quality and productivity. Reduction in process variation and continuous improvement may be achieved by the use of Statistical Quality Control and other typical Quality Circle techniques.

Manufacturing Capability: This aspect of QS 9000 is concerned with optimising and quality assuring the processes, resources and facilities. One example of this could be such as fool-proofing equipment to ensure that mistakes cannot be made when operating the equipment. In Japan this is known as Poka-Yoke.

Customer Specific Requirements

The Customer Specific Element of QS 9000 is concerned with issues key to that individual customer's needs. For example in Ford's case, one of the main requirements is the introduction of a *Quality Operating System* (QOS). This is a very simple technique and one which employs techniques which are well known but in an immensely powerful way.

The Quality Operating System is a simple problem solving tool which can be used to drive the continuous improvement programme. It is based

Supplier Quality Assurance
Based on QS-9000

ISO9000 Based Requirements

Sector Specific Requirements

Customer Specific Requirements

Figure 77 Customer Specific Requirements

on collecting and analysing data in a consistent way and can, in certain circumstances, be used as an alternative to Statistical Quality Control (SQC). Some organisations have great difficulty in applying SQC to their processes. (The sheer volume of processes or variables to monitor, is usually cited as the most difficult problem).

QOS can be broken down into four phases: Measurement & Targets, Pareto Analysis, Action Planning and Performance Monitoring. There is nothing new in these phases but applied consistently it provides a common method of assessing quality improvement projects progress. Also this assessment can be contained on one sheet of paper and be quickly understood and analysed by almost anyone.

Figure 78 Phase One - Measurement & Targets

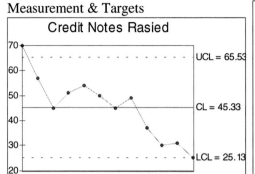

Table 32 Phase Three - Action Plan

Problem	Action	% Completed				Date
		¼	½	¾	1	
Misinterpretation	Training for Sales men	█	█	█		Jul 94
Price Error	Create Pricing Procedure	█	█	█	█	Mar 94
Wrong Customer Details	Up date data base	█				Jul 94

Figure 79 Phase Two - Pareto Analysis

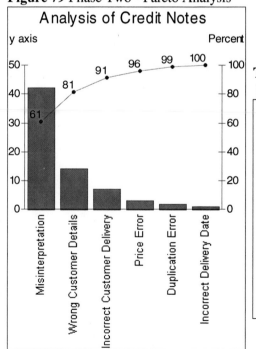

Table 31 Phase Four - Performance Monitoring

Jan	Feb	Mar	Apr	May	Jun	Jul	Aug	Sep	Oct	Nov	Dec
42	34	27	31	33	30	27	30	22	18	19	15
14	12	9	11	11	10	9	10	8	6	6	5
7	6	5	5	6	5	5	5	4	3	3	3
3	3	2	2	2	2	2	2	2	1	1	1
2	2	1	2	2	1	1	1	1	1	1	1
1	1	1	1	1	1	1	1	1	0	0	0
69	56	45	52	55	44	45	49	38	29	30	25

Figure 78 and **Figure 79** and **Table 32** and **Table 31** show an example of a completed QOS sheet. Phase one, the measurement and targets, shows the monitoring of performance with time. In this case the number of credit notes issued monthly. Phase two, is a Pareto analysis of credit note data to identify the important few reasons for raising credit notes. From this Pareto analysis, an Action Plan (Phase three) has been established in an attempt to reduce and eliminate the specific causes for issuing a credit note. Phase four is the raw data collected on a monthly basis detailing the breakdown of the reasons for issuing credit notes. Phase four row data labels (not shown) are the same as the horizontal axis in Phase two - Pareto Analysis. Flags can also be included in phase four, which indicate that one of the items on the action plan has been implemented. The effect of this action should be seen (hopefully positively) on the measurement and targets chart.

Implementing QS 9000

To see QS 9000 as an overall process **Figure 80** has been drawn. The figure represents typically the sequence that could be followed in achieving QS 9000 (assuming ISO 9000 certification has already been achieved). The stages consist of initially determining the customer's requirements and the critical features of the design by the use of Quality Function Deployment QFD and Failure Mode and Effects Analysis FMEA. Next the information from the these two techniques (QFD & FMEA) is used to generate the Quality Plan for the product or service. This Quality Plan can now be very much more accurate and reliable as the plan will be based on the QFD and FMEA information.

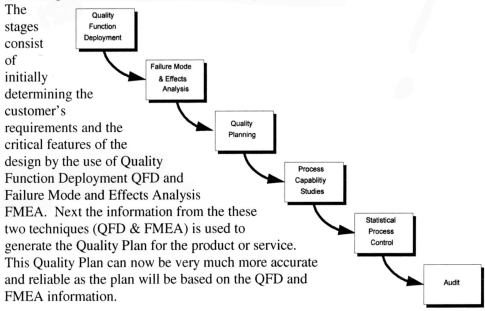

Figure 80 Supplier Quality Control Steps

The Quality Plan can detail the quality control elements and records that will be needed at each stage in the production of service process. Examples of the sort of controls specified in the Quality Plan may be Process Capability Studies or Statistical Quality Control (variable or attribute control charts) etc.

Finally, instead of what may be considered a rather nebulous audit as required by ISO 9000, a product or process based specific audit can be performed against the precise requirements of the Quality Plan.

Quality Function Deployment: As a project or design progresses, the greater the chance that specific customer's needs and expectations are overlooked or not satisfied. In order not to neglect or overlook *"the voice of the customer,"* the technique Quality Function Deployment (QFD) has been developed. The aim for QFD is to identify the key customer needs and translate these needs into controls. This control is achieved by establishing what the customer requires and through the various stages of QFD how these requirements will be achieved. (See section on Quality Function Deployment).

Failure Mode and Effects Analysis: This technique is used to identify and eliminate possible causes of failure. The technique requires a sequential, disciplined approach by engineers to assess systems, products or processes. The technique involves establishing the modes of failure and the effects of failure on the system, product or process. This ensures that all possible failure modes have been fully identified and ranked in order of their importance. (See section on FMEA).

Quality Control Planning: Having completed the QFD and FMEA, an excellent understanding of the customer needs and expectations will have been gained. Any potential system or product failures will also have been identified. Consequently, the process or project can be properly planned.

Process Capability Studies: Processes can be subject to variation. This variation may be small and insignificant. Alternatively, the variation could be excessive allowing products to be manufactured outside the specification. It is therefore important to understand the extent to which a process will vary before starting manufacture, thereby avoiding costly scrap or start/stop manufacture.

One method of determining a process's ability to meet specification is by conducting a Process Capability Study, where the process is statistically evaluated for the processes ability to conform to specification. (See section Statistical Quality Control).

Statistical Quality Control (SQC): Having determined the process's ability to meet specification, controls need to be applied which continually monitor the process for quality and to make continuous improvements to product quality. This involves taking regular measurements of process variation and comparing these observations with predetermined control limits of variation. This comparison can best be accomplished graphically on control charts. The application of SQC gives the opportunity to implement operator quality control, assisting in reinforcing the operator's responsibility for the quality of their own work and gives a sense of pride in their work. (See section on Statistical Quality Control).

Problem Solving: The use of the seven stage approach is a powerful tool in problem solving:

i.	Use the team approach.
ii.	Understand the problem.
iii.	Implement and confirm provisional corrective action.
iv.	Establish and verify the root cause.
v.	Confirm the viability of permanent corrective action.
vi.	Implement permanent corrective action to prevent recurrence of the problem.
vii.	Recognise the team's achievements.

Assessment, review and evaluation: Having established a product specific Quality Control Plan, then perform an audit to confirm compliance with the agreed Quality Plan including the application of SQC. Review and evaluate the results of the assessment to identify any areas for possible improvement.

As can be surmised, time resource for such a programme is considerable, but the final analysis must be - how seriously is supplier quality assurance to be taken.

SECTION 4 - QUALITY AUDIT

System Review and Evaluation

"I kept six honest serving men they taught me all I know. Their names are: what, where, when, why, how and who and the seventh is show me"

Rudyard Kipling

These questions can be successfully used in a number of circumstances (problem solving) but they can be particularly helpful when auditing. The questions could form the basis of audit questions: What procedures are required for this task? Where are the procedures kept? When are the procedures used? Why are the procedures necessary? By who and how are the procedures used? Possibly the most important question would be - can you show me the procedures?

Quality Audit

Definition: Quality Audit, a systematic and independent examination to determine whether the quality activities and related results comply with the planned arrangements and whether these arrangements are effectively implemented and are suitable to achieve objectives. (BS 4778, ISO 8402)

An Audit: is the study of actual practice against some concept of good practice, carried out by someone independent of or having no direct responsibility for the conduct of the activity undergoing audit. The audit would be carried out by someone trained or experienced in auditing techniques and skills. Scheduling of the audit should be done in advance rather than in response to a crisis and conducted with the prior knowledge and participation of those whose area or work is being audited.

Different Levels of Audit

Figure 81 shows diagrammatically the different levels of audit from the accreditation body, National Accreditation Council of Certification Bodies (NACCB), accrediting the certification bodies. The certification body, e.g. BSI, independently assessing other organisations to approve these organisations under a registration scheme such as ISO 9001. Customers

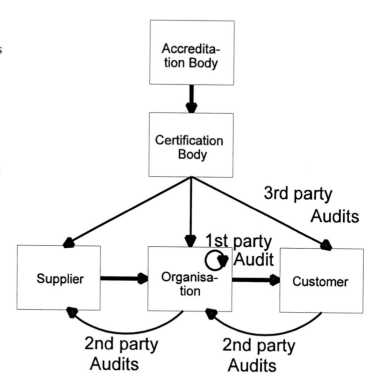

Figure 81 Levels of Audit

auditing suppliers to determine the suitability and effectiveness of their QMS. Finally, the organisation's own internal audits to ensure continued implementation of the documented QMS.

External Certification (3rd party): An external certification audit generally consists of a two-tier assessment.

a)   Adequacy audit - assessment of the quality system documentation against the 'Goal', e.g. ISO 9001.

b)   Compliance audit - assessment of the implemented quality system against the system documentation or the 'Goal', i.e. assessment of the system in practice.

External Audit (2nd party): An external audit is an assessment of a supplier or sub-contractor's quality system by the customer. The basis for this type of audit may be a recognised standard such as ISO 9001 or the customer's own standard. The audit may be performed by auditors from within the customer's own company or they may call on a professional auditor to provide this service.

Internal Audit (1st party): An internal audit is carried out by a company on its own systems, procedures and activities. The audits are generally conducted by company staff, however, on occasion there may be professional auditors engaged to act on behalf of the company. The key difference between an external or third party audit is that the third or second party audits are against a standard (ISO 9000) whereas an internal audit is against the organisation's own procedures and systems. The results of these audits are recorded in a similar way to an external audit and used as a basis for the company to develop and improve its operation.

Some of the following sections describe in more detail the differences in approach between internal and external audits.

Accreditation of Certification Bodies

The United Kingdom Accreditation Service operates accreditation schemes for Certification Bodies. Namely the National Accreditation of Certification Bodies (NACB) for the accreditation of Certification Bodies and the National Measurement Accreditation Service (NAMAS) for accreditation of Calibration Laboratories or Test Houses. In the case of the NACB, it uses the EN 45000 series to accredit Certification Bodies that certify organisations using the BS EN ISO 9000 series of standards. In the case of NAMAS, it uses the EN 45001 (M10) as the basis for its accreditation.

Diagrammatically the hierarchy of these Bodies would be as shown in **Figure 82**.

The National Accreditation of Certification Bodies (NACB)

The NACB operates a system of accreditation of Certification Bodies such as BSI, Lloyds, Bureau Veritas Quality International, United Register of Systems etc. which certify organisations using the BS EN ISO 9000 series.

The purpose of NACB is to assess the independence and technical competence of UK certification bodies to the requirements of EN 45011/2/3.

EN 45011 is the standard for certification bodies when issuing certificates of product conformity.

EN 45012 is the standard for the certification bodies own Quality Management System

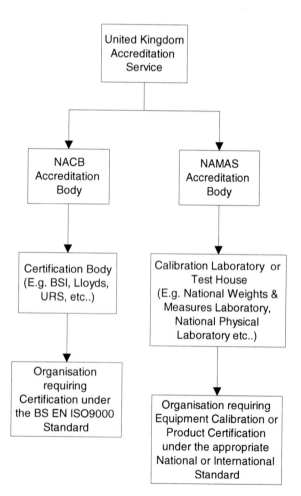

Figure 82 Accreditation Bodies

usually based on ISO 9001, i.e. the Certification Bodies' Quality Manual, Quality Manager, Internal Audit procedure etc.

EN 45013 is used to assess the competence of the certification bodies own personnel (assessors).

Together these standards cover the structure, operation and management of the certification body.

Once the certification body is accredited, it is granted the right to use the Tick and Crown symbol. It is this symbol which denotes the authority of the certification body in any particular industrial sector, as not all certification bodies are accredited in all industrial sectors. For example, some certification bodies are not accredited by the NACB in the medical or software sectors. In this situation, certification bodies may still assess and certificate companies working in the medical and software industrial sectors. However, the certificates issued cannot carry the Tick and Crown.

National
Accreditation
of
Certification
Bodies

The accreditation process is very similar to the ISO 9000 certification process with application, preassessment, adequacy audit, full assessment and, if successful, accreditation.

Once a certification body is accredited by the NACB then any organisations certificated by that body can appear in the DTI QA register of approved companies. Together with the certification bodies' own guide, e.g. BSI Buyers Guide.

Certification
Body Number

Figure 83

The National Measurement Accreditation Service (NAMAS)

The purpose of NAMAS, the National Accreditation Service, is for the assessment, accreditation and the monitoring of testing and calibration laboratories. The value of this accreditation is based on the need to ensure that products are produced to specification and that products are safe. Note; product certification not management system certification. NAMAS accredited laboratories can provide this necessary assurance of the competence of calibration and testing houses. It is this competence which will avoid the need for multiple assessment of calibration and testing laboratories. NAMAS certificates of calibration and test reports have now been recognised by organisations such as British Telecom, Ministry of Defence, Rolls Royce etc. NAMAS is also involved with gaining agreement on the recognition of other National Schemes and, as a consequence, International acceptance of the competence of the accredited laboratory.

Following the stringent examination to the requirements, usually of the standards M10 and M11[16], laboratories would then be authorised to use the formal certification and reports to record the results of any measurements and tests taken. These standards are very similar to ISO 9001 but with reference to calibration.

The method of certification is also very similar to the approach that would be adopted by the NACB or any other accreditation body. There is an application, the laboratory documentation is examined, there is a pre-assessment and then a full assessment of the laboratory.

Non-compliances to M10 and M11 would then be raised (if any were found). Corrective action would be taken and on satisfactory completion of these corrective actions NAMAS would offer the laboratory accreditation. The NAMAS certificate would then be issued and the surveillance visits would commence on a regular basis. Once certificated the accredited laboratory services would be publicised through the NAMAS directory of accredited laboratories.

These accredited laboratories can include commercial calibration laboratories and test houses as well as laboratories forming part of larger organisations such as a manufacturing company, University, or Government organisation.

Only laboratories accredited by NAMAS may use the NAMAS logo in conjunction with their accreditation number. This is an important distinction and one which is carefully guarded by NAMAS to the extent that forging of these NAMAS certificates has resulted in custodial sentences for the misuse of these certificates.

---

[16]   M10 & M11 are similar to BS 7500 series, EN 45001 & EN 45002 and ISO Guides 25 & 54. These documents cover the accreditation standard, the measurement & calibration system and the regulations

A typical example of one of these NAMAS certificated reports is shown in **Table 33.**

Table 33 Typical Calibration Certificate

CERTIFICATE OF CALIBRATION

Issued by the Quality Management & Training Laboratory
Date of Issue: 13 July 1995   **Serial No: 1234**

NAMAS

Quality Management & Training Laboratory   **CALIBRATION NO:**
P O Box No 172   **Approved Signatories**
Guildford Surrey GU4 7GS   Mr F Tickle BA Ceng MIQA
                                                    Signed **F Tickle**
Tel: 01252 344454   Mr G Vorley MSc MIQA
Page 1 of 1 pages   Signed **G Vorley**

CUSTOMER: Vakes Ltd Benley Park Guildford
DESCRIPTION: 1 off Micrometer to measure 0 to 25mm ± 0.01mm
SERIAL NO: 12345
DATE OF CALIBRATION: 13 July 1995
                              REPORT
BASIS OF TEST: A specified tolerance of ±1%
DIMENSIONAL: The gauge was measured for pressure at seven positions across the
                         range of the equipment using the Butenburgh testing rig. Serial No
                         123456.

                         The results were taken at 20°c +/- 2°c

MEASURING POSITIONS		RESULTS (mm)
1	0 mm	0
2	5	5.001
3	10	9.995
4	15	15.008
5	20	19.996

                         Uncertainty of measurement ± .5%
                         All measurement values were within the tolerance specified above
                                   Signature **F Tickle**
The uncertainties are for a confidence probability of not less than 95%.

This certificate is issued in accordance with the conditions of the accreditation gained by the National Measurement Accreditation Services which has assessed the measuring capabilities of the laboratory and is traceable to recognised National Standards and for the units of measurements realised at the corresponding National Standards Laboratory. Copyright of the certificate is jointly owned by the Crown and issuing Laboratory and may not be reproduced in full except with the prior written approval of head of NAMAS and the issuing laboratory.

Different Types of Audit

Management Reviews or Management Audits; Management audits are a review of the company's operation. The particular areas for review are allocation of responsibilities, efficient deployment of resources - both personnel and plant, effective communication, possible streamlining and simplification of the paperwork systems and operational procedures. These audits are generally done at Board of Director level.

Adequacy Audit (Desk study): This audit involves comparing the organisation's documented Quality Assurance System (QAS) against an appropriate Quality Assurance Management Standard (ISO 9001). For each paragraph of the Quality Standard (ISO 9001) there needs to be some reference in the documented QAS which addresses and fulfils the requirements of the standard. This adequacy audit can be against the standard (ISO 9000) or alternatively the check list below may be employed.

a. Is the procedure clear and complete?
b. Can the procedure be worked to or followed?
c. Is the procedure up to date (version level) and current (in line with current working practices)?
d. Does the procedure correctly reference other documents?
e. Is the input information (etc.) to complete the task specified?
f. Are the outputs from the task specified?
g. Are the resources to complete the task defined?
h. Are any checks, approvals or monitoring of the procedure or tasks defined?

This list is not exhaustive and the answers to these question need not be yes!

Systems Audits (Vertical Audits): System audits are a review of all company procedures relating to quality. Increasingly, the quality of work depends on the quality of written procedures and the degree to which operators are aware of, understand and adhere to such procedures. The aim of a systems audit is to examine the effectiveness of the specified system procedures.

Project Audits (Horizontal Audits): Communication is a common problem in many organisations. One method of examining the effectiveness of communication is by conducting a project audit across departments. This is a very searching technique and can uncover some strange anomalies. A project audit is conducted by following a project through departments, reviewing all the documentation, materials, etc. applicable to the chosen product or project. Project audits aim to establish the extent to which the projects comply with the contractual or specified customer requirements.

Procedural Audit: Audits against a specific procedure or work instruction. Procedural Audits usually start with an adequacy audit of the procedure or work instruction. Adequacy audits were described previously.

Once the procedure has been reviewed for adequacy, the audit aspects of the procedure can be identified. This can be achieved by reading the procedure and underlining all elements of the procedure that need to be audited. Below is an extract from an Enquiry/Quotation Review procedure with the elements that can be audited underlined.

On receipt of a customer enquiry or specification: when the enquiry is special (e.g. away from the standard price list) the Salesperson concerned completes an enquiry form/check list detailing the customers requirements. (See appendix). On completion of the enquiry form the form is signed by the reviewer and where appropriate submitted to the Manager for approval. If the enquiry is acceptable to the organisation and the customers requirements are understood, a quotation is raised on the basis of the information contained within the enquiry form.

This is possibly the most powerful method of auditing and is more extensively employed when procedures are in more common use. It ensures compliance with procedures (which is the most important) rather than the standard ISO 9000.

Improvement Audits: It may be considered that all audits should be improvement audits or what is the point of auditing? However, improvement audits can be specifically aimed at particular area for improvement.

N   Project Improvement - This could be an audit after project completion, to identify lessons learnt. These audits need to be sensitively handled as they can be quickly seen as a blame laying exercise. It is important the audit objective and positive outcomes are established and communicated before embarking on the audit. The audit can encompass all aspects of the project from sales and the suitability and prudence of the order, to the feedback from Installation, Service and the Customer. During the audit, factual information (rather an anecdotal) can be obtained regarding documentation and dates of document availability. When was the order received? When was the order acknowledged and accepted (they are different)? Was a project plan recreated before promising a delivery date? If necessary - how, who and when was bad news communicated to the customer? This information can best be presented in a table see below.

Project details	Project A	Project B	Project C
Project Name/Leader	3001/JC	1847/BA	3056/DD
Order date	36356	36269	7 Sept 99
Contract review /date	36371	36317	7 Oct 99
Delivery Date Promised/ Actual	Pro. 23 Dec 99/ Act. March 00	Pro. 4 June 99/ Act. Sept 99	Pro.23 Dec 99/ Act. Mar 00
Project Mobilisation review /date	Available /14 Oct 99	Available /28 June 99	Available /6 Oct 99
Project Plan/ date	Available /Mid Oct 99	Available /Aug 99	Available /2 July 99
Release to installation/date	14 Oct 99	36361	5 Nov 99
Test Specification/date	OK	OK	OK
User manual	OK	OK	OK
CE mark	OK	OK	OK

Examination of some of the dates in the table above may be revealing. What steps and action would be appropriate in these circumstances? (See Project Quality Assurance)

N   Process Improvement - The audit could be an audit of a process to establish performance criteria such as process; definition, owner, measurement, targets, etc. (See Benchmarking and Business Process Analysis)

N   Areas for improvement - The audit could simply entail discussion with the auditee to examine areas where they feel improvement could be made, e.g. the filing system, clear definition of responsibilities, better communication, etc.

N   Use a different Quality System Model - It may be appropriate to use a different model to audit against. Usually ISO 9001 will have been employed as the audit model but there are alternatives that could be employed such as the European Quality Award (EFQM), Deming prize or Malcolm Baldrige Award. (See Quality award Schemes).

Product Audit: These audits are very different to the above audits as they generally involve performing actual measurements or tests on a product to determine if the product (in all respects) meets the specified requirements or possibly an appropriate International or National product standard (e.g. the product standard for an electrical plug). This audit can necessitate the stripping down of the product into its individual parts and checking each part against a drawing. This product audit may also include some reliability or durability tests.

ISO 10011 Auditing Quality Systems

This international standard has been developed to provide guidelines for personnel carrying out internal or external audits. The standard is in three parts:

ISO 10011-1   Guidelines for Auditing Quality Systems Part 1: Auditing
ISO 10011-2   Guidelines for Auditing Quality Systems Part 2: Qualification Criteria for Quality Systems Auditors
ISO 10011-3   Guidelines for Auditing Quality Systems Part 3: Management of Audit Programmes.

ISO 10011-1 Guidelines for Auditing Quality Systems Part 1: Auditing. This section establishes basic audit principles, criteria and practices. It also provides guidelines for establishing and planning the audit and the methodology for performing audits and how audits should be documented. The standard contains certain definitions:

Quality System:	The organisational structure, responsibilities, procedures, processes and resources for implementing quality management.
Auditor (quality):	A person who has the qualification to perform quality audits.
Lead Auditor:	An auditor designated to manage a quality audit.
Client:	A person or organisation requesting the audit.
Auditee:	An organisation to be audited.
Observation:	A statement of fact determined as part of the audit process and substantiated by objective evidence.
Objective evidence:	Qualitative or quantitative information, records or statements of fact pertaining to the quality of an item or service or existence and implementation of a quality system element, which is based on observation, measurement or test and which can be verified.
Non conformity:	The nonfulfillment of specified requirements.

The objectives of an audit are defined as 'to determine conformity with the recognised and agreed standard'. The audit needs also to determine effectiveness of the Quality Management System in controlling quality and to provide the opportunity for quality improvement. The audit can also confirm compliance with a specified regulatory requirement, with a view to permitting entry in a recognised listing in a register.

The roles and responsibilities of auditors, audit teams and lead auditors are explained in the standard. They include the qualification for the auditor and their authorisation to carry out the audit. The need for the auditor to be independent, objective and at all times ethical in their approach to auditing.

The client and the auditee also have certain responsibilities with regard to ensuring that all relevant employees are informed of the intended audit and that they are briefed and appropriate guides are appointed. The client and auditee need to establish that there are adequate resources provided and that access and cooperation will not be a problem. Lastly and possibly most importantly that for any non-conformances appropriate agreed corrective actions are initiated.

The Audit organisation's responsibilities are identified as determining the scope and frequency of audits. This together with preparing the audit plan and executing the audit following an agreed pattern, described in these guides to auditing.

ISO 10011-2 Guidelines for Auditing Quality Systems Part 2: This section of the standard details the qualification criteria for quality systems auditors and to provide guidance in the selection of auditors. There are no specific educational standards, however, being able to demonstrated oral and written fluency in the officially recognised language would be necessary. The auditors would need to be adequately trained and knowledgeable in understanding the standards against which quality systems audits may be performed. The training could include the assessment techniques of examining, questioning, evaluating and reporting the audit findings. Additional skills required for managing an audit could include planning, organising, communicating and directing the audit and audit team members. Examination of the competence to be an auditor should be demonstrated through written or oral tests and other suitable means. The auditor should have a minimum of four years full-time appropriate practical workplace experience and at least two years in quality assurance with at least four audits totalling not less than 20 days. The personal attributes of an auditor should include open mindedness and maturity. The auditor will need to possess sound judgement, analytical skills and have the ability to perceive situations in a realistic way. To understand complex operations from a broad perspective and to comprehend the role of individual units within the overall organisation.

To meet the criteria for the selection as a Lead Auditor the auditor will need to have completed at least three complete audits as qualified auditor and have demonstrated competence and ability.

ISO 10011-3 Guidelines for Auditing Quality Systems Part 3: Management of Audit Programmes. This part of the standard gives guidelines for managing quality systems audit programmes. The guidelines include the identification of the department within organisation which has the responsibility to plan and carry out the series of programmed quality audits. Thus ensuring that this department is independent of implementation of quality system. The department needs also to set up a method of monitoring and maintaining auditors performance, to ensure that the audits are achieving the consistency required. This could be achieved by:

"   holding auditor training workshops
"   making auditor performance comparisons
"   reviewing of audit reports
"   holding performance appraisals
"   rotating the auditors between teams.

Logistical and operational factors and facilities required to perform audits needs to have been considered. The commitment of resources, the establishment of auditing and corrective action procedures, etc.

The Need for and Benefits of Internal Quality Audits

a)   Once a job is understood by an individual there is generally no further need to refer to documented procedures etc. and consequently the supervisor may not monitor the process.

b)   A Supervisor has many jobs and his monitoring/auditing of operating practices may not be as frequent as they ought to be.

c)   A deviation created in an emergency may become common practice.

d)   What the management believe in good faith is happening, frequently differs from what is actually happening.

e)   The policy and goals of the company can be audited to ensure that they are being met, allowing for changes in targets etc.

f)   Audits improve communication and understanding at all levels.

g)   Auditors tend to be less severe as they themselves are subject to audit.

h)   Audits enable individuals to 'air' existing problems that are evident within their area but the solution is outside their control.

i)   Auditing can be a powerful tool for training people in the requirements of the procedures and standards.

What does Auditing involve? There are four basic questions to be answered before conducting an audit; those being:

What?   Before starting an audit it is important to determine what is to be audited, i.e. the area and the scope of the audit. This can be decided on a departmental basis, e.g. Purchasing, Sales, Manufacturing etc. or on a functional basis such as document control or training which may involve several departments.

When?   Audits should be scheduled in advance and the relevant areas and personnel notified beforehand. The timing of the audit should ensure that it does not infringe upon normal company activities such as the regular Monday morning production progress meetings towards the end of the working day as this could cause problems such as availability of personnel. The frequency of the audits may be based upon a 'Pareto' type analysis where functions or departments may be identified as being the source of quality failures. The frequency depends on the stability of the procedures and confidence established by track record. The generally accepted frequency is that any function or department is audited at least once per annum. An Audit Programme or Audit Timetable needs to be created. The following table below shows the typical content of such an audit timetable. Included on the audit time table are the scheduled dates for the internal and supplier audits and the Management Review. As each of the audits are completed half the box can be shaded, when all the corrective actions have been concluded then the full box can be shaded.

Table 34 Audit Time Table

Audit Time Table												
Months / Area/Item	J	F	M	A	M	J	J	A	S	O	N	D
Internal Audits												
Contracts	*				*							
Purchasing		*				*						
Processing			*					*				
Dispatch				*					*			
Management Reviews					*					*		
External Audits												
Supplier A	*											
Supplier B					*							
Supplier C											*	
Approved by:				Date								

Who?   Audits should be conducted by personnel independent of the function being audited. These personnel should also be experienced and/or have had training in auditing techniques. Many larger companies employ full-time auditors to carry out audits and continuously monitor follow-ups. It frequently falls upon the Quality Manager to perform the auditing function but more commonly now, companies are using the 'mutual auditing' method where departmental managers audit each other's departments. Professional auditors are also sometimes employed to conduct audits on behalf of the company. Remember, it is like the old joke; "What is the difference between a Quality Auditor and a terrorist? You can negotiate with a terrorist!" So if the auditor and audit is perceived in this way (and some are) perhaps a change of style is required.

How?   An auditing procedure should be available which details the method to be adopted when carrying out an audit, e.g. method for notifying the department concerned, conducting of an opening meeting, how to record the results etc.

Figure 85 shows a Typical Audit Sequence, from *determining the need to perform an audit*, through to, *the follow up action*, having completed the audit. Below, each of the stages/boxes in the flow diagram are explained.

The need to conduct an audit may be determined from the audit time table. Alternatively, Purchasing may wish to use a new supplier whose products will have a significant effect on quality and a supplier audit may be required.

The Audit will then require planning - the next section headed "Audit Organisation and Planning", describes some of the actions necessary in planning a successful audit. The section also includes the possible format for communication advising the auditee of the forthcoming audit.

Before commencing the compliance audit an adequacy audit of the quality documentation may be necessary. An adequacy audit can be appropriate either in the

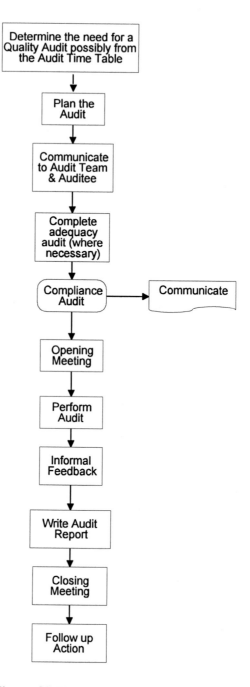

Figure 85 Flow Diagram of a Typical Audit Sequence

case of a new supplier or if the quality document has been significantly changed. Adequacy audits are also useful for; the creation of the audit check lists, determining the shape of the audit and in completing an audit schedule (See **Table 38**).

To complete a compliance audit an opening meeting will be required. It is advisable to conduct an informal opening meeting with the department head not only in the case of an external audit but also in the case of internal audits.

The section 'Gathering the Information' describes the various means by which audit information can be gained.

Once the audit has been completed, an audit report needs to be completed and a closing meeting held at which the corrective action can be agreed and subsequently confirmed. Each of these stages will now be explained in more detail.

Once the information has been gathered, it is important that it is agreed with the supervisor or manager of the area being audited. This ensures that the information is correct and that when the report is issued there is no opportunity for argument or disagreement.

Audit Organisation and Planning

Audits can be undertaken by teams of two or more[17]. One of the team is appointed to be the team leader whose job it is to:

A.   Decide how much work is involved; department or organisation size, structure, documentation etc.

B.   Determine the team size and composition. **Table 35** may be helpful as a guide.

Table 35 Audit Resource

Quality Standard	ISO 9001 (with Design)			ISO 9001 (without Design)		
Organisation size	1500-600	400-100	60-15	1500-600	400-100	60-15
Number of man days	8-5	6-4	4-3	6-4	4-3	3-2

C.   Preparation of a draft audit schedule (See **Table 38**).

D.   Allocate tasks to team members

E.   Ensure that team members are fully prepared for the audit, including an audit timetable of the areas to be visited and on which day

F.   Advise the auditee of the date and duration of the intended audit

If this was an internal audit then it would be necessary to detail; Date & time of the audit, are department's personnel aware that the department is being audited? Ensure that the department head or nominated representative will be available. That the auditor's role will be to determine; has the department a Quality Management System? Is the department working to the Quality Management system? Is the QMS effective in preventing poor quality?

G.   Run the audit

H.   Present a report of the auditor's findings

---

[17]   Audits can be performed by more than one individual

The Role of the Auditor

The auditor's role is to collect information and report on the findings. It is not for the auditor to accuse, criticise or apportion blame. The auditor must observe, question, listen and record the observations in an objective manner. This report should mirror what has been seen, heard and learnt about the activities and operation of the function being audited. The auditor should be appropriately dressed for the area/function that is to be audited.

Opening Meeting

An opening meeting, *in the case of an external audit,* can be a formal meeting between the auditor and the auditee. During this meeting it is necessary to complete the introductions (audit team, guides etc.), advise the auditee of the conduct of the audit and determine the local requirements of the company.

The auditor should advise the auditee that the audit is confidential and confirm with the auditee the scope of the audit (e.g. ISO 9001). The audit areas, time table, the audit reporting method and the audit sequence (conduct the audit, write report, closing meeting) should be described. The status of the quality documentation (quality manual) needs to be determined (it may have changed since the adequacy audit). It may be necessary to confirm the lunch arrangements and that employees are aware of the audit. The auditor should determine if there are any no go areas, special clothing or health requirements etc.

The duration of this opening meeting needs to be as short as possible (more time spent in the opening meeting means less time auditing) - 10 minutes if possible.

An opening meeting, *in the case of an internal audit,* can be less formal but will still need to cover the key elements described previously. The emphasis may be geared more towards putting the auditee at ease, reassuring the auditee that the audit is intended to be positive and that there will be an informal feedback to the departmental head before the written audit report is completed.

Gathering the Information

There are a number of methods that can be employed when comparing practice against written procedures. The most common is by the use of check lists. Checklists are a series of questions designed to test compliance with the key procedural requirements. The check lists require careful compilation and consideration to ensure that attention is being paid to important activities. Examples of ready made checklists can be found in Appendix A of Parts 4, 5 and 6 of BS 5750 1979 (prior to the issue of the latest ISO 9000 series). Although, obviously now not up to date they still can be of value for reference purposes. Checklists should be used as a basis for questioning and not become inhibitors to alternative questions which have the potential to provide a valuable insight into system weaknesses. They should be used as a guide and aide-memoire rather than a questionnaire.

A second source of questions for the check list can be the quality manual or the local procedures. The question compilation process involves scrutinising the quality manual for particular activities that should be completed or possibly records that need to be maintained. The audit can then involve simply stepping through each question in turn to determine conformance to the agreed procedures.

The concept of auditing is to gather information and there are several ways to do this:

Observation: Observing people at work can often be used as a means of comparing practice against written procedures and work instructions. Handling, storage and protection can be observed and compared against acceptable standards.

Interview: Questioning people about the activities they are conducting reveals information about problems they have encountered and what actions they have taken to solve them. It is frequently found that the most naive of questions can lead to the most basic non-compliance with procedures etc.

Examination: The examination of documentation, drawings, registers, records, batches of work etc. can reveal where there may be areas for concern. For example drawings may be found to be at an incorrect issue, there may be incorrect products being used or tested and possibly inspection stamps are not being recorded.

Sampling: A method which can be employed to ensure a full examination, is by the use of sampling. Sampling is very useful to confirm procedures are being reliably and consistently observed. Taking one example or sample is not statistically reliable. It is better that a number of observations or samples are taken, as this will provide a greater degree of confidence that procedures are being followed. An example of this could be in the Purchasing Department. The first thing to determine is what to sample? In Purchasing this probably would be Purchase Orders. To determine the sample size to take, sampling tables like BS 6001 can be used, alternatively taking a sample of 10% may be satisfactory. Just taking a sample ten items (Purchase Orders) may be all that is required. What is each of the samples examined for? Well in the case of Purchase Orders the following Table shows the results of such an Audit Sample. The second column shows what the Purchase Orders were checked against. The third column shows the results. Note; although only five orders were not approved this would imply that some 50% of all the Purchase Orders have not been signed.

Table 36 Audit Sample Check List

AUDIT SAMPLE CHECK LIST													
#	Question	Purchase Order Number										Result Num. NOK	%
		1	2	3	4	5	6	7	8	9	10		
1	Has all the Purchasing Order been completed correctly?												
1a	Precise identification of what is being ordered (title, specification, drawings etc.)?	✔	✔	✔	✔	✔	✔	✔	✘	✘	✘	3/10	30%
1b	Delivery Date Correct?	✔	✘	✘	✔	✔	✔	✔	✔	✔	✔	2/10	20%
1c	Inspection & Test instructions included?	✔	✔	✔	✔	✔	✘	✔	✘	✔	✔	2/10	20%
1d	Terms & Conditions included?	✔	✔	✔	✔	✔	✔	✔	✔	✔	✔	0/10	0
2	Has the Purchasing Order been approved?	✘	✘	✘	✔	✔	✔	✘	✔	✘	✔	5/10	50%
3	Is the Purchase Orders filled in correctly (in sequence)?	✔	✔	✔	✔	✔	✔	✘	✔	✔	✔	1/10	10%
4	Is a requisition available?	✔	✔	✔	✔	✔	✔	✔	✔	✔	✔	0/10	0
5	Is the supplier on the Approved List of Suppliers?	✔	✔	✔	✔	✔	✘	✔	✘	✔	✔	2/10	20%

Other samples that can be taken could be contracts, drawings, stores items, inspection results etc.

Sequence of the Gathering Information

Having compiled the Audit Schedule (for the department or section under investigation) and established a set of questions derived from the Quality Manual and the audit standard[18], there is a danger of the assessor immediately starting to audit without first understanding the role, tasks and duties of the department being audited. Assessors who only audit by following the book or set questions are in danger of overlooking key issues which may only be discovered by understanding the department or process. It may be better to follow the sequence shown in **Figure 86**.

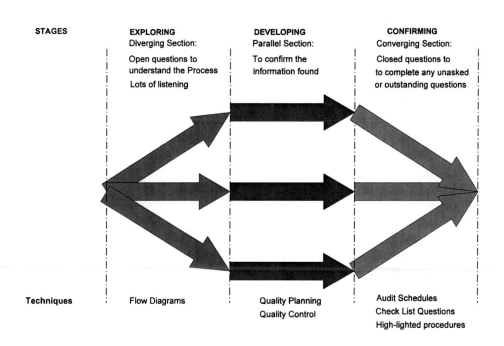

Figure 86 Audit Question Sequence

The first stage is to understand the process, section or department main roles, tasks and responsibilities. The process may be quite simple, such as an assembly process, but the process could equally be quite complicated such as modelling the way radioactive materials decay, using a very high speed computer. The approach to quality controlling these two processes would be quite different and the expected and operational methods of verification and validation of these processes needs to be understood. It is not

---

18   This audit standard could be ISO 9001 but there are many other standards which can be audited against ISO TS 16949, AS 91000, etc.

possible to audit in a vacuum and the assessor needs to understand the process to determine whether the controls are complete and satisfactorily applied. So the first stage is to *understand the process*. The techniques that can be employed to understand the process can be to draw a flow diagram of the sequence of typical departmental tasks or to simply list out the tasks of a department.

The next stage is to follow through any specific issues uncovered by understanding the process. It may be that the:

"   Assembly operation is not foolproof, which would not have been uncovered without discussion with the operator.
"   Computer model has not been validated or verified. Methods of validation and verification could include a review by other appropriate engineers or by the creation of an alternative model or method.

It is important to remember to follow any issues which may be seen to be discrepancies, through to a logical conclusion. This is to ensure that the issues of concern really are discrepancies not just a misunderstanding. So the middle stage is *follow through*. The techniques that may be appropriate to use are quality planning or to establish the expected quality control methods that would normally be applied to such tasks and activities.

The final stage is *confirmation*. This is to clear up all of the outstanding questions, i.e. questions not yet asked from the check list of questions and audit schedule. During this stage it may be more beneficial to asked specific closed or yes/no type questions. These closed questions are where the auditee is only expected to confirm with evidence the existence for records etc. See Questioning Skills on page 267.

A technique that may now be employed is the use of the audit schedule (See **Table 38**), where the audit schedule table (which was completed before starting the audit) can be employed. This audit schedule identified the paragraphs of the ISO 9001 standard that the department being audited needs to comply with. The list of questions compiled before the audit can be asked.

Procedural Audit - the quality manual or procedure can be examined prior to the audit and key activities (such as record keeping) can be identified or highlighted. This is so that these key activities can be confirmed as satisfactorily taking place. During this confirmation stage it may be more beneficial to ask specific closed or yes/no type questions. An example could be where the auditee is only expected to confirm (with evidence) the existence of records - can you show me the records of contract review? See Questioning Skills on page 267.

Informal Feedback

It is essential that the auditor completes an informal feedback to the department head confirming the audit findings. That is not to say that all the findings will result in discrepancies but to confirm the findings are accurate and factual. This helps put the auditee at ease - there should be no nasty surprises in the audit report, thus avoiding arguments at the closing meeting about the accuracy of the report.

Social Skills Required of an Auditor

From the above it is apparent that auditing requires special skills and attributes. These are achieved by careful selection and training.

Desirable attributes of an auditor include: Ability to communicate, Unbiased, Patient, Articulate, Diplomatic, Inquiring mind, Interested, Industrious, Professional, Open minded, Analytical, Listener, Thorough, Polite.

Negative attitudes which undermine the effectiveness of an audit can include: Critical, Nit-picking, Argumentative, Opinionated, Gullible, Egocentric, Cynical, Shallow, Condescending, Emotional.

Questioning Skills

Leading questions: If you make a point of studying a television interviewer, you will notice that they ask "leading" questions. In other words, questions which lead the person to respond with an explanation, description, recollection or further "tit-bits" of information rather than a yes/no response. Interviewers are trained in this technique and it is easy for them to manipulate people's answers to say what they want the audience to hear. An auditor should, however, avoid putting words into people's mouths.

Informative and interested questions: If a person detects a lack of interest then they will not be very forthcoming, therefore, ask questions out of genuine curiosity or from information already gained.

Open questions: Questions where it is not possible to answer yes or no - used when trying to understand the process. "What are the main tasks you perform?"

Closed questions: Questions that only allow a specific or yes/no answer - useful when the auditee is procrastinating or avoiding the point. "Do you have inspection and test records for this item?"

Quality Audit

Naive questions: It is often surprising how a simple question can bring forth the most significant information. Questions which nobody asks for being thought ignorant or the answer is generally taken for granted can open up new avenues of information.

Why? Why? Why? Very often the first response given to a question does not give the necessary information. It may merely be the answer they think you want to hear, or it may be an assumption or guess because the person does not know the answer, they may even have been briefed on the answers to give. It is often worthwhile repeating the question until you are satisfied with the answer. It is, however, important to be careful not to alienate or belittle the person. If they do not appear to know the answer make it easy for them to say so rather than have them inventing answers to avoid looking foolish.

Association of ideas: Use the information gained to guide you to further questions but not to the extent that you are misled or follow a "red herring." Adopt a theme to act as a thread in a line of questioning.

Taking notes: Excessive note-taking means that you will miss what the speaker is saying, on the other hand, not taking notes at all will certainly mean that important key facts will be forgotten or remembered incorrectly. When taking notes it is useful for the auditee to see what the auditor has written and also confirm with the section head before leaving the section. This is not that the findings or notes necessarily indicate a discrepancy but rather to confirm that the notes are correct.

Check your understanding: There are approximately 600,000 words in the English language, the average person uses 2,000 of them and 500 of the more commonly used words have an average of 28 meanings. If in doubt ask the question in a different way and perhaps a little later in your discussion.

Table 37 Typical Audit Form

Internal Audit Report			Report No.		
Organisation:			Date:		
Standard: ISO 9001	Requirement:		Discrepancy Category		
			A	B	C
Assessor:	Section Head:		Dept:		
Discrepancy:					
Action Recommended					
Action taken:					
Discrepancy A Significant non-compliance with the standard B Significant number of minor non-compliancies with the standard C Minor problem area that warrants attention.					
Signature:			Date:		

Reporting the Findings

The findings of the audit are frequently presented in the form of a series of audit report discrepancy forms and a summary sheet produced stating the main findings of the audit. The report can only contain the non-compliancies but sometimes it is worth including the compliancies. The compliancies can be used to ensure that subsequent audits do not unnecessarily repeat any audit trails previously followed. The final written report is normally issued to the company's management for their consideration. An approach to compilation of an audit report can be:

"   Examine the audit notes and identify any possible discrepancies
"   Rephrase, reword or clarify as necessary each discrepancy statement

" Determine the appropriate Quality Standard (ISO 9001) paragraph number and discrepancy category - A, B or C. See **Table 37**.

Closing Meeting

A closing meeting is often held between the supervisor, departmental manager and auditor. During the meeting the audit findings are presented and discussed. The aim of the meeting is to agree the findings and determine the action proposed to correct the discrepancies. It is important to remember that it is not the auditors' brief to determine what that action should be, but they can be asked to advise on recommended action. The implications of any proposed corrective action should be evaluated at this stage as it is a well known fact that a solution to one problem often leads to the emergence of another problem elsewhere.

A typical format and sequence of a closing meeting could be:
" Introduction:
Remind the meeting attendees of the reason and scope of the audit. Thank the auditees for any help and assistance (don't mention any problems). Auditing only tends to identify the bad points, it is often worth noting the good aspects as well.
" Request that questions are withheld until after the report has been presented (other than possibly questions regarding clarification of the audit report).
" Present the audit report:
Remind the meeting attendees that the audit findings were either witnessed by the guide or reported to the section head at the time of audit. Hand over a written copy of the audit report. If there are a number of discrepancies it may be appropriate to only identify certain key issues - (e.g. no final inspection and test inspections) rather than totally de-motivate with a huge list of discrepancies.
Present each report in turn detailing the appropriate quality standard (ISO 9001) paragraph name, the category A, B or C and the discrepancy. The discrepancy report needs to be as clear as possible, with, wherever possible, examples; quality manual reference, part or procedure numbers, location etc. The report needs to be sufficiently clear so that suitable corrective action will be taken, if the report is not clear then wrong or no action may be taken.
" Summarise the findings (See **Table 38**).

Table 38 Typical Audit Schedule

Audit Schedule	Report Number:			
Department/ Company	Date:			
Requirement	Checked	A	B	C	D
Management system					
General requirements					
Documentation requirements					
Management responsibility					
Policy					
Planning					
Responsibility, authority & communication					
Management review					
Resource management					
General requirements					
Human resources					
Information					
Infrastructure					
Work environment					
Product and/or service realisation					
General requirements					
Customer-related processes					
Design and development					
Purchasing					
Production and service operations					
Control of measuring and monitoring devices					
Measurement, analysis and improvement					
General requirements					
Measurement and monitoring					
Control of nonconformity					
Analysis of data					
Improvement					
Report Summary: **"D"** means no evidence of non-compliance					
Name (Auditor)	Date:			

"   Request and record the corrective action to be taken (what, when, how, who).
"   Make a note of the attendees and close the meeting.
"   Distribute copies of the audit report.

Action after the Audit

Implementation of corrective action: Having agreed the corrective action to be taken it is important to ensure that everyone affected by the change is properly informed. Any modifications to procedures or manuals should be carried out and issued to the relevant parties in the shortest possible timescale.

Follow up: Now that the agreed corrective action has been agreed and implemented, is that it? The trouble with human nature is that if we are not monitored we tend to fall into bad habits. This can be true for new procedures and amendments to existing procedures, they can fall into disuse as a result of neglect. To remove the chances of this happening it is necessary to carry out what are called 'follow up' audits. These are normally conducted after an agreed time and are intended to verify that those new procedures are being adhered to and that they are effective with regard to removing the non-compliance. These audits are only intended to check on those areas where non-compliance was found and are not to check on areas that were not covered in the original audit.

SECTION 5 - LAW

Quality Assurance and the Law

The law has always been concerned with quality by specifying what standard should be set and by providing means of enforcement. Legal attention has now widened to the process or system of controlling quality and the overall responsibility of management to provide safe, high-quality goods and services.

The relevance of the law to Quality Assurance is two-fold. Firstly, everything happens according to law and as a corollary there is no such thing as an accident. In fact the systematic approach of QA is an acknowledgement of that very truth. Secondly, and more conventionally, the law establishes a system by which duties and responsibilities may be identified and enforced.

The Criminal Law is a means of protecting society from the dangers of poor quality and deterring or punishing those who fail to achieve their public duty. Civil Law is a means of enforcing private responsibilities and recompensing those who suffer damage as a consequence.

Thus the law concerns us all, for whatever our situation, at work or outside, we need to rely on the safety and reliability of other people's designs, products and services.

It is well known that ignorance of the law is no defence, and today it seems that inaction is no defence either. Society is not prepared to accept failures in quality or safety, as witnessed by public reaction to recent tragedies, for example in rail, sea and air transport. More and more the individuals concerned and the companies for which they work are being held responsible and liable by the courts. At the same time there is a continual stream of new laws, regulations, codes and directives, which seek to protect society and indeed improve the quality of our lives.

Criminal Law

Statutes or Acts of Parliament, may establish a criminal responsibility as a deterrent or punishment for bad quality. Penalties may include fines, the loss of a trading licence or even imprisonment. It is a crime to sell certain goods, which are not approved by an Independent agency and marked by them, e.g. Hall-marking, or other products which are not marked as conforming to British Standards, e.g. crash helmets. Offences may be committed under the Weights and Measures Acts, Food and Drugs legislation and the Trade Descriptions Acts. It is a

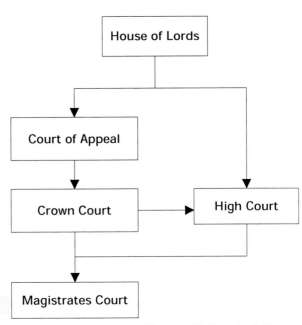

Figure 87 Criminal Courts

defence under the last mentioned Acts to have taken reasonable precautions and exercised due diligence to avoid committing an offence. In 1989 one company pleaded this defence and cited its QA system and BS 5750 registration as proof. (Note pre-ISO 9001) However the prosecution was successful, thus indicating that the British Standard assessment may fall short of what the law requires. **Figure 87** shows the hierarchy of criminal courts and appeals process.

Trade Description Act 1968: Providing false or misleading description. The act states that "Any person who in the course of trade or business:

    a.   applies a false description to any goods or

    b.   supplies or offers to supply any goods to which a false trade description is applied shall be subject to the provisions of the act, be guilty of an offence"

Quality assurance issues include; a duty of due diligence and care. Product inspection, testing and trials confirming (and providing documentary evidence) that the product complies with all the stated specifications. Checking the accuracy of product advertisements, product claims and specification sheets. Possible defence could include that it was a genuine mistake.

Weights and Measures Act 1985: Primarily concerned with physical properties such as length, volume, mass, etc.
Quality assurance issues include:

i)   The consistency and reliability of the measuring equipment
ii)   The calibration status of the measuring and its control
iii)   The sampling frequency, quantities, procedures, training and records

Food Safety Act 1990: This act has five basic aims to ensure that:

1.   food is on sale is safe to eat
2.   food Is not misleadingly represented
3.   proper legal powers and penalties were available
4.   the United Kingdom could meet its role within the EU
5.   continuity was maintained by environmental change

There is no defence if at fault - product or service at fault. However, proving not to blame or not your fault would be considered a defence.

The quality assurance duty of care is to adequately test, provide proper controls and records and ensure adequate training, storage and instructions.

The Health and Safety at Work Act, 1974: This act laid down duties on the designers, manufacturers, importers and suppliers of substances and articles for use at work. Since 1988 these duties have been extended to include liability for the misuse of items where that was foreseeable. Chairs and tables are often used to stand on and screwdrivers are commonly employed to open tins of paint! Another amendment means that producers and suppliers now have an extended duty under the Act. There is a continuing duty to revise information and warnings about a product when anything gives rise to a serious risk to health and safety. Responsibilities are ongoing, and there is no simple answer as to when, if ever, they cease. Executives can be personally liable under the Act if consent, connivance or neglect is proved against them. The possibility of a manslaughter charge is no idle threat today.

Since the Consumer Protection Act 1987 it is now a criminal offence "to supply consumer goods which are not reasonably safe having regard to all the circumstances". One defence would be compliance with an approved standard. Trading Standards Officers have been given greater powers of investigation, testing, seizure and prohibition, in the interest of public safety.   BSI safety Hawk.

More recently, new regulations have been introduced to control the quality of the work environment, namely the Control of Substances Hazardous to Health, Noise at Work and Electricity at Work Regulations. Other E.C. Directives also cover the Safety of the workplace, and work equipment. A common feature in all these Regulations and

Directives is the need for a systematic approach to ensure assets, materials and services are assessed, evaluated and maintained properly. In short the risks involved must be well managed.

Civil Law

There are three areas of civil law which are concerned with the quality of goods and services. They are the law of Contract, Negligence and Strict Liability. These laws apply whether or not any criminal offence has occurred. **Figure 88** shows the hierarchy of civil courts and appeals process.

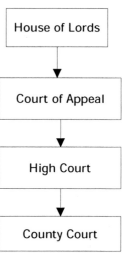

The Law of Contract

A contract is a legally binding agreement, whether in writing or not, by which the parties acquire rights and undertake responsibilities. The quality of the subject matter may be expressly stated in a specification. There may even be an insistence that a particular QA system is in operation. Terms as to quality may also be implied by custom or by statute.

Figure 88 Civil Courts

The essential features of a valid contract are:

i) *Offer*: One party makes an offer that the other party accepts, e.g. a specification, the price, the delivery date. Issues - contract terms.

ii) *Acceptance*: Acceptance of the offer made by the other party. There are two elements to acceptance, "fact", the moment at which the contract was made and "communication", receipt of acceptance by the offeror.

iii) *Consideration*: This distinguishes a contract from a promise as in this case money or a consideration is exchanged.

iv) *Intention*: That the parties intended the contract to be legally binding, e.g Commercial agreements both parties usually intend a binding agreement.

v) *Legality*: There cannot be a contract to do something illegal.

vi) *Capacity*: The parties concerned have the mental capacity to understand the contract.

The Sale of Goods Act 1979 implies the following terms into business contracts:

(1) Goods must fit their description. This may refer to quantity, quality, size, measurement, packing, labelling and so on.

(2) Goods must accord with their sample.

(3) Goods must be of merchantable quality. This term is being replaced now by "acceptable quality".

(4)   Goods must be fit for the purposes requested.

One question that often arises is: for how long should quality last? Case law may provide some guidance. In **Crowther & Shannon (1975)** the dealer was still liable for the engine seizure of a second-hand Jaguar that he sold - with 80,000 miles on the clock.

Terms as to the quality of a service are implied by The Supply of Goods and Services Act 1982. In the absence of specific terms a service should be to a reasonable quality, at a reasonable price and performed within a reasonable time. The definition of reasonableness is what could be expected according to the circumstances of the particular case. Ultimately it may require an arbitrator or judge to decide.

Legislation has also been found necessary to stop parties contracting out of their responsibilities by the use of exclusion clauses or disclaimers. Under the Unfair Contract Terms Act 1977, such clauses must pass the test of "reasonableness". As between businesses it is possible to exclude liability via specially agreed non-standard terms, for example, that an item is not warranted as suitable for incorporation into some other assembly.

Contractual Chains. This inter-relationship between contracts merits further consideration. **Figure 89,** Contractual Chain, illustrates how many parties may be involved in the quality of an item from its initial conception

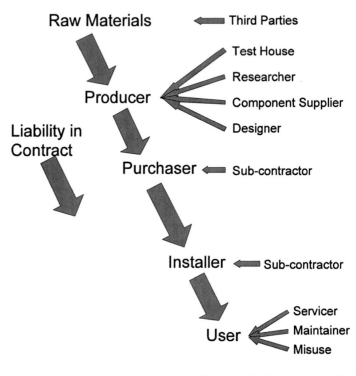

Figure 89 Contractual Chain

through to its use or even misuse. Links in the contractual chain can be identified at various stages. Each party therefore has legal responsibilities towards its immediate partner.

However, the advent of Product Liability (see section on The Law of Strict Liability) has increased the exposure of all these parties to legal redress. Not only can the 'chain' be short-circuited with a direct action by anyone suffering damage, but as the liability is now 'joint and several' one party may be answerable for the liability of another, who, for example, has become insolvent. The contractual device that is now being used is to obtain an indemnity in the contract to prevent that liability being transferred. This in turn necessitates an insurance obligation to ensure the party responsible is able to pay. Concern about the capability, financial or otherwise, of a trading partner, has been a key factor in the development of QA itself.

The Law of Negligence

In the diagram "Contractual Chain" reference is made to "Third Parties", who are outside the "contractual chain". Without a remedy in law - Contract third parties can only sue for damages under the Tort of Negligence. A "tort" is simply a civil wrong. To be successful a victim has to prove that he is owed a duty of care, that the duty was broken, and that the resultant damage caused his injury. This is well illustrated by the famous case of **Donoghue v Stevenson**, in 1932, when the non-purchaser of a bottle of ginger ale was made ill by the drink which also contained the remains of a snail. It is interesting to note that the retailer of the drink was not liable because he could not inspect the opaque, sealed bottles. Hence it was the manufacturer who was negligent in not having an adequate system for production and quality control.

The duty of care under Negligence can be very far reaching. Anyone involved in the design, production, inspection and marketing of a product or service may be liable. The Tort of Negligence has evolved to include liability for careless statements, even negligent certification of the quality of a product. After a recent Chinook helicopter crash in the U.S.A. both the Boeing inspector and the F.A.A. representative were charged with negligence. A QA system is evidence that an organisation is attempting to fulfil its duty of care. On the other hand it may be easier to point out a failure by reference to such a system. So it may be a two-edged sword with the advent of more professional organisations seeking to be quality assured, warnings have been sounded again. An engineer's duty of care is based on reasonable skill and care, but the public may be entitled to a higher standard if the engineer is certified. However QA is evidence of the 'state of the art', and unless there was an alternative equivalent system, that might be evidence of a breach of duty too.

The apparent ease of suing in negligence is however tempered by the need to prove fault. Without such proof the defendant is not liable. This difficulty reached a high-water mark with the Thalidomide tragedy. The drug manufacturers pleaded that they were not at fault in failing to foresee the consequences of the product they developed. In turn this tragedy precipitated a movement to introduce No-fault Liability, more accurately termed: Strict Liability.

The Law of Strict Liability

An E.C. Directive gave rise to the Consumer Protection Act 1987, which introduced into the U.K. a system of strict liability for products. Now any person injured by a defect in a product may sue any person responsible for its production or supply (including importers and 'own branders') and without the need to prove fault. Therefore the onus is thus on the party sued to prove who else was responsible for the defect if they are to escape liability. Furthermore, as the

Table 39 Consumer Protection Act Overview

i)	Producer or supplier	
	i)	Liable for damage (whether knew or not)
	ii)	Producer means importer or seller
	iii)	If two people then joint liability
	iv)	Product defect when used for intended purpose
ii)	Producer or supplier not liable if:	
	i)	Did not circulate
	ii)	Not defective when distributed
	iii)	Not indented for distribution
	iv)	Damage means death property etc.

liability is joint and several one party's inability to pay may render another liable for the whole damage. This was referred to earlier as the cause for indemnity and insurance terms in contracts. It illustrates the importance of quality in procurement, servicing, maintenance and so on.

As victims had discovered to their cost before, it is not easy to prove that another party is to blame. One prerequisite is to be able to trace the product origin, hence traceability and accurate record systems are essential, and these records may be required for up to twenty-five years after initial circulation. Traceability will be vital too if a dangerous product has to be recalled. Recent examples involving baby food and mineral water show the importance of emergency recall procedures which should be laid down, rehearsed and fully effective. The damage to business reputation here is verging on the irrecoverable.

Under the new law it is still incumbent upon the claimant to prove that there was a defect in the product. However the definition of a defective product is quite wide, i.e. "where the safety of the product is not such as persons generally are entitled to expect". It is not the expectation of the designer, producer or marketing manager nor the user. Thus, if people expect screwdrivers not to fracture when opening tins of paint, that indicates a defect in the screwdriver and cannot be dismissed as misuse. This has given rise to a few surprising cases on 'reasonable misuse', (although not as bizarre as several American equivalents). It is not unreasonable to stand on a packing case, nor to crawl across a ladder suspended across some open floor joists. The warnings and instructions for product use take on added significance here, for they are deemed to be part of the product. Such literature must be in the appropriate languages, unambiguous, and be to hand even long after initial circulation. For all these points the importance of feedback, via prototype testing, market research, customer complaints, records of accidents and near-misses assume added significance.

The so-called "defect" may also manifest itself in the handling, storage, packaging or delivery of an item. Nor are these stages limited to the control of the producer or supplier, for the user may need to be warned too. This is another example of the continuing responsibility even long after handover which was referred to under the Health and Safety at Work Act (See section on Criminal Law - Health and Safety at Work). In fact a

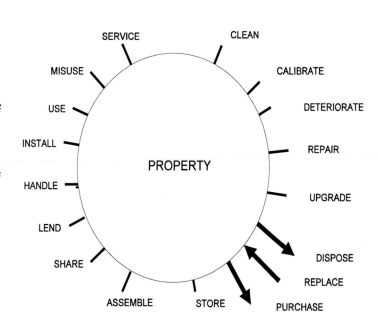

Figure 90 Product Life Cycle (After Sale)

product in its life "may play many parts", as illustrated by **Figure 90**, Product Life Cycle (after sale). At any of the stages on the circle a defect may arise for which the designer, producer or supplier could be sued. The onus is then on them to prove otherwise. It should be noted that this potential liability may continue and include the safe disposal of the product. Designers of buildings may be liable if decommissioning cannot be carried out safely. Under another E.C. Directive, which was implemented in 1991, strict liability applies to anyone who produces, stores, transports or disposes of waste. A QA system would seem to be indispensable.

The law is becoming more involved in how goods are processed or services are provided rather than just being concerned with the quality of the end product. It seems right to look at the causes not just the effects. It will also mean a safer workplace and environment for the staff and the community. The principle is that prevention of harm is better than the cure and QA helps to achieve both. Lately management systems have come in for heavy criticism whenever tragic accidents have occurred. Public opinion demands more accountability and the punishment of companies and individuals who fail in their duties. Individual claims for damages can now even exceed £1M. The consequences for the reputation, even survival, of a business are immense. It is no accident that Insurance Companies are offering premium reductions to firms that can show evidence of the assessed capability of their Quality Management Systems.

CE Marking

Introduction

The European Union (EU) or E.C. has a series of Directives on General Safety and Product Liability. These Directives were agreed by all Member States and will affect all businesses that design, manufacture or export into the European Union. The purpose of these directives is to:

CE

" Create a legal requirement for all the Member States to adopt these agreed, common and harmonised technical standards.

Figure 91
The CE
Mark

" Prohibit the supply of goods which do not conform to these technical standards. The CE mark is shown in the **Figure 91** and is used to declare that a product complies with all relevant standards.

" Promote free trade within the EU by removing local or national technical standards that may have been a barrier to free trade. The CE mark is the guarantee that the product will not be challenged at national boundaries.

Listed in **Table 40** are the Directives adopted since the resolution of May 1985.

Table 40 EU Directives

Title	Directive
Acoustics	90/270/EEC
Active Implantable Medical Devices	90/385/EEC
Appliances Burning Gaseous Fuels	90/396/EEC
Cable-Way Installations	94/C70/07
CE Labels	91/C160/07
Construction Products	89/106/EEC
Electrical Equipment designed for use within certain voltage limits	73/23/EEC
Electromagnetic Compatibility	89/336/EEC
Machinery	89/392/EEC
Medical Devices	93/42/EEC

Title	Directive
New Hot-Water Boilers fired with Liquid or Gaseous Fuels	92/42/EEC
Non-automatic Weight Instruments	89/384/EEC
Personal Protective Equipment	89/686/EEC
Pressure Equipment	93/C246/10
Recreational Craft	92/C123/07
Safety of Toys	88/378/EEC
Satellite Earth Stations	3/97/EEC
Simple Pressure Vessels	87/404/EEC
Telecommunications Terminal Equipment	91/263/EEC
VDU Ergonomics	90/270/EEC 91/2303

It is a criminal act to supply goods which do not conform to the harmonised standard and consequently the penalties are quite severe. They include the supplier being required to remove all similar products from the EU. The persons found guilty will have a criminal record and can be imprisoned for up to three months and fined £5,000 per offence.

Outlined below are some typical steps necessary to ensure designs and products meet the CE marking requirements and any other appropriate national or international regulations and directives. There are some reference documents which include:

    Outline Technical Construction File Contents
    Outline Declaration of Conformance
    Outline Declaration of Incorporation

The procedure below, embraces the sequence of events necessary to ensure compliance with Directives or Regulations. (This needs to include both new or modified product or production equipment and other modified purposes such as production.) The procedure also needs to include the steps necessary when incorporating other suppliers' equipment into a company's own products.

There may be a need to review existing Purchasing and Goods Inwards Inspection Procedures to ensure that they adequately cover the CE marking requirements and do not need enhancement.

CE Marking
Procedure Guidelines

Introduction: Figure 92, CE Marking

Overview, indicates the general shape to addressing the CE mark requirements. CE marking is self-certification and does not usually involve third party registration. In other words the supplier is claiming compliance with a particular requirement as supported by their own checks, tests, approvals etc.

The left-hand side is a list of all of the supplier's products. At the top is a list of any

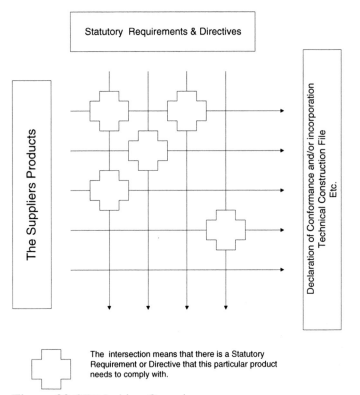

Statutory Requirements & Directives

The Suppliers Products

Declaration of Conformance and/or incorporation
Technical Construction File
Etc.

The intersection means that there is a Statutory Requirement or Directive that this particular product needs to comply with.

Figure 92 CE Marking Overview

applicable requirements, regulations or directives. The output from this analysis will be the central matrix showing where a Product or Design needs to show compliance with a requirement, then certain documentation will need to be produced. Namely the creation of a design Technical Construction File which provides evidence of compliance with the necessary requirements. Together with the Declaration of Conformance and/or Incorporation (in the case of the supplier's products being incorporated in another product). I.e. documentation that goes with the product to show compliance.

Input to the CE Marking Process: A current, new product[19] or significant design change to a new product must be reviewed to ensure that it complies with all current directives and regulations. Any modification to production or other types of equipment will also need to be reviewed to ensure compliance with all directives and regulations. Reviews will need to include any new directives or where the directives have become mandatory[20], i.e. the transition period has ended.

---

[19]   A product referred to here is a generic product not an individual variation. I.e. the individual product variation does not impact on the essential requirements of a directive or is not covered in an existing Technical Construction File.

[20]   The technical expression is *Transition Ends* - the period between in force and mandatory.

Quality Management (Principles & Practice)

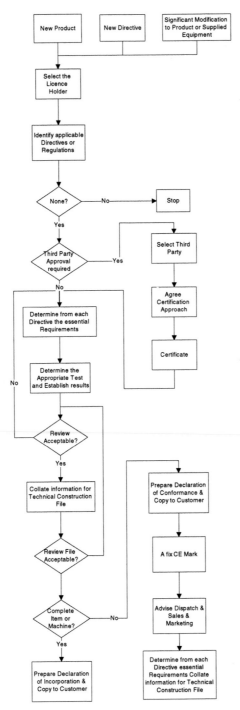

Figure 93 CE Marking Sequence

CE Marking Sequence: See **Figure 93**. Firstly, it is necessary to identify a Product Licence Holder[21]. Once the person has been established, then a review can take place.

Review 1: Identify any directives or regulations which are applicable, e.g. Electrical Equipment, Simple Pressure Vessels, Electromagnetic Compatibility and Machinery. Taking due account of any directives which are in force and transition has ended. See **Table 40** for guidance.

If Third Party Certification[22] is required (only as a result of the directive) e.g. Pressure Vessels, then the certification body will need to be selected. Next the test standard and certification approach[23] will need to be agreed with the certification body.

Having established the appropriate directives then each of the requirements needs to have been addressed. One way in ensuring complete coverage of the directives' requirements is by copying[24] the Directive, then adding and completing three columns, headed; Requirements, Test and Results. The following table shows the Directives Requirements (in normal print) and adjacent to each requirement (in script) the tests carried out to confirm compliance, together with the test results.

---

[21]   The person responsible for compliance

[22]   A Notified Body such as BSI can provide an E.C. type examination certificate

[23]   Samples Tested by an Independent Testing Body, Audit by an Independent Body, Testing by the suppliers etc.

[24]   Copying is acceptable

Table 41 Typical Example (for the Machinery Directive) of part of a Completed Directive Review

Requirement	Test	Result
The suppliers Designed Items		
1.1.4 Light Suitable	Visual	OK
1.2.1 Safety & Reliability of the Controls	Visual Enclosure Test	OK OK
Subcontract Sourced Items		
1.5.1 Electrical Supply	Add Declaration of Incorporation required from Suppliers to Purchase Order	Added Declaration of Incorporation Provided

Review 2: The above information is then examined by the Licence Holder and possibly the Department Head and if appropriate the Buyer. If acceptable the last page could be signed by the Licence Holder.

The information detailed in the Table of Contents for the Technical Construction File can then be compiled. See Appendix, Technical Construction File Contents List.

Review 3: All of the information in the Technical Construction File can then be examined and reviewed by the Licence Holder and the Departmental Manager. If the same person then a peer. If acceptable then archive information for a minimum of ten years after cessation of manufacture. If the product is a complete machine then a Declaration of Conformity needs to be completed and a copy sent to the customer. A CE mark can then be added to the machine (usually adjacent to the rating plate). Sales & Marketing can be advised that the sales literature can be updated to indicate that the product conforms to specified directives. The dispatch documentation will usually need to carry the same information.

If the product is not a complete item (e.g. a sub-assembly) then a declaration of incorporation can be produced and a copy sent to the customer.

Note: Every piece of equipment that is to be sold for use in the European Community must be affixed with a CE mark. This mark must be affixed to one or more of the following:

i)   The equipment
ii)   The equipment packaging
iii)   The equipment instructions for use
iv)   The equipment guarantee certificate.

Typical Technical Construction File Contents List:

1   Contents List
2   Copy of Directive which includes the tests and results essential to show compliant with the directive
3   Drawing List (including issue status) and Drawings
4   Calculation List and Calculations
5   Manuals (User, Operation, Maintenance, Installation, Commissioning etc.)
6   Any Quality Plans or ISO 9000 records
7   Copy of the Declaration of Conformance or Certificate of Adequacy of equipment supplied
8   Bibliography of the Standard Used

Specific requirements associated with the Medical Devise Directive.

This directive applies to all medical devices sold or placed on market within the EC. Note place on the market could infer manufactured or modification for example by the NHS. The directive states:

"Any instrument, apparatus, appliance, material or other article, whether used alone or in combination, including the software necessary for its proper application intended by the manufacturer to be used for human beings for the purpose of:
diagnosis, prevention, monitoring, treatment or alleviation of disease,
diagnosis, monitoring, treatment, or alleviation of or compensation for an injury or handicap, investigation, replacement or modification of the anatomy or of a physiological process, control of conception and which does not achieve its principal intended action in or on the human body by pharmacological, immunological or metabolic means, but which may be assisted in its function by such means."

For example, Medicine measuring cups, Syringes, Dental instruments, Stethoscopes, Thermometers, Prescription spectacles and contact lenses, Bandages and splints, Dental treatment chairs, Wheelchairs, Condoms, First aid kits.

The directive classifies the requirement into three risk levels:

Class	Interpretation
Class I - Low risk	Devices are subject to the following requirements: Registration, (manufacturers or agents) typically in UK to MDA and appoint Representative Demonstrate design verification Perform risk assessment Demonstrate clinical evidence of effectiveness of device Implement procedure for post market surveillance Complete a Declaration of Conformity Maintain a product technical information file CE mark the product or packaging
Class II - Medium risk	Devices are subject requirements above plus possibly the introduction of a ISO 9001system and registration and an audit of their production quality assurance scheme by a notified body. They will also need to meet the following safety requirements: A general requirement for safe design Minimisation of risks from contamination Compatibility with materials with which they are likely to come into contact Minimisation of hazards of infection and microbial contamination Provision of sufficient accuracy (for devices with a measuring function) Protection against radiation Adequate product marking Adequate user instructions Conformity Assessment
Class III - high risk	As Class II plus design dossier Vigilance procedures

Product Recall

In the case of safety critical products, e.g. food manufacturing, electrical goods etc. it may be appropriate to establish procedures in the event of a product recall being necessary. Not only is this acting with due diligence and good preplanning (hopefully unnecessary) but also because it can possibly lead to a reduction in the insurance premium.

Definition: A product recall is an action taken to remove a product from the market. The action may be ordered by the government or initiated by the supplier or manufacturer.

Typically product recalls can be divided into six main categories;. There are a number of International, European and governmental organisations which monitor and regulate these categories.

These organisations can include:

Category	Agency
Food and Drugs	World Health Organisation (WHO) Food and Drug Administration (FDA)
Consumer	Trading Standards Organisation National Consumer Council US Consumer Product Safety Commission (CPSC)
Automotive	UK Department of Transport USA Department of Transportation (DOT)
Aerospace	CAA - Civil Aviation Authority FAA - Federal Aviation Administration
Environmental	Environmental Protection Agency (EPA)

Many of these agencies have the authority to issue or demand recalls, safety alerts and warnings.

A guide to product recall and disaster recovery procedures

These procedures can become very large documents. However, one organisation found that size was no indication of usefulness - if fact the disaster recovery document was (due to its size) found to be unworkable and eventually resulted in a slimmed down, user friendly document. Unfortunately this was not done until after the organisation had experienced a disaster. Which indicates the need for testing the procedures associated with disaster recovery and product recall.

Product Recall, Disaster Recovery or Safety Alert Procedure

1. Recall Objectives: The objectives of a recall is to effectively remove, eliminate or minimise the effect of products that may represent a health hazard to the consumer or user. This is action taken by a manufacturer, distributor, or importer to carry out their responsibility to protect the public.

2. Definitions: A product recall is an action taken to remove a product from the market. The action may be ordered by the government or initiated by the supplier or manufacturer.

3. Determine the seriousness (risk analysis) of the problem, where possible the likely effect on health and safety, fit and function, aesthetics etc.

   a. Class I Recall, there may be a reasonable probability that the use of or exposure to a product will cause serious injury or death.

   b. Class II Recall is a situation where use or exposure to a product may cause temporary or medically reversible injury.

   c. Class III, a Safety Alert is issued in situations where a product may present an unreasonable risk of substantial harm.

   Determine the most appropriate corrective action; recall, rectification, check, alerts, etc.

4. Communication: Circulate a note to key members of the company, including the Managing Director, indicating the situation and proposing the following action. After consultation within the organisation and confirmation of the findings it may be necessary to consider what governmental organisations need to be notified.

5. Establish the extent of the problem

   a. Product name and identifying model

   b. Serial numbers, code, lot or batch number and any other means of identification.

   c. The total quantity of the recalled product originally in his possession.

   d. The total quantity of the recalled product distributed and in the organisation.

   e. Area of the distribution of the recalled product by county and country.

   f. The quantity of the recalled product.

   g. The reason for initiating the recall.

6. Recall Strategy: The recall strategy will need to take account of:

   a. The level of risk

   b. Ease in identifying the product.

     c.   The degree to which a faulty product is obvious to the consumer or user.

     d.   The degree to which the product will remain unused in the market place.

     e.   The availability of essential products.

     f.   Depth of recall; Consumer or user level, Retail level, Wholesale level.

7.   Recall communications: Determine the most appropriate method for notifying customers or users of the suspect items and the action they should take (e.g. return item to factory for replacement). Hazard or advisory notice to all customers either by letter or in the form of a press release.

     a.   Public warning; general news media, national or local as appropriate.

     b.   Professional warnings; Trade or ethnic press, or to specific segments of the population such as physicians, hospitals, aircraft repairers, etc.

8.   Effectiveness checks: Determine the most appropriate method of monitoring the effectiveness of the corrective action. Also the success with which the customers affected have been contacted and items affected have been located. This could include personal visits, telephone calls, letters, etc.

9.   Recall Plan: All of these tasks will require a programme and plan detailing the steps (this procedure), responsibilities an time scales.

10.   Corrective action: Action taken to ensure the problem never happens again.

11.   Recall test: Tests of this procedure are necessary to ensure its effectiveness, waiting until a disaster happens is probably not a good idea. The recall or disaster recovery test needs to detail the test method, frequency, recording the results and analysis.

SECTION 6 - CUSTOMER FEEDBACK

Customer Satisfaction or Market Driven Quality

Note: This section is concerned with the external customer[25], not the internal customer[26]. See Quality Management Tools & Techniques) Departmental Purpose Analysis for an approach concerning internal customers.

It is very important to establish the customers' perception of the quality of product and service provided. This may be in some part determined from customer complaints or warranty returns but it is often stated that the customer rarely complains, they just don't come back. When this statement is balanced with the amount of investment (financial and resource) that is being placed on identifying and gaining new customers (i.e. increasing market share) against the investment on retaining old customers. Then, maybe the effort and resource is being placed in the wrong area. If old customers are being lost, possibly at the same or higher rates as gaining new customers, then a new approach is required. It may be worth considering investing money on retaining existing customers. On this basis customer loyalty is worth ten times the price of a single purchase, as a loyal customer will return to make further purchases.

Le Boeuf suggested that organisations spent six times more obtaining new customers than keeping old customers.

A study detailed by Le Boeuf on the reasons why customers no longer dealt with a particular supplier gave the following results:

i)   3% move away giving no reasons,
ii)   5% develop other supplier relationships,
iii)   9% leave for competitive reasons,
iv)   14% are dissatisfied with the product,
v)   68% quit because of an attitude of indifference toward the customer by the owner, manager, or some employees.

A successful Sales Director of one organisation believes that if customers like their service, they will tell three people. If they don't like their service, they will tell eleven people. This illustrates the effect of a customer complaint over customer praise and how

---

[25]   External Customer; People or departments outside the organisation who receive the output from the supplier department.

[26]   Internal Customer; People or departments inside the organisation who receive the output from the supplier department.

quickly news of bad information over good information spreads. (What sells newspapers good or bad news? - a newspaper that was launched, specifically to tell only good news quickly failed).

One organisation thought that the way to measure customer satisfaction is to examine the number of customer complaints. The problems with this method is that it is reactive. It only responds (if at all) after the event and it does not really measure satisfaction only dissatisfaction. Monitoring complaint levels does not really tell if the customers are any more or less satisfied with the product or service. For example, consider how many times you have been dissatisfied with a product or service - say once a month. Now how many times have you written to complain - say never or possibly once. Managers and Directors often say "if our customers are unhappy they soon tell us". Well do they? If on a personal level you rarely write to complain, what happens at a company level - is it different? Here is an example of an organisation basing its customer satisfaction strategy on levels of customer complaints and getting badly misled. In a Warehousing organisation that I know, customers were unable to obtain products (spares, consumables, etc.) from the newly relocated, reorganised and centralised warehouse. Deliveries were often late or wrong if they arrived at all. The customer complained verbally but being unable to obtain their spare or consumable, spent their time looking for an alternate supplier rather than wasting their time complaining. Customers could not afford the time to complaint, they were too busy avoiding their processes from stopping by sourcing the required items from another supplier. The Warehouse turnover plummeted. "If our customers are unhappy we'll soon know about it" said management - well they didn't, at least not until it was too late and they had lost 90% of their customers. A situation which is still continuing.

The issues associated with customer satisfaction that may need to be considered are:

a.   To *"Understand Customer Needs and Requirements"*. See page 298.
b.   To examine various factors which can be used to determine levels of Customer Satisfaction (and dissatisfaction), *"Measures of Customer Satisfaction"*. See page 302
c.   To measure the levels of customer satisfaction - *"Measuring Customer Satisfaction"*. See page 304

Next each of these three key issues is discussed, clarified and explained. Associated with each explanation are some possible approaches that could be adopted in improving levels of customer satisfaction.

a.　Understanding Customer Needs and Requirements

There are a number of approaches that can be employed to ensure the customer needs, requirement and expectations are understood.

- N　Contract Review - See section on Quality Management Systems.
- N　Quality Function Deployment "Voice of the Customer" - See section on Quality Function Deployment.
- N　SMART
- N　Using Customer Satisfaction Surveys - See Customer Satisfaction questionnaires.
- N　Gap Analysis.

SMART

How are customer requirements established? There are a number of means.

- N　*State and re-state*: State the requirements to the customer and await their response. Following their response, restate back to the customer what they have just told you. State and restate, either written or, more likely, verbal.
- N　*Customer need defined:* Is there a written specification of what the customer expects? Should there be?
- N　*What did the customer say?* Listen to the customer, do not ASSUME. (It makes an ASS out of U and ME).
- N　*Customer schedule:* Have the requirements been defined in a separate document?
- N　*Customer Input:* What is the customer input to the requirements, if just the salesman view then how can this be substantiated?

Clear and Unclear Requirements. Any instruction or need can be communicated in a clear or unclear manner. Below are some examples of unclear requirements, which are confusing instructions.

"Go and get some orders"
"Design a new order entry system"
"Review employee performance"
"Clean up the files"
"Run a trial to prove the theory"

These unclear requirements can be categorised by being, vague and general. They do not provide any limits (including time) and are possibly unreasonable and not particularly well thought out.

Here the instructions are made clearer:

> "Get orders from six new accounts for the ABC product within the next six months"
> "Prepare an inventory report, definition P101, by the fifth working day of the following month"
> "Use the Corporate Guidelines to review the job performance of your employees every twelve months"

What has made these instruction clearer? SMART - What are the characteristics of clear requirements?

Specific

Measurable - Success Criteria Established, with clearly defined start and end point

Action Oriented, i.e. Specifies the problem not the solution

Realistic - Achievable, e.g. Within the team's capability

Time Limits Set and allows for short term interval success

Which type of specification is best? A tight specification or loose specification?

On the face of it a tight specification is the one to choose. A statement by a Project Manager; *"With a tight specification, change is my friend"*. What is implied is the project manager has much greater power - if the customer now makes changes then the (cost, time, etc.) implications are clearer to describe and discuss. Although there are certain situations (e.g. research projects) where a loose specification which can be changed, may be of benefit. *"With a loose specification I have freedom to chose my own direction"*.

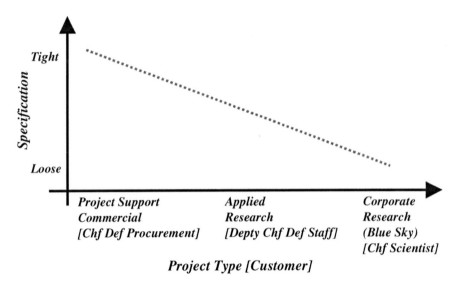

Customer Satisfaction

Figure 94 Tight or Loose Specification?

Possible though this research example is relatively unusual and SMART still rules.

Gap Analysis

As explained previously, it is very important to establish the customer's perception of the quality of the product Improving customer satisfaction may be achieved by clearer understanding of the customer needs and expectations. Dissatisfying, satisfying and delight factors can all be identified by using a customer satisfaction survey. A customer satisfaction survey is a way of determining the customer needs and expectations and whether the current product or service lives up to these needs.

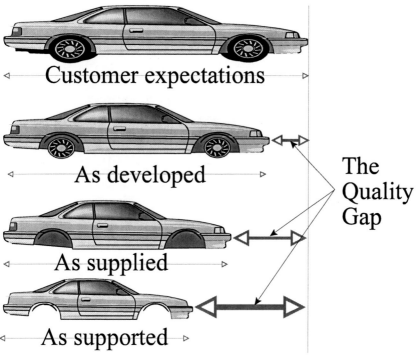

Figure 95 Gap Analysis

Gap analysis, as the diagram suggests, is an exercise in determining peoples' perception of the expectations of a product or service.

This can be achieved by:

1.   Identifying two or three slumbering products or service ranges/types
2.   Identifying a typical end user/customer, key person in the distribution chain, key supplier.
3.   Getting each to describe their view of the customer needs

b. Measures of Customer Satisfaction

Delighting the Customer

The idea of delighting the customer can sometimes grate on British ears. It has a ring of jargon and hype surrounding the phrase - *"Delighting the Customer"*. Unfortunately, there doesn't appear to be another appropriate phrase. Even reference to a thesaurus does not provide a better word than *delight*, other than possibly *enthra*, but that seems over the top and doesn't convey the correct meaning. So it appears we're stuck with this phrase. What is possibly more important is to examine the background to the concept.

In a price sensitive market, where organisations do not wish to embark on a price war, what will distinguish their product or service from its competitors? E.g. mobile phone industry. Advertising may be one (expensive) way, but as already explained, does this only replace customers lost though poor quality? Quality of Service may be seen as a more cost effective route. Delighting the customer - in this situation it can

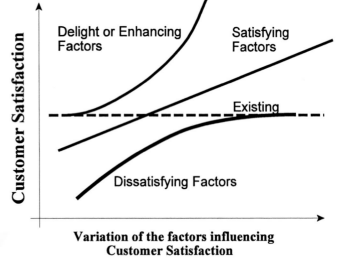

Variation of the factors influencing Customer Satisfaction

Figure 96 Variation of the Factors Influencing Customer Satisfaction

bring enormous rewards in improving market share. Even if a price increase was contemplated, it may not be possible unless the customer sees that the product or service is in some way superior.

Dr. Noriaki Kano provides a model for understanding different types of customer requirements. Reference to **Figure 96** shows diagrammatically the factors influencing customer satisfaction: Dissatisfying Factors, Satisfying Factors and Delighting Factors.

Dissatisfying Factors: These are the factors which bring about a negative or adverse reaction from the customer. Things which the customer does not expect to happen, which, when they do occur, decrease a customer's satisfaction with the product or service. Dissatisfying factors can make a customer less satisfied but the total absence of dissatisfaction factors does not make a customer more satisfied. This is because these factors are the standards of quality and grade normally expected by the customer - the industry norm. Examples of dissatisfying factors are: first time use failures, delivery problems, unhelpful or uncooperative staff, being kept waiting, lack of support, lack of understanding, customer complaints, etc. Addressing these issues will return the organisation to the industry norm but will not take the product or service beyond this point. Issues which influence satisfaction and delight will need to be identified and improved to increase customer satisfaction further from this point.

Satisfying Factors: These are the factors which can provide the customer with greater satisfaction with the product or service provided. These factors are proportional to the level of customer satisfaction. Examples of these factors can be reduction in price, increase in the number of features or enhancements to the product or service, better value for money, reduced lead or response time, etc. As the number of factors are identified and provided, then the greater the customer satisfaction. However, satisfying factors cannot compensate for dissatisfying factors, e.g. low price is no use if the service is slow or the product fails on first time use.

Delight Factors: These are the factors which, when provided, elicit a very positive or surprise reaction from the customer. Such features or enhancements were not expected when purchasing the product or service. These factors invoke a feeling of even better value for money as these features were neither expected nor specified. Examples of these factors are: a bouquet of flowers on the back seat of a newly purchased or serviced car, the receptionist of the hotel knowing and calling you by your name, being able to provide an immediate flat battery service from the Hotel or Car Park.

Delight factors could be established by the use of techniques such as Quality Function Deployment, although this technique also helps with customer satisfaction.

All of these factors (dissatisfaction, satisfaction and delight) are extremely dynamic and the consequence of some of these actions needs to be considered. Often delight features, with time, become satisfaction features and eventually the absence of these features could become a dissatisfaction factor.

c.   **Measuring Customer Satisfaction**

i)   Credit Notes
ii)   Customer Loyalty
iii)   Customer Complaints & Feedback (including internet)
iv)   Customer Focus Groups
v)   Mystery Customer
vi)   Customer Liaison (Visits & and Tours)
vii)   Customer Satisfaction Surveys

Credit Notes: (A measure of dissatisfaction not satisfaction) There are a number of performance measures that can be established to determine levels of customer satisfaction. The obvious method is numbers of customer complaints but often these are not recorded for a number of reasons; time, not in the writers interest, blame, etc. So how can the true picture be established? One method frequently over looked is the number of credit notes raised. A credit note is the accountant's method of repaying the customer. A credit note may be raised when an invoiced customer is to be reimbursed. Such circumstances may be; over changing due to incorrect price list, under delivery, faulty goods or the customer has had to carry out some rectification. In all the cases listed, the supplier has an unhappy customer on their hands and a customer complaint should have been raised. This may cause the number of customer complaints to increase - good, now at least the extent of the customer dissatisfaction is known. If it is not measured it cannot be improved!

Customer Loyalty: Lost Customers (possibly a measure of both satisfaction and dissatisfaction). "Customers do not complain, they just do not come back". It is difficult to measure customer loyalty. Overall figures cannot always provide the information (how many are new) and the exercise requires careful analysis of the customer database. Possibly a job for the computer.

Customer Complaints and Feedback: (Complaint - a measure of dissatisfaction not satisfaction). When Customer Complaints are raised this provides a good picture of the key problem areas. The use of a computer database is obvious. The major difficulty having raised the customer complain is gaining some action. The one person who should never be responsible for resolving a Customer Complaint is the Quality Manager. All too often the Quality Manager is seen as the person to investigate, take action and close the complaint, when in fact they have no knowledge of the problem and are only resolving other peoples mistakes. These people (who in their ignorance of the havoc they have caused) will happily continue making the same mistake again and again. Unless the person responsible for the mistake is actively involved in its

esolution then no lessons will have been learnt *"There's taught nous[27] and bought
ous but there's nothing as clear as bought nous"*.

Should the phrase customer complaint or feedback be used? The word complaint can
be seen as negative and possibly bring about a defensive response. For this reason
often organisations will use the word "feedback". This could be seen as just playing
with words but it does encourage both customers and employees to log this vital
information. Often people ask what do we mean by a customer complaint? (There is
a definition below in the procedure). Well the definition needs to be sufficiently wide
ranging to stimulate customer facing staff (support line, service engineers, reception,
sales, etc.) to record this invaluable information. Customer facing staff are frequently
reluctant to complete or provide this customer feedback information either because:

i)   Not encouraged to record
ii)   Activity discouraged from recording
iii)   Too many to record or they are all the same *(where is my delivery it
        was promised last week?)*
iv)   Too busy
v)   Too much bureaucracy and more paperwork
vi)   No action taken or feedback given when customer complaint registered
        previously
vii)   Fear (of causing problems and being seen as a trouble maker)
viii)   Blame culture prevails

Means of motivating and stimulating this feedback needs to be found, possibly by
reward or just explaining the importance of the information and promising and activily
demonstrating that follow up, corrective and preventive action is taken. Use of the
internet has shown to be one successful way of logging, transmitting and providing
(sometimes automatically) immediate feedback that the complaint has been registered.
website http://www.customer-satisfaction.co.uk is such an example. However, this
alone is not going to resolve the feedback or complaint, for this a process or procedure
needs to be established. One simple and successfully employed customer complaint or
feedback procedure is detailed below.

Customer Complaint or Feedback Procedure

Definition: A Customer Complaint (CC) is any communication which, in the view of
the receiver, necessitates the completion of a CC form is a Customer Complaint.

Sequence:
        i.   Customer Complaint received from the CC originator.

---

27   Knowledge

ii. The Customer Complaint receiver takes the next number from the Customer Complaint Log.

iii. CC receivers completes a customer complaint form.

iv. Email the CC form as attachment to the CC recipient (person identified by the CC receiver as appropriate to take the corrective action) and the Quality Manager.

v. The CC recipient, on completion of the corrective and prevent action emails the up dated Customer Complaint form to; the Quality Manager, the original receiver of the CC and possibly the CC originator.

Note, in this system the Quality Manager's role is to monitor, not action. The customer complaint receiver determines who (not the Quality Manager) should be the recipient. They are rarely, if ever, wrong in this judgement and it works. Consideration also needs to be given to communication with the CC originator and corrective and preventive action. Often the CC recipient completes the rectification with the CC originator but does not consider any corrective action. Clearly, also poor preventive action was taken (otherwise why is there a CC). See section definitions.

Mystery Customer (possibly a measure of both satisfaction and dissatisfaction). A method often employed in the service industry to determine how well the customer is treated is the mystery customer. Not strictly speaking a means of determining customer satisfaction although possibly by inference. The method comprises an employee of the organisation posing as a customer and monitoring and recording how the staff respond. The mystery customer may even in certain circumstance play certain roles; Mr Angry, Mr Moaner, Mr Pushover, etc.

Customer Focus Groups (possibly a measure of both satisfaction and dissatisfaction). A synergistic means of obtaining from a selected group of customers their views, thoughts and novel ideas. The logistics associated with organising and facilitating customer focus groups should not be underestimated. Not only getting the difficulties in getting the group together and "gelling" but also developing the open ended (possibly even provocative) questions and facilitating discussion. Another approach could be to organise customer tours of the organisation, demonstrations or from exhibitions. In this case the customer focussed group would be random and it does provide the opportunity to build customer confidence and loyalty. Sometimes this approach can be combined with customer observation monitoring, examining (possibly videoing) the customer reaction to the product or service. This may reveal frustrations, difficulties and anxieties the customer has with the product or service, which either may or may not be immediately apparent, or the customer is reluctant disclose.

Customer Satisfaction Surveys (possibly a measure of both satisfaction and dissatisfaction). It seems that all assessment schemes now have a customer satisfaction element (see European Quality Award, Malcolm Baldrige Award and ISO 9001:2000) which require measures, results and action regarding customer satisfaction performance. This is not surprising when considering the never ending demand for better quality products and higher quality services. The use of questionnaires is one means of determining levels of Customer Satisfaction. Next is described an approach to conducting a Customer Satisfaction survey with the objective of determining levels of customer satisfaction. Discussed are the:

a. Reliability of such methods
b. The various sampling techniques available
c. The methods that can be employed to increase response rates
d. Examples of Customer Satisfaction questionnaires

Two methods of determining what makes a customer satisfied, are described by *Bob Hayes in "Measuring Customer Satisfaction"*. These are:

1. Key Quality facet development process - Here the approach is for the provider of the product or service to establish the key quality facets; identifying the facet and then defining them with examples. There are different types and number of quality facets depending on the product or service provided. Five facets for quality of service could be; tangibles, reliability, responsiveness, assurance and empathy. Trade journals are one excellent source for identifying quality facets. Another is the organisation's own staff. An example of four quality facets and their definitions are provided in the table. See Quality Function Deployment and Understanding Customer requirements.

Table 42 Examples of Quality Facets

Quality Facet
i) *Responsiveness* - ability to respond to the customer's needs e.g. promptness of the response to a request for service or changes in order levels or requirements.
ii) *Availability* - the immediacy with which the item or service is available or the time taken to deliver (response and lead time.).
iii) *Completeness* - ability to meet the stated or implied job requirements.
iv) *Professionalism* - personal behaviour and level of support provided to the customer.

2. Critical Facet technique - This technique uses the customer to define the key quality facets. It focuses on obtaining information from customers about the

product/service received. A critical facet is a specific example of either positive or negative performance. To obtain the information from the customers an interview technique may be used, either in a group or individually. The interview should include a number of (five to ten) negative and positive questions. It is useful to use quantitative rather than qualitative descriptions, e.g. not 'the service was nice' - but 'the response was quick'. The results of the interviews can be grouped, bringing similar facets together. Each of the facets can then be awarded satisfaction points and the agreement between them checked. As a means of checking that all the facets have been identified, initially do not include ten per cent of the responses in the analysis. Once the initial analysis has been completed and all the critical quality facets identified. Then confirm this analysis by demonstrating that the ten per cent of responses left out can be readily and easily placed into the critical quality facet categories. If they cannot then some facts have not been identified and further interviews may be necessary. An example of such a questionnaire can be found below.

To establish the reliability and validity of the critical quality facets the following tests can be performed.

- ○ Repeating the same survey with the same customers. The issue associated with this is the duration between the two surveys. Too short and the person surveyed may remember the answer. Too long and there may have been a change in the service performance provided.
- ○ Asking the same question but in a different way:
  Question 1. "The procedures documented in the Quality Manual accurately reflect what actually happens on a project?"
  Question 2. "It does not matter which project I am on, the process is still the same?"
- ○ Other issues that will affect survey accuracy include sample size and number of questions per item. (It is difficult to establish a customer view with one question).

Creating a Customer Satisfaction Questionnaire

Generally there are four elements to the creation of a customer satisfaction questionnaire:

1.   *The questions to be used.*   The questions should be clear, unambiguous, short and to the point. There should only be one issue per question.
2.   *The response format,* e.g. multiple choice, written response, scoring (like to dislike using the scale 1 to 5), yes/no.
3.   *Introduction to the questionnaire,* e.g. "As a valued and trusted customer you have been selected as.........." An explanation as the questionnaires aims and objectives, the benefits in completion, confidentially, analysis of the results, time to complete.
4.   *Final review of the completed questionnaire* (Its look and feel). The initial impression the questionnaire makes, is important in obtaining the correct level of response. Desk Top Publishing, proof reading, length, question style etc.

Sampling - distribution of the questionnaire

○   The questionnaires are unlikely to be sent to every customer, therefore some form of representative sampling will need to be completed.

○   Sampling methods include;
The whole of the customer base (OK with small number of major customers). Statistical sampling random, stratified, e.g. income, each age range, gender, etc. cluster - from a particular geographical location or office.

Obtaining a Response

Consideration needs to be given to the manner in which the information is obtained. By post - the problems are; Will the questionnaire be completed? Will the questions be understood? Will a response be obtained from the most valuable customers? However, it will speed up the data gathering exercise.

By the manager having face to face discussion with the customer. Although, this could be a less efficient way of gathering the information it may be an important marketing and personal relationship exercise which provides more information than from a questionnaire. These questions may be used as a guide to the customer discussion process.

By the service person, (possibly the service engineer) having face to face discussions with the customer. This may be an opportunity for the service provider and the customer to see the service person's role in a different light, extending the service person's role and the service provided.

The responded rate is not good, typically a ten per cent return is very good. To improve on this return ratio there are some methods to cajole the customer into responding:

- An incentive - enter into a prize draw.
- Reason for the questionnaire - how it will help improve our service.
- Ease of return; email, prepaid reply envelope, etc.
- Use of a impartial third party.

Examples of questionnaires can be found in the section on Customer Satisfaction Survey Questionnaires.

Data analysis

See section on Statistical Quality Control. How will the information obtained be analysed and, most importantly, will action be taken to correct any shortcomings? Who should receive the results of the customer satisfaction survey; managers, service providers, the customer, etc.? How will the results be communicated?

The data can then help identify areas for improvement such as whether the induction and training programme has been effective.

Improving Customer Satisfaction - Action Planning:

- " Reduce dissatisfaction
- " Increase satisfaction
- " Provide delight features

The first stage is to identify and eliminate or minimise the dissatisfaction factors. No increase in the satisfaction and delight factors is going to improve customer satisfaction without first resolving dissatisfaction. Customer complaints monitoring, analysis and corrective action will help identify key dissatisfaction factors. (See section on Quality Management System - ISO 9000). Often organisations will plot graphs to monitor trends and compare performance against the target. Establishing a customer call escalation system or product support system is also a necessary prerequisite to understanding and reacting in a timely manner to customer problems.

Improving customer satisfaction may be achieved by clearer understanding of the customer needs and expectations. A customer satisfaction survey is a way of determining the customer needs and expectations and whether the current product and service lives up to these expectations.

Customer Satisfaction Survey Questionnaires

Following are some examples of customer satisfaction surveys. They are obviously biased towards a particular industry and may be in need of conversion for use in other industries. The format of the questions is important and in certain circumstance it may be necessary to make the questions positive, not negative. If the questions are negative, the questionnaire may emphasise the bad points instead of building on the good.

Negative: What do you dislike about our service?
Positive: What do you like about our service?

A Questionnaire successfully used by a Service and Repair organisation.

Name:		Position:	
Organisation:		Date:	
#	Question		Response
1.	**Service offered:**		
a.	Are you aware of the range of services offered? (*Lists the services provided*)		
b.	Are you aware of the procedure of requesting our services? (*Describe the procedure*)		
c.	What other services would you like to see offered?		
d.	Would a visit be helpful to describe the services offered?		
2.	**Performance:**		
a.	What is it about the service provided that satisfies you most?		
b.	In what way could the service be improved?		
c.	Have you any complaints regarding the service provided?		
d.	The response to requests for service should be (*detail response time*) Is this response time adequate?		
e.	If not, what response time would be adequate?		
f.	In your view is the response time met?		
g.	The completion time for the service provided should be (*detail		
h.	completion time*) Is this completion time adequate? If not, what completion time		
i.	would be adequate?		
j.	In your view is the completion time met?		
k.	Is the service provided carried out as effectively as possible?		
l.	If not how could the service be more effective & efficient?		

#	Question	Response
3.	**Managing the problem:**	
a.	During the service - if a permanent solution could not be achieved was an alternative or temporary solution offered?	
b.	Was concern shown if the service was not achieving the required objectives?	
c.	Are you advised of the service person's presence?	
d.	Are you advised of the service being completed?	
e.	If the service was interrupted are you advised of the reason?	
f.	Generally, are preventive measures taken to avoid any recurring problems?	
g.	Are there any discussions regarding preventing the problem recurring?	
4.	**Attitude:**	
a.	Are the service providers courteous? In what way were the service providers most helpful?	
b.	Are the service providers interested? In what areas were the service providers most help?	
c.	Are the service providers suitably dressed?	
d.	Were constructive comments made?	
5.	**Customers Questions:**	
a.	Is there any thing you wish to bring to our attention?	
b.	What is the single most important change that you would like to see that could improve our service?	

THANK YOU FOR YOUR HELP IN IMPROVING OUR SERVICE TO YOU

A questionnaire to determine the value of the Quality Management System in Project Management Organisation.

Introduction

You have been specially selected to assist in assessment of the capability of our organisations Project Control related processes. The objective of this questionnaire is to provide information regarding our capability in managing Projects and satisfying the customer's needs. The information will also provide an indication of areas or projects which require greater focus in a subsequent in-depth assessment.

Please answer the following questions in relation to recent experience within the organisation, so that the information may be used to gain an overall impression of the current project management processes used.

The information will be kept confidential to the assessment team, only the analysis of all questionnaires will be reported and reporting will be non-attributable to individuals.

Quality Management (Principles & Practice)

Do not spend too long answering any one question. If you don't know what the question is asking, just leave it and move on to the next. The whole questionnaire should take less than 20 minutes to complete. If you have any difficulties, or it is taking significantly longer than 20 minutes, please contact the Quality Department - see below.

Please return the completed questionnaire to the Quality Department.

#	Statement	Regarding your role and responsibility you do				
		Strongly Agree	Agree	Disagree	Strongly Disagree	Not Know
1.	Documented procedures (quality manual) accurately reflect what actually happens on a project.	G	G	G	G	G
2.	We satisfactorily control customer specifications.	G	G	G	G	G
3.	The team's tasks are clearly defined in the Project Handbook.	G	G	G	G	G
4.	Only projects with strong Project Leaders will succeed.	G	G	G	G	G
5.	Data is regularly provided on completion of tasks.	G	G	G	G	G
6.	Design and project reviews take place, and minuted actions agreed.	G	G	G	G	G
7.	It does not matter which project I work on, the process is still the same.	G	G	G	G	G
8.	Bad news is always transmitted to the customer.	G	G	G	G	G
9.	Data from previous projects is readily available when making estimates.	G	G	G	G	G
10.	The quality of the customer deliverables is consistently good.	G	G	G	G	G
11.	Number and severity of faults or errors identified on all projects can be tracked.	G	G	G	G	G
12.	We know when a project is going wrong by analysing the project's data.	G	G	G	G	G
13.	Project's progress can be determined by reference to the project programme.	G	G	G	G	G
14.	Methods such as Contract Review are used to assess the quality of the customer's requirements.	G	G	G	G	G
15.	Communication routes are well understood, used and managed?	G	G	G	G	G
16.	Customer's preference or other pressures cause 'Quality' practices to be compromised.	G	G	G	G	G

Customer Satisfaction

#	Statement	Regarding your role and responsibility you do				
		Strongly Agree	Agree	Disagree	Strongly Disagree	Not Know
17.	Our organisation and projects suffer from 'initiative fatigue'.	G	G	G	G	G
18.	We have adequate project resources.	G	G	G	G	G
19.	Plans are reviewed and updated on a regular basis.	G	G	G	G	G
20.	When things sometimes go wrong, someone is always held accountable.	G	G	G	G	G
21.	Our estimates accurately reflect the actual time and effort spent on projects.	G	G	G	G	G
22.	Where training is required it is provided.	G	G	G	G	G
23.	The risks we face are addressed in the planning stage of the project.	G	G	G	G	G
24.	Customer coordination is well managed.	G	G	G	G	G
25.	Interfaces e.g. Inter Office, Suppliers, Contractors, etc. are well managed.	G	G	G	G	G

Note: The questions are only meant as a guide to assist discussion regarding establishing the most appropriate questions.

A questionnaire to determine the value of an organisation's Quality Management System can be found on page 219.

Performance Measurement & Benchmarking

Introduction:

All organisations need to establish and quantify the key factors with which to monitor their quality performance. It is not enough to believe that the organisation's quality performance has always been satisfactory. Agreement needs to be reached as to what the key factors are by which to judge the organisation's quality performance. What is the organisation's current performance against these factors and how can the current quality performance be improved? If measures of Quality Performance are not established and monitored, then adverse and possibly catastrophic trends may not be identified with possible dire consequences for the organisation concerned. Juran talks about breakthrough and control to new levels of quality performance; organisations that can achieve this objective will always be successful because they will continually be making never-ending improvements.

Quality Performance measures need to be established, not only at a corporate level but at all levels throughout the organisation, even down to an individual unit or person. Quality Performance measurement is one of the most important ways of improving the quality performance of organisations. If the current quality performance is not known then improvements can only be subjective and not quantifiable.

Having established and measured an organisation's or department's performance indicators these values need to be compared (benchmarked) against recognised leaders or pacesetters. This is to determine if the current performance is of the correct standard (*World Class*).

Guidelines for Benchmarking:

Firstly, there is a need to agree the necessity for establishing quality performance measures with senior management. The necessity of establishing quality performance measurement then needs to be communicated to all levels throughout the organisation to gain commitment and understanding for the need to continually make improvements in quality performance. Departmental Purpose Analysis and Customer/Supplier investigations can be used to help convince personnel of the need for quality performance measurement. The TQM team needs to agree the performance measurement.

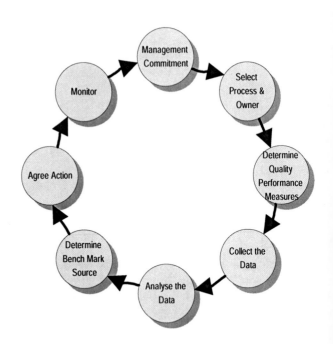

Figure 97 A Benchmarking Sequence

Next, the actual processes that need to be monitored have to be established and agreed. Having established the process to be monitored then the factors critical to success need to be determined.

These critical success factors or quality performance measurements should be:

i)   Suitable for the particular process, department or organisation evaluated.

ii) Consistent, so that there is no doubt about the method of calculation of the performance measure and so that the data for performance measurement can be accurately and reliably obtained.

iii) Clear and owned by a particular group or cell so that responsibility or ownership for achieving the performance criteria understood.

iv) Easily and regularly calculated, usually numbering between 3 and 7 performance measures.

v) Clearly defined start and finish.

vi) Defined direction not a solution.

vii) Achievable and within the group's capability.

viii) Possibly determined from the customer/supplier relationship and the department's purpose analysis.

The performance measurement categories can be broken down into two main categories, quantifiable "Hard Standards" and non-quantifiable (subjective) "Soft Standards". These categories can be broken down still further in terms of:

N customer satisfaction; product and service performance, reliability, complaints and claims

N process efficiency; scrap, rejects, wasted time, change, rework, labour and process utilisation

N environmental losses; pollution, unsatisfactory performance, disposal and decommissioning, waste of resources both human and energy.

"Hard Standards" are measurable such that an agreed performance target can be set. Examples of such standards could be:

Cost	a.	Costs per item, transactions per employee
Quality	b.	Number of rejects, failure rates, complaints
Service	c.	Average response and down time, lead time, delivery time

"Soft Standards", although not always directly measurable, are equally important as hard standards. These soft standards can make the difference between an existing customer returning, obtaining a new customer or placating a dissatisfied customer.

An example of soft standards could be the way in which the service engineer deals with the customer. This can often make the difference between the customer renewing their service contract and the customer advising possible new customers of the excellent service the customer has received. Or alternatively, the poor service the customer has received which may result in the customer not returning and advising potential future customers of the unsatisfactory service.

Benchmarking

Soft Standards can include:

Personnel style	a.	Friendly, helpful, positive approach
Efficient Service	b.	Anticipate needs, be flexible, provide clear information, professionalism
Concern	c.	Manage problems - when troubles do occur understanding the customer's difficulties and help to resolve the problem.

Data collection: Having determined the quality performance standards that need to be monitored, the next stage is to agree how to quantify the current performance level and to start to collect the data on a regular basis. The data collected could include:

N   customer satisfaction; which could be quantified by surveys of both existing and potential customers (see example of the customer satisfaction survey). Surveys of competing products and services. Analysis of service and product performance in terms of reliability, numbers and types of complaints and claims.

N   process efficiency; by monitoring scrap, rejects and rework levels. Analysis of processes to determine wasted time, labour and process utilisation, examination of the number of changes. (See Cost of Quality).

N   environmental losses; waste of resources, human and energy, could be quantified and monitored by employee surveys, interviews (e.g. exit or leaving interviews) and energy audits.

Analysis: With the current performance level determined, the TQM team or departmental personnel need to agree new targets. These new targets can either be agreed with the customer (internal or external), or alternatively, the targets may be based on other recognised leaders or pacesetters - the organisations that are seen as being World Class or best in class. This information can be obtained from; surveys (customer and competition), technical journals, review of advertisements etc.

Obtaining the Benchmark Source: There are a number of possible benchmark sources. *Internal Benchmarking;* against a similar national or international division. This is the easiest, as access to the required information should be relatively straightforward. *Industrial Benchmarking;* against the competition. This is obviously more difficult as competitors are unlikely to be keen on releasing commercially sensitive information. However, Trade Associations can be helpful but information scientists can provide useful information. Alternatively, recruiting staff from the competition could provide more effective route. There are also best practice clubs now available, which share approaches and information.

Action Plan & Monitoring: Having obtained what is seen as being a suitable target then work can commence towards establishing an action plan for improving the performance to meet the new performance criteria.

Benchmarking

Exercises - Customer Satisfaction:

1. Facilitate group discussion on why customers no longer deal with us and capture the factors for this on a flip-chart. *Reasons why customers do not come back is explained in the Kano Model.*

2. Kano

   a. Dissatisfaction factors; Expected or Implicit Needs, The Industry Norm. 302

      Can we provide any examples of this?

      How do we measure dissatisfaction?

   b. Satisfaction factors; Normal or Expressed Need, Features, Value for money

      How do we describe the satisfying factors?

      How do we identify the satisfying factors?

      Who is responsible for identifying these factors?

   c. Delight factors; Latent Needs or Attractors, Unexpected features

      How do we identify these latent factors?

      Who is responsible for identifying these factors?

      Can we identify any existing or new latent factors?

3. Convert the Customer Satisfaction Survey table into one suitable for your industry.

4. Management have committed to measure levels of Customer Satisfaction describe:

   a. The adopted approach (include reasons for your adopted approach)

   b. The implementation plan

   c. How the results will be validated and verified

   d. Consider what action could be taken after results analysis

SECTION 7 - QUALITY PHILOSOPHY

Quality Philosophy

"To lose one parent, Mr. Worthing, may be regarded as a misfortune; to lose both look like carelessness."

Lady Bracknell from *"The Importance of being Earnest"* by Oscar Wild

The idea is - making one mistake is forgivable, repeating the same mistake may be see as carelessness. However, making the same mistake for the third time may be seen a incompetence? What would be even better, is to prevent the mistake being made in th first place!

Quality Philosophy: There are a number of influential figures in the field of Qualit Assurance. Although this list is not exhaustive possibly the best known are:

> Philip B. Crosby - Zero Defects
>
> W. Edwards Deming - 14 Points
>
> P Drucker - Management by Objectives
>
> A. V. Feigenbaum - Total Quality Control
>
> K. Ishikawa - Quality Circles
>
> Joseph M. Juran - Breakthrough and Control
>
> Claus Møller - Time Management
>
> Tom Peters - Passion for Excellence
>
> Shigeo Shingo - Poke-Yoka and Zero Quality Control
>
> Genichi Taguchi - Taguchi Technique (Analysis of Variance) and Los Function

Although they all share a common ambition - 'the attainment of quality', they each have their own very individual style or approach to achieving the ambition. However, there are some issues which do tend to occur in all of their approaches:

"   Management Commitment is essential for success.

"   Cost of Quality - Identification of the critical quality problems or issues.

"   Understanding of the processes and characteristics that require control indicating what to change and how to measure performance.

"   Prevention rather than detection.